FOOD ANALYSIS

The Authors

Dr. (Mrs.) Neelam Khetarpaul presently working as Dean, College of Home Science at CCS Haryana Agricultural University, Hisar is the recipient of many awards viz., Distinguished Teacher Award-2000, Young Investigator Award, Ms. Manju Utreja Gold Medal and cash award for doing the best research work in the University and Best Research Paper Award by AFST (I) Hisar Chapter. She is the recipient of various Visiting Fellowships abroad funded by different national and international agencies and visited USA, Australia, UK, Hungary, Ecuador, Ghana and Netherlands for academic pursuits. She is country Coordinator of Indo-Netherlands Tailoring Biotechnologies project programme being funded by the Department of Biotechnology, Ministry of Science & Technology, Govt. of India and the Wageningen University, The Netherlands. She has published more than 214 research papers in various journals of national and international repute and 18 books in the discipline of Food Science and Human Nutrition.

Dr. Darshan Punia is presently working as Scientist in the Department of Foods and Nutrition. She was the Principal Investigator of National Agricultural Technology Project funded by ICAR. She is the recipient of ICAR Ch. Devi Lal Outstanding All India Coordinated Research Project (AICRP) Team Award, 2003. She also received Best Research Paper Presentation Award during the year 1998. She had been the convenor and co-convenor for poster presentations at International Conferences. She has published about 50 research papers in national and international journals of repute. Presently, she is the Incharge of All India Coordinated Research Project in the Department of Foods and Nutrition, CCS Haryana Agricultural University, Hisar.

FOOD ANALYSIS

Dr. Neelam Khetarpaul
Ph.D. (Foods and Nutrition), FICN
Dean (COHS)
CCS Haryana Agricultural University

Dr. Sudesh Jood
Ph.D. (Foods and Nutrition)
Associate Professor
CCS Haryana Agricultural University

Dr. Darshan Punia
Ph.D. (Foods and Nutrition)
Sr. Scientist
CCS Haryana Agricultural University

Daya Publishing House®
A Division of
Astral International Pvt. Ltd.
New Delhi - 110 002

First Published, 2011
Reprinted, 2018

ISBN: 978-81-7035-687-5 (PB)

Published by : **Daya Publishing House®**
A Division of
Astral International Pvt. Ltd.
– ISO 9001:2015 Certified Company –
4736/23, Ansari Road, Darya Ganj
New Delhi-110 002
Ph. 011-43549197, 23278134
E-mail: info@astralint.com
Website: www.astralint.com

Preface

The science of food analysis has grown tremendously in its scope in recent years. New analysis techniques are being developed and existing techniques optimized. Moreover, there is a growing demand from students of various disciplines including Foods and Nutrition, Food Science, Food Technology, Soils, Agronomy, Horticulture, Agricultural Sciences, Dairy manufacturing etc. to acquire training in the fundamentals of quantitative and qualitative analysis with sufficient laboratory techniques to equip them for research work in these different specialized fields. To meet the demands and interests of such students has been one of the objects of this book. The needs of this group of students have been considered in preparing this book.

There is an increasing awareness of hazards posed to both human and animal health by mycotoxins in foodstuffs and feeds. This has led to the development of methods of analysis for these toxins. In this context, fluorescence techniques in food analysis have got much more importance which have been discussed in very detail in the book.

Flavour is another major concern of great interest to the food scientists because it is a significant factor influencing the food purchase behavior and decisions of the consumers and its perception of food quality. Hence, the book consists of a number of topics, showing how real food aroma problems have been resolved through the use of modern analytical instruments and olfactometry.

This book also provides information on general topics like sampling and sampling procedures and solvent extraction also which is very essential prior to application of various techniques needed to analyze foods in laboratory experiments. Other topics covered include information on the basic principles, procedures, advantages, limitations, and applications of gas liquid chromatography, high performance liquid chromatography, fluorescence techniques, fluorescence microscopy, fluorescence spectroscopy, atomic absorption and emission spectroscopy, multivariate calibration etc. from the perspective of their use in the chemical analysis of foods.

We hope that this book shall be ideal for undergraduate and postgraduate courses in food analysis and also an invaluable reference to professionals in the food industry. We shall consider our efforts amply regarded if the book is received with enthusiasm.

Neelam Khetarpaul

Sudesh Jood

Darshan Punia

Contents

Chapter 1

Sampling and Sampling Procedures

Introduction

To control food quality and acceptance within satisfactory limits, it is important to monitor the vital characteristics of raw products, ingredients and processed foods. This could be done by evaluating all foods or ingredients from a particular lot, which is feasible if the analytical technique is rapid and non destructive. However, it is usually more practical to select a portion of the total product volume and assume the quality of the selected portion is typical of the whole lot. Obtaining a portion, or sample, that is representative of the whole is referred to as sampling, and the total quantity from which a sample is obtained is called the population. Adequate sampling technique helps to ensure that sample quality measurements are an accurate and precise estimate of the quality of population. By sampling only a fraction of the population, a quality estimate can be obtained more quickly and with less expense and personnel time than if the total population were measured. The sample is only an estimate of the true value of the population, but with proper sampling technique it can be a very accurate estimate. A laboratory sample for analysis can be of any size or quantity.

Selection of Sampling Procedures

1. General Information

It is important to clearly define the population that is to be sampled. The population may vary in size from a production lot, a day's production, to the contents of a warehouse. Population may be finite, such as size of a lot, or infinite, such as in the number of temperature observations made of a lot over time. For finite populations, sampling provides an estimate of lot quality. In contrast, sampling from infinite populations provides information about a process. Regardless of the population type, that is, finite or infinite, the data obtained from sampling are compared to a range of acceptable values to ensure the population sampled is within specifications.

Data obtained from an analytical technique are the result of a stepwise procedure from sampling, to sample preparation, laboratory analysis, data processing, and data interpretation. There is a potential for error at each step and the uncertainty, or reliability, of the final result depends on the cumulative errors at each stage. An estimate of uncertainty is the variance. The total variance of the whole testing procedure is equal to the sum of variances associated with each step of the sampling procedure and represents the precision of the process. Precision is a measure of the reproducibility of the data. In contrast, accuracy is a measure of how close the data are to the true value. The most efficient way to improve accuracy is to improve the reliability of the step with the greatest variance. Frequently, this is the initial sampling step. The reliability of sampling is dependent more on the sample size than on the population size. The larger the sample size the more reliable the sampling. However, sample size is limited by time, cost, sampling methods, and the logistics of sample handling, analysis, and data processing.

2. Sampling Plan

Most sampling is done for a specific purpose and the purpose may dictate the nature of the sampling approach. The International Union of Pure and Applied Chemistry (IUPAC) defined a sampling plan as "a predetermined procedure for the selection, withdrawal, preservation, transportation, and preparation of the portions to be removed from a lot as samples". A sampling plan should be a well-organized document that establishes the required procedures for accomplishing the program's objectives. It should address the issues of who, what, where, why and how. The primary aim of sampling is to obtain a sample, subject to constraints on size that will satisfy the sampling plan specifications. A sampling plan should be selected on the basis of the sampling objective, the study population, the statistical unit, the sample selection criteria, and the analysis procedures. The two primary objectives of sampling are often to estimate the average value of a characteristic and determine if the average value meets the specifications defined in the sampling plan.

3. Factors Affecting Choice of Sampling Plan

Each factor affecting the choice of sampling plans must be considered in the selection of a plan. When the purpose of the inspection, the nature of the product, the test method, and lot to be sampled are determined, a sampling plan can be developed that will provide the desired information.

4. Sampling for Attributes or Variables

Sampling plans are designed for examination of either attributes or variables. In attribute sampling, sampling is performed to decide on the acceptability of a population based on whether the sample possesses a certain characteristic, for example, *Clostridium botulinum* contamination in canned foods. Attribute sampling provides data that are in dichotomous form, *i.e.*, data for which there exist two possible alternatives, such as present or absent. The statistical distribution of such a sampling plan is hypergeometric, binomial or poisson. In variable sampling, sampling is performed to estimate quantitatively the amount of a substance (*e.g.*, salt), or a characteristic (*e.g.*, colour) on a continuous scale. The estimate obtained from the sample is compared with an acceptable value (*i.e.*, previously determined) and the deviation measured. This type of sampling usually produces data that have a normal distribution such as in the per cent fill of a container and total solids of a food sample. In general, variable sampling requires smaller sample size than attribute sampling.

There are three basic types of sampling plans; single, double, or multiple. Each may be used for evaluation of attributes or variables, or a combination of both. Single sampling plans allow accept/reject decisions to be made by inspection of one sample of a specified size. Double sampling plans require the selection of two sample sets. If the first sample indicates the lot is of intermediate quality, a second sample set is taken. A decision on the acceptability is then based on analysis of data from both sample sets. The cost associated with multiple sampling plans can be reduced by rejecting low-quality lots and accepting high-quality lots quickly. The amount of sampling depends on the overall lot quality.

5. Risks Associated with Sampling

There are two types of risks associated with sampling which should be considered when developing a sampling plan.

1. The *consumer risk* describes the probability of accepting a poor quality population. This should happen rarely (<5% of the lots) but the actual acceptable probability of a consumer risk depends on the consequences associated with accepting an unacceptable lot.
2. The *vendor risk* is the probability of rejecting an acceptable product. As with consumer risk, the consequences of an error determine the acceptable probability of the risk. An acceptable probability of vendor risk is usually 5-10%. A sampling plan should be simple and flexible, protect both the consumer and the vendor, and provide for utilization of rejected lots.

Sampling Procedures

The reliability of analytical data is compromised if sampling is not done properly. The general considerations to be taken into account when obtaining a sample for analysis are:

1. Homogeneous vs. Heterogeneous Populations

The ideal population would be uniform throughout and identical at all locations. Such a population would be homogeneous. Sampling from such a population is simple, as a sample can be taken from any location and the analytical data obtained will be representative of the whole. However, this occurs rarely, as even in an apparently uniform product, such as sugar syrup, suspended particles and sediments in a few places may render the population heterogeneous. Therefore, the location within a population where a sample is taken will affect the subsequent data obtained.

2. Manual vs. Continuous Sampling

To obtain a manual sample the person taking the sample must attempt to take a "random sample" to avoid human bias in the sampling method. Thus, the sample must be taken from a number of locations within the population to ensure it is representative of the whole population. For liquids in small containers, this can be done by shaking prior to sampling. When sampling from a large volume of a liquid, such as that stored in silos, aeration ensures a homogeneous unit. Liquids may be sampled by pipetting, pumping or dipping. However, when sampling grain from a rail car, mixing is impossible and samples are obtained by probing from several points at random within the rail car. Such manual sampling of granular or powdered material is usually achieved with triers or probes that are inserted into the population at several locations. Errors may occur in sampling, as rounded particles may flow into the sampling compartments more easily than angular ones. Similarly, hygroscopic materials flow more readily into the sampling device, than does non hygroscopic material. Horizontal core samples have been found to contain a larger proportion of smaller-sized particles than vertical ones. Continuous sampling is performed mechanically. This should be less prone to human bias than manual sampling.

3. Statistical Considerations

(*a*) Non Probability Sampling

Non probability sampling is performed when a representative sample of a population cannot be collected. In certain cases of adulteration such as rodent contamination, the objective of the sampling plan may be to highlight the adulteration rather than collect a representative sample of the population. This type of sampling can be done in many ways, but in each case the probability of including any specific portion of the population is not equal because the investigator selects the samples, without estimating sampling error.

Judgement sampling is solely at the discretion of the sampler and therefore is highly dependent on the person taking the sample. This method is used when it is the only practical way of obtaining the sample. It may result in a better estimate of the population than random sampling if sampling is done by an experienced individual.

Convenience sampling is performed when ease of sampling is the key factor. The first pallet in a lot or the sample that is most accessible is selected. This is also called "chunk sampling" or "grab sampling". Although this sampling required little effort, the sample obtained will not be representative of the population, and therefore is not recommended.

Restricted sampling may be unavoidable when the entire population is not accessible. This is the case if sampling from a loaded box car, but the sample will not be representative of the population.

Quota sampling is the division of a lot into groups representing various categories, and samples are then taken from each group. This sampling method is less expensive than random sampling but also is less reliable.

(*b*) Probability Sampling

Probability sampling plans provide a statistically sound basis for obtaining representative samples with elimination of human bias and therefore are the most desirable. The probability of including any item in the sample is known and sampling error can be calculated.

Simple random sampling requires that the number of units in the population be known and each unit is assigned a number. A specific quantity of random numbers between one and the total number of population units is selected. Sample size is determined by lot size and the potential impact of a consumer or vendor error. Various sampling plans are used, including random number tables and computer-generated random numbers. Units corresponding to the random numbers then are analyzed as an estimate of the population.

Systemic sampling is used when a complete list of sample units is not available, but when samples are distributed evenly over time or space. The first sample is selected at random and then every n^{th} unit after that. However, the variance is difficult to determine.

Stratified sampling involves dividing the population in to overlapping subgroups so that each subgroup is as homogeneous as possible. Group therefore differs from each other as much as possible. Random samples are then taken from each subgroup. The procedure provides a representative sample because no part of the population is excluded and it is less expensive than simple random sampling.

Cluster sampling entails dividing the population into subgroups, or clusters, so that the clusters' characteristics are as identical as possible, *i.e.*, the means are as similar as possible. Any heterogeneity occurs within each cluster. Clusters should be small with a similar number of units in each cluster. The clusters are sampled randomly and may be either totally inspected or sub sampled for analysis. This sampling method is more efficient and less expensive than simple random sampling, if populations can be divided into homogeneous groups.

Composite sampling is used to obtain samples from bagged products such as flour, seeds, and larger items in bulk. Two or more samples are combined to obtain one sample for analysis that reduces differences between samples.

(c) Mixed Sampling

Mixed sampling combines random and non statistical sampling. The population is subdivided by the investigator and items from the groups are selected randomly.

(d) Optimum Sampling Size and Statistical Analysis

Statistical analysis, using the t-test provides important information regarding the optimum sample size needed to obtain a reliable population estimate. The sample size is dependent on how accurate the estimate needs to be, *i.e.*, the sample size depends on the degree of accuracy required. A larger sample size is needed to obtain a population estimate that is plus or minus 5% of the true value than would be needed to obtain an estimate that is plus or minus 25%. The following equation shows how the optimum sample size for a certain degree of accuracy can be found using t-=values.

$$T = \frac{\chi - \mu}{SD / \sqrt{n}}$$

where

χ: Sample mean

μ: Population mean
SD: Standard deviation of the sample
n: Sample size

To find the probability that the sample and population means are different, the calculated t-value can be compared to a t-distribution with degrees of freedom one less than the sample size.

4. Problems in Sampling

Unreliable data can be obtained by non statistical factors such as poor sample storage resulting in sample degradation. Samples should be stored in a container that protects the sample from moisture and other environmental factors like heat, light and air. To protect against changes in moisture content, samples should be stored in an air tight container. Light sensitive samples should be stored in containers made of opaque glass, or the container wrapped in aluminium foil. Oxygen sensitive samples should be stored under nitrogen or inert gas. Refrigeration or freezing may be necessary to protect chemically unstable samples. Freezing should be avoided when storing unstable emulsions. Preservatives can be used to stabilize certain food substances during storage. Mislabeling of samples causes mistaken sample identification. Samples should be clearly identified by markings on the sample container in a manner such that markings will not be removed or damaged during storage and transport. For *e.g.*, plastic bags that are to be stored in ice water should be marked with water-insoluble ink. If the sample is an official or legal sample the container must be sealed to protect against tampering and the seal mark easily identified. Official samples also must include the date of sampling with the name and signature of the sampling agent. The chain of custody of such samples must be identified clearly.

Preparation of Samples

1. General Size Reduction Considerations

If the particle size or mass of the sample is too large for analysis, it must be reduced in bulk or particle size. To obtain a smaller quantity for analysis the sample can be spread on a clean surface and divided into quarters. The two opposite quarters are combined. If the mass is still too large for analysis, the process is repeated until an appropriate amount is obtained. For *e.g.*, raw sugars should be mixed thoroughly and rapidly with a spatula. Lumps are to be broken by a mortar and pestle or by crushing with a glass or iron rolling pin on a glass plate.

2. Grinding

Grinding is important for sample preparation prior to analysis and for food ingredient processing. Various mills are available for reducing particle size to achieve sample homogenization. To homogenize moist samples, bowls cutters, meat mincers, tissue grinders, mortars and pestles, or blenders are used, while mortars and pestles and mills are best for dry samples. Some foods are more easily ground after drying in a desiccator or vacuum oven. Grinding wet samples may cause significant losses of moisture and chemical changes. In contrast, grinding frozen samples reduces undesirable changes. The grinding process should not heat the samples, and therefore the grinder should not be overloaded because heat will be produced through friction. Contact of food with bare metal surfaces should be avoided if trace metal analysis is to be performed.

To break up moist tissues, a number of slicing devices are available; bowl cutters can be used for fleshy tubers and leafy vegetables while meat mincers may be used for fruit, root and meat. Addition of sand as an abrasive can provide further subdivision of moist foods. Blenders are effective in grinding soft and flexible foods and suspensions. Rotating knives (25,000 rpm) will disintegrate a sample in suspension. In colloidal mills, a dilute suspension is flowed under pressure through a gap between slightly serrated or smooth surfaced blades until they are disintegrated by shear. Sonic and supersonic vibrations disperse foods in suspension and in aqueous and pressurized gas solution. The Mickle disintegrator sonically shakes suspensions with glass particles and the sample is homogenized and centrifuged at the same time. Alternatively, a low shear continuous tissue homogenizer is fast and handles large volumes of sample.

Application for Equipment

Mills differ according to their mode of action, being classified as a burr, hammer, impeller, cyclone, impact, centrifugal, or roller mill. Methods for grinding dry materials range from a simple pestle and mortar to power driven hammer mills. Hammer mills effectively grind cereals and dry foods, while small samples can be finely ground by ball mills. A chilled ball mill can be used to grind frozen foods with predrying. Dry materials can be ground using an ultra centrifugal mill by beating, impact and shearing. Large quantities can be ground continuously with a cyclone mill.

Particle Size

Particle size is controlled in certain mills by adjusting the distance between burrs or blades or by screen mesh size (*i.e.*, the number of openings per linear inch of mesh). The final particles of dried foods should be 20 mesh for moisture, total protein, or mineral determination. Particles of 40-mesh size are used for extraction assays such as lipid and carbohydrate estimation. In addition to reducing particle size for analysis of samples, it is also important to reduce the particle size of many food ingredients for use in specific food products.

There are a variety of methods for measuring particle size. The simplest way to measure particle sizes >50 µm is by passing the sample through a series of sieves with increasing higher mesh number. The mesh number is the number of square screen openings per linear inch. As the mesh number increases, the apertures between the mesh are smaller and only finer and finer particles pass through subsequent sieves. Sieve sizes have been specified for salt, sugar, wheat flour, corn meal, semolina and cocoa. However, this method only provides an approximation of particle sizes. To obtain more accurate size data for smaller particles (<50 µm), characteristics that correlate to size are measured, and thus size is measured indirectly. Surface area and zeta potential (electrical charge on a particle) are characteristics that are commonly used. Optical and electron microscopes are routinely used to measure particle size. The most widely used technique for particle analysis is dynamic light scattering. These instruments determine particle size and even the molecular weight of large molecules in solution. This is achieved by measurement of frequency shifts of light scattered by particles due to Brownian motion. This method can be used for particles as small as a few nanometers in diameter. Particle size measurement is useful to maintain sample quality but care must be taken in choosing an appropriate method and interpreting the data.

3. Enzymatic Inactivation

Food materials often contain enzymes that may degrade the food components being analyzed. Enzyme activity therefore must be eliminated or controlled using methods that depend on the nature of the food. Heat denaturation to inactivate enzymes and freezer storage (-20°C to -30°C) for limiting enzyme activity are common methods. However, some enzymes are more effectively controlled by changing the pH, or by salting out. Oxidative enzymes may be controlled by adding reducing agents.

4. Lipid Oxidation Protection

Lipids present particular problems in sample preparation. High fat foods are difficult to grind and may need to be ground while frozen. Unsaturated lipids are sensitive to oxidative degradation and should be protected by storing under nitrogen or vacuum. Antioxidants may stabilize lipids and may be used if they do not interfere with the analysis. Light-initiated photo-oxidation of unsaturated lipids can be avoided by controlling storage conditions. In practice, lipids are more stable when frozen in intact tissues rather than as extracts. Therefore, ideally, unsaturated lipids should be extracted just prior to analysis. Low-temperature storage is generally recommended to protect most foods.

5. Microbial Growth and Contamination

Microorganisms are present in almost all foods and can alter the sample composition. Likewise, microorganisms are present on all but sterilized surfaces, so sample cross-contamination can occur if samples are not handled carefully. The former is always a problem and the latter is particularly important in samples for microbiological examination. Freezing, drying, and chemical preservatives are effective controls and often a combination of these is used. The preservation methods used are determined by the probability of contamination, the storage conditions, storage time, and the analysis to be performed.

Chapter 2
Solvent Extraction

Aqueous Samples

Aqueous samples are available from a number of sources. Industrial plant operations may yield such products. Carbonated beverages, fruit juices, and caffeinated beverages can often be extracted directly. Fruits and vegetables can be homogenized with water, treated with a pectinase enzyme to destroy the pectins, and filtered through a bed of diatomaceous earth to remove particulates.

When relatively large amounts of aqueous samples are available, then separatory funnels or commercial liquid-liquid extractors may be employed. A large number of solvents have been summarized by Weurman and reviewed by Teranishi *et al.*

The solvents most commonly used today are diethyl ether, diethyl ether/pentane mixtures, hydrocarbons, freons, and methylene chloride. The latter two have the advantage of being nonflammable. Solvent selection is an important factor to consider, and the current status has been summarized by Leahy and Reineccius. In general, the following suggestions can be made. Nonpolar solvents such as freons and hydrocarbons should be used when the sample contains alcohol. Diethyl ether and methylene chloride are good general purpose solvents. Ether can form explosive peroxides, and for that reason contains inhibitors (*e.g.*, BHT), which will show up in gas chromatography/mass spectroscopy (GC/MS) analysis. It has been found that methylene chloride is a satisfactory general purpose solvent, particularly for flavor compounds with an enolone structure (*e.g.*, Maltol and Furaneol). It is somewhat toxic and is an animal carcinogen. To aid in extraction, sodium chloride may be added to the aqueous phase to salt out the organics when low-density solvents are employed.

If the sample contains any particulates, it should be filtered. A convenient way to filter samples is through a syringe filter (*e.g.*, Gelman Sciences, Ann Arbor, Mich.) of the type recommended for HPLC sample preparation. These filters have a pore size of 0.45 μm and are solvent resistant. Microtypes with low solvent hold-up are available.

Continuous extractors have been described in the literature for solvents more dense and less dense than water and are available commercially (*e.g.*, ACE Glass, Vineland, NJ; Supelco, Inc, Bellefonte, Pa) for $200–600. These are a pleasure to use (providing there is no solvent loss and that emulsions don't occur) since they will operate relatively unattended. They are normally operated for 2–4 hours, but may be operated overnight.

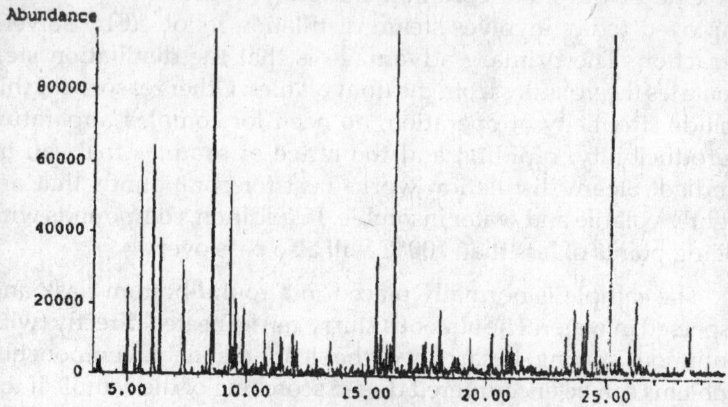

Figure 2.1: Total Ion Chromatogram (TIC) of Brewed R&G Coffee Extracted with Methylene Chloride

Liquid carbon dioxide was recommended as an extraction solvent as early as 1970. It has the advantages of being nontoxic and inexpensive. Liquid carbon dioxide is reported to have solvent properties similar to diethyl ether and to be particularly selective for esters, aldehydes, ketones, and alcohols. If water is present, it will be removed also.

A commercial liquid carbon dioxide Soxhlet extractor is commercially available. The vessel holds a sample of 2.5 g. This apparatus seems to have achieved only limited use, perhaps because of its cost ($1500 plus accessories) and limited sample size. Moyler discussed a commercial liquid carbon dioxide system and reported such extracts to be more concentrated than the steam distillates or solvent extracts. More important, he reported that the character was "finer."

Supercritical carbon dioxide has been employed recently as an extraction solvent. When using supercritical carbon dioxide, it is necessary to balance temperature, pressure, and flow rate, which requires complex instrumentation. Several instrument vendors produce supercritical fluid extractors in the price range of $25,000–90,000. Again, sample capacity is relatively limited.

The Steam Distillation of Samples

One of the most common sample-preparation techniques employed today involves steam distillation followed by solvent extraction. The primary advantage is that the distillation step separates the volatiles from the nonvolatiles. Other reasons for this include simplicity of operation, no need for complex apparatus, reproducibility, rapidity, and the range of samples that can be handled. Steam distillation works best for compounds that are slightly volatile and water insoluble. In addition, compounds with boiling points of less than 100°C will also pass over.

The sample is normally placed in a round-bottom flask and dispersed in water. The aqueous slurry can be heated directly (with continuous stirring) to carry over the steam-distillable components. Problems can be encountered due to scorching of the sample if too much heat is applied, and in addition bumping may occur when the sample contains particulates. Stirring may prevent these problems. Foaming is another potential problem. Many food products contain surface-active agents and will foam during distillation; addition of anti foams (*e.g.*, DC polydimethyl siloxanes) may prevent this problem, but these silicones usually end up in the distillate.

Indirect Steam Distillation

Indirect steam distillation has many advantages over the direct technique. It is more rapid and less decomposition of the sample occurs since the sample is not heated directly. The steam may be generated in an external electrically heated steam generator or in a round-bottom flask heated by a mantle. It is even possible to use laboratory house steam, in which case the steam must be passed through a trap that allows removal of condensate and any particulates that may come out of the line. It is imperative that blank samples be run, since house steam may be highly contaminated. Even so, this technique has the great advantage of being rapid and easy. The steam and volatiles are usually condensed in a series of traps cooled with a succession of coolants ranging from ice water to dry ice/acetone or methanol.

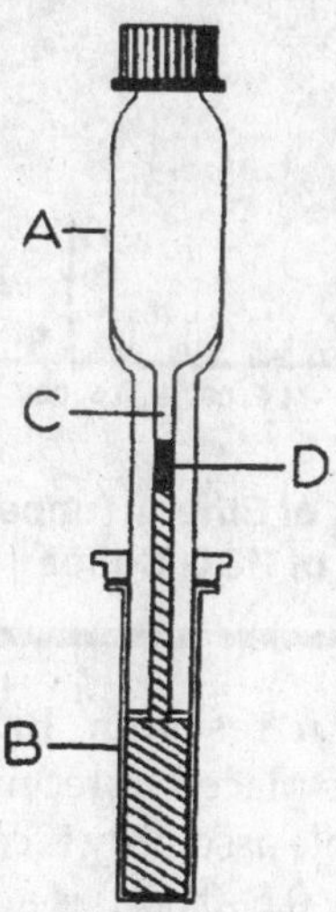

Figure 2.2: Mixor Apparatus for the Extraction of Aqueous Samples

If sample decomposition remains a concern, then the steam distillation may be operated under vacuum. In this case inert gas should be bled into the system to aid in agitation. A number of cooled traps should be in line to protect the pump from water vapor and the sample from pump oil vapors. Another simple method to generate; a condensate under vacuum is by use of a rotary evaporator. Bumping is normally not a problem in this case. The higher-boiling components do not distill as efficiently as they do under atmospheric pressure.

Use of Mixor has been described by Parliment and its utility described in a number of publications. These extractors are available with sample volumes ranging from 2 ml to 100ml. The 10-ml capacity extractor is

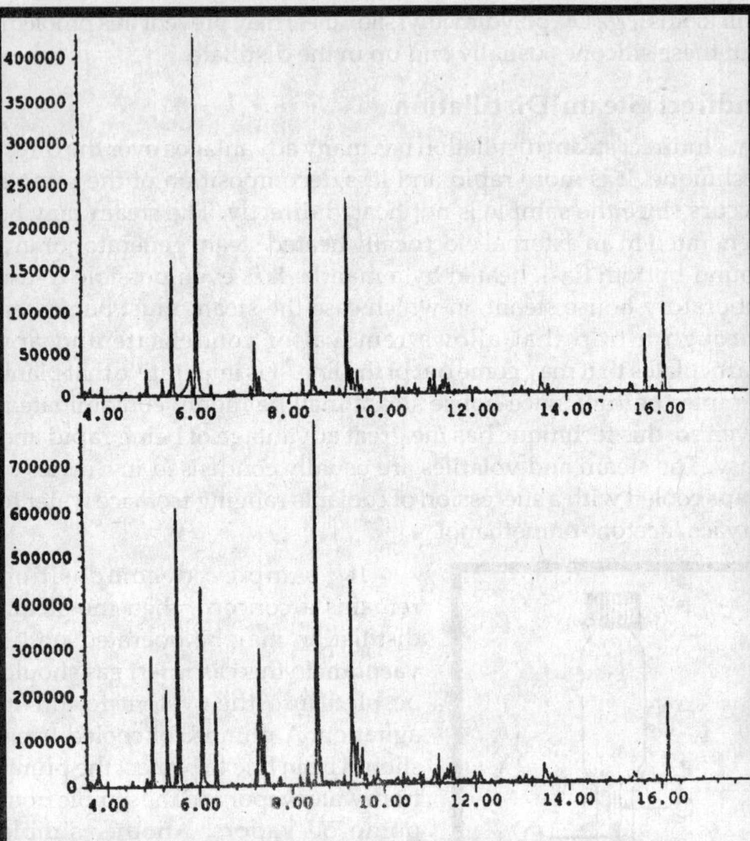

Figure 2.3: Comparison of Chromatograms of Etheral (upper) and Methylene Chloride (lower) Extract of R&G Coffee

particularly convenient capacity for flavour research. Briefly, approximately 8 ml of aqueous condensate is placed in receiver B and saturated with sodium chloride. The whole assembly is cooled and then a quantity of diethyl ether (typically 0.5–0.8ml) is added. The ether may contain an internal standard. The system is extracted by moving chamber A up and down a number of times. After phase separation occurs, the solvent D is forced into an axial chamber C, where it can be removed with a syringe for analysis. Percent recoveries for a series of ethyl esters from an aqueous solution are essentially quantitative even at the sub-ppm level.

A less sophisticated alternative also exists. The sample may be placed in a screw-capped centrifuge tube and a small amount of dense solvent added. After exhaustive shaking, the tube can be centrifuged to break the emulsion and separate the layers. The organic phase can be sampled from the bottom of the tube with a syringe. Methylene chloride works well in this application.

Roasted and ground coffee was indirectly steam distilled at atmospheric pressure and a condensate collected. The upper curve in the figure represents the ethereal concentrate prepared via the Mixor technique; the lower curve is the methylene chloride extract. Pattern differences are apparent. The largest peak in the ethereal extract (Rt = 6.0) is furfuryl alcohol; the largest peak in the lower curve (Rt = 8,5) is 5-methyl furfural.

Simultaneous Steam Distillation

One of the most popular and valuable techniques in the flavor analysis field is the simultaneous steam distillation/extraction (SDE) apparatus first described by Likens and Nickerson. The apparatus provides for the simultaneous condensation of the steam distillate and an immiscible organic solvent. Both liquids are continuously recycled, and thus the steam distillable-solvent soluble compounds are transferred from the aqueous phase to the solvent. The advantages of this system include the following:

1. A single operation removes the volatile aromas and concentrates them.
2. A small volume of solvent is required, reducing problems of artifact buildup as solvents are concentrated.
3. Recoveries of aroma compounds are generally high.
4. The system may be operated under reduced pressure to reduce thermal decomposition.

The sample flask has a 500 ml to 5 liter capacity and contains the sample dissolved or dispersed in water so that the flask is less than half filled. Agitation is advisable if suspended materials are present to prevent bumping. As with all distillations, the pH of the sample should be recorded (and adjusted if necessary) prior to distillation. Heat may be supplied by a heating mantle or (better if solids are present) a heated oil bath with stirrer. The solvent is normally contained in a pear-shaped flask of 10–50ml capacity.

Many solvents have been employed. In one model system study, Schultz *et al.* compared various solvents as the extractant. They reported that hexane was an excellent solvent except for lower-boiling water-soluble compounds, where diethyl ether was considerabiy better. Use of methylene chloride has been recommended in a modified Likens-Nickerson extractor. Currently, most researchers appear to be using pentane-diethyl ether mixtures.

Regardless of which solvents are used, boiling chips should be added to both flasks to ensure smooth boiling. The distillation is generally performed for 1–3 hours. After the distillation is completed, the system is cooled and the solvent from the central extraction U tube is combined with that of the solvent flask. The solvent is dried over an agent such as sodium sulfate and the concentrated by slow distillation.

An impressive sample of the use of a Likens-Nikerson extractor is shown in Figure 2.4. This figure shows the gas chromatogram of a green and a roasted Kenyan coffee and shows how aromatic compounds are generated in the roasting process.

Vacuum versions of the SDE system have been described. These have the advantage of reducing the thermal composition of the analyte. Leahy and Reineccius report that vacuum operation had a slightly negative effect upon recovery compared to atmospheric operation. Experience of some scientists is that operation under vacuum is quite complex since one must balance the boiling of two flasks, keep the solvent from evaporating, and hold the pressure constant.

Distillation of Lipids

The lipid material may be steam distilled at atmospheric pressure or under vacuum, and subsequently subjected to solvent extraction. Alternatively, a modified Likens-Nickerson extractor has been described, which permits the introduction of steam into the system. Recoveries of model compounds from lipid systems were not as satisfactory as for aqueous samples.

When large amounts of lipid materials are present, the sample may be subjected to a falling film molecular still. The apparatus utilizes the principle of vaporization of the flavor from a heated thin film of the oil under high vacuum. One such apparatus is shown in Figure 2.5. Several hundred milliliters of oil are placed in vessel A

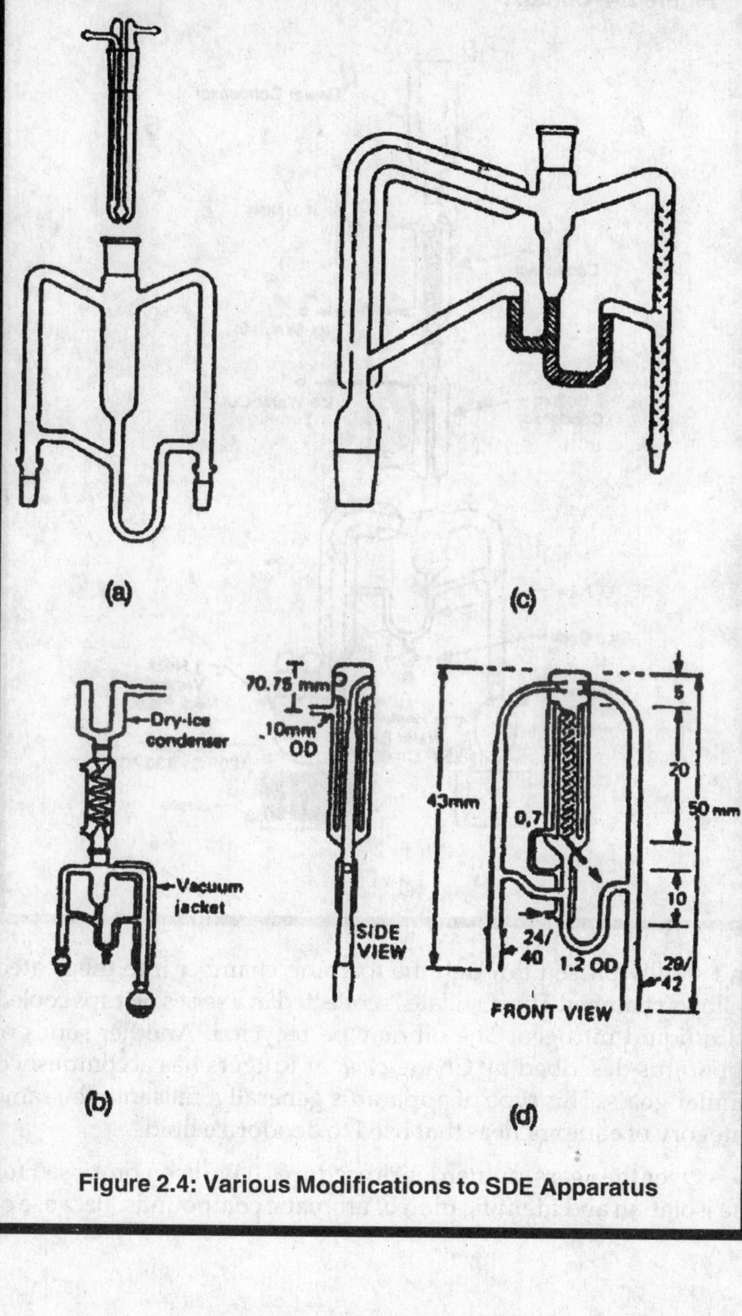

Figure 2.4: Various Modifications to SDE Apparatus

Figure 2.4–Contd...

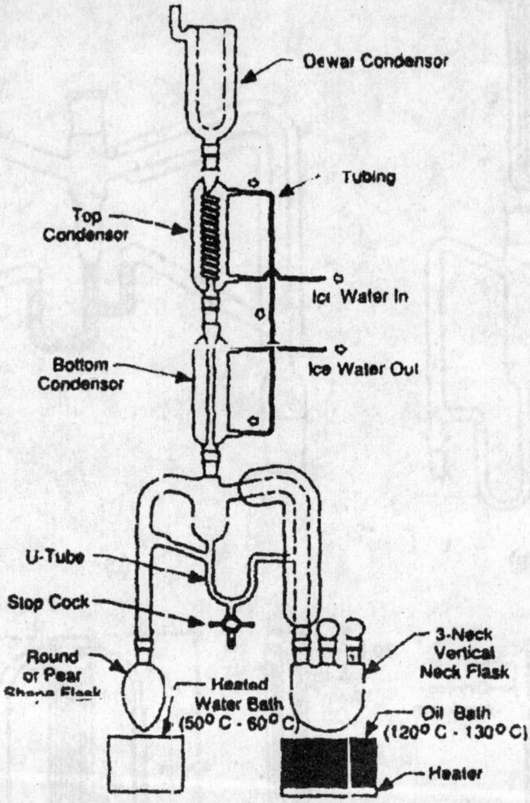

(e)

and slowly passed through the foaming chamber into the heated bellows chamber. The distillate is collected in a series of traps cooled with liquid nitrogen. The oil may be recycled. Another series of apparatus described by Chang *et al.* at Rutgers has accomplished similar goals. This type of apparatus generally, falls into the same category of equipment as that used to deodorize lipids.

Over the years, numerous procedures have been proposed for the isolation and identification of aromatic compounds. Because of

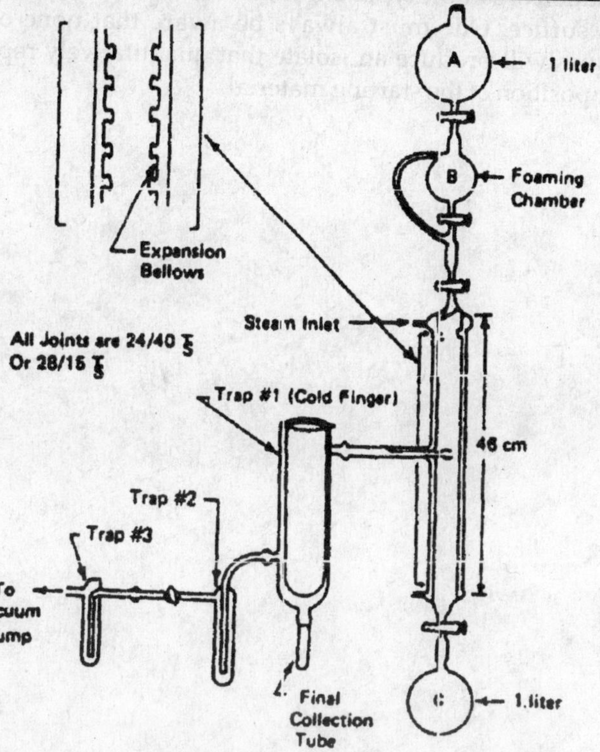

Figure 2.5: Falling Film Molecular Still for the Removal of Volatile from Lipids

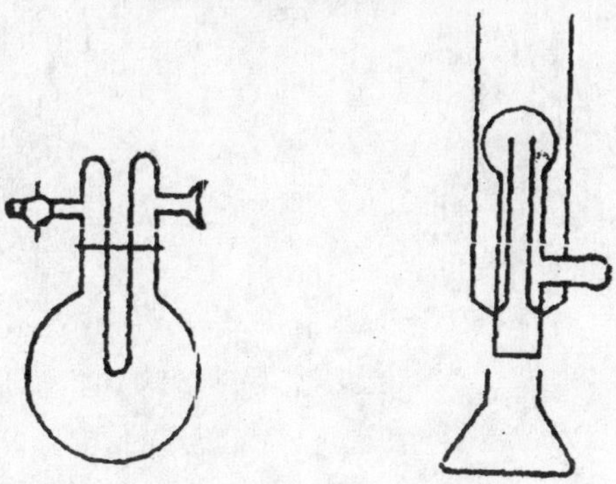

Figure 2.6: Apparatus for the Removal of Aromatics from Lipids

the variation of sample types encountered, no single technique will always suffice. One must always be aware that none of these techniques will produce an isolate that quantitatively represents the composition of the starting material.

Chapter 3

Basic Anatomy of Olfaction

Introduction

Each individual has a unique, genetically determined scent. This olfactory identity is coupled with a remarkable ability to distinguish thousands of odours. The basic anatomy of olfaction has been understood for long time. In mammals, an odour is first detected in the upper region of the nose at the olfactory epithelium. In this region, millions of neurons (signalling cells) provide a direct physical connection between the external world and the brain. From one end of each neuron, cilia (hairlike sensors) extend outward into the nasal cavity. As part of the cilia, receptors can bind odorants. At the other end of the neuron cell, an axon (fiber) runs into the olfactory bulb in the brain. In the bulb (the connection of nose and brain), axons converge at the glomeruli; from there signals are relayed to other regions of the brain, including the olfactory cortex, which then projects to higher sensory centers in the cerebral cortex, the area of the brain that controls thoughts and behaviours.

When an odour interacts with an olfactory receptor, signalling proteins (G proteins) are activated to initiate a cascade of events resulting in the transmission on an electrical impulse along the olfactory sensory axon. Around 1000 different receptors are encoded by 1000 different genes. This means that nearly 1 per cent of all genes are devoted to the detection of odours, making this the largest gene family thus far identified in mammals. At least 10,000 odours can be detected; consequently, each of the 1000 different receptors must respond to several odour molecules, and each odour must bind to several receptors. It is believed that various receptors respond to discrete parts of an odorant's structure and that an odorant consists of several functional groups each of which activates a characteristic receptor. To distinguish the smell, the brain must then determine the precise combination of receptors activated by a particular odorant. Theoretically, mammals should be able to detect an extraordinarily large number of odors. Because odors interact with multiple receptors rather than with individual ones, the possible combinations exceed by several orders of magnitude the number of odors that animals can actually detect. The remaining question–how the olfactory cortex is decoding the signals provided by the olfactory bulb-is one of the central and most elusive problems in neurobiology.

Sensorily active compounds have to fulfill several molecular and physical prerequisites to initialize an olfactory receptor signal:

1. A certain vapor pressure for the ability to reach the olfactory epithelium
2. A minimal solubility in water to penetrate the aqueous layer of the membrane as well as low polarity (surface-active properties; highly polar compounds odourless)
3. A lipophilic behaviour to penetrate the fatty layer of the neuronal cells
4. A molecular weight that is not too high (the highest molecular weight of an odorant is 294)

However, several organic compounds that exhibit all of these properties still do not initialize any olfactory impression. For instance, vanillin has a sweet-floral flavour; its isomer isovanillin, differing only in the spatial arrangement of the same substituents, does not smell. A weakly polar region and a strongly hydrophobic region in the molecule, associated with a certain molecular shape, are most probably the minimum requirements of sensory activity.

Today, we witness an intense era of molecular biology research in various fields, including receptor ligand interaction and signal transmission. It is important to keep this perspective while looking back to the more or less empirical models of olfaction established in the past. On the other hand, we should not forget that only the signalling process via G proteins is relatively well known, whereas the mechanisms of recognition of an odorant by one or several receptors are still not fully elucidated.

The very first olfactory theory is more than 2000 years old. The Roman doctor Galenus discovered the olfactory nerves, and the Roman poet and philosopher Titus Lucretius Carus described various odorants. According to Carus's theory, pleasant odorants had a spherical shape, whereas slinking substances were acute and prickly particles; an olfactory sensation would need molecules that are able to pass through a slot of the complementary sensory organ.

More than 20 different theories have since been developed. Some of these are clearly not valid, such as the penetration and puncturing theory of Davies, the chromatographic theory, and the information theory. Other hypotheses, created for an empirical description of the olfactory system of insects, cannot be transferred from the pheromone field to olfaction by mammals. Only receptor-related theories may be complementarily used in different fields of research.

The vibrational theory of Wright is based on the assumption that a certain odor is recognized as such by distinct molecular vibrations in the frequency range of 50–400 cm^{-1} (infrared range), the olfactory cell being stimulated by a synchronous "throbbing" of the odorous molecule and the receptor site. For example, compounds having a musky smell were related to four characteristic bands of absorbance frequency. To overcome the apparent short-coming in explaining odor differences of mirror image isomers (in the following called "enantiomers"), Wright suggested that enantiomeric molecules have the same vibrational frequencies only if they are not perturbed by an external agency and that such a perturbation could arise from a close approach of a stimulus molecule to a chiral receptor site. This idea is inspired by Hayward's theory of dispersion-induced optical activity in olfaction.

The principle "similar profile, similar odor" stands behind the profile functional group theory established by Beets. Here the functional group with the highest tendency to interact with a receptor site would orient itself towards the receptor, similarities in the profile of the rest of the odorous molecule, thus determining similarities in odor; specialised receptors do not occur in this picture.

Following the principles established for substrate recognition by enzymes, Amoore developed his stereochemical theory. He suggested complementary acceptor sites ("pits" and "sockets") for particularly shaped regions of odorant molecules. Five "primary odors" (camphoraceous, musty, minty, floral, ethereal) could be associated with five groups of compounds classified on the basis of their molecular shape and dimensions, while functional groups were not taken into consideration. For mixed odours, the odorant would fit into two or more different types of receptors. A modified theory presumes that olfactory substances supposed to cause an "anosmic defect" would interact with specific receptor sites and thus, produce the primary odors.

Randebrock postulated a molecular theory based on the assumption that the odorant would specifically interact with an amide group of the α-helix of a receptor protein located in the olfactory cilia. Here, the hydrogen-bonding network constituted by three continuous chains around the α-helix would form a vibrational system that could be thermally excited. These vibrations were influenced by attached odours substances in two directions, longitudinal as well as transversal, depending on two factors: (a) the molecular mass of the odorant and (b) the direction of the interaction.

The Enantiomers of Odorous Compounds

The first hint that enantiomers of odorous compounds might differ in their smell dates back to 1874. The odor of two essential oils containing (+)- and (–)-borneol, respectively, revealed distinct differences, as outlined in Table 3.1. The last decade of the nineteenth century witnessed a general tendency to treat this problem from an increasingly scientific perspective.

A major shortcoming of the early research in this discipline was the lack of good qualitative and quantitative criteria. In 1925, Richter attempted to improve this situation by introducing a terminology suited to describe differences in odor. One year later, von Braun and Haensel criticised earlier reports in as much as these had erroneously compared a single enantiomer with the racemate instead of with the antipode. Moreover, it is desirable to have the two enantiomers isolated from the same source, although this is normally not easily accomplished. In the absence of the sharp analytical tools available today (as compared with polarimetric measurements), many of the results reported up to the 1960s suffer from possible interference of odorous impurities with the odor of the test compounds. In some cases, the researchers failed to consider all possible stereoisomers. Another group of molecules investigated does not smell because of the high molecular weight of over 400 far beyond the aforementioned limit of 294.

A prominent compound listed in Table 3.1 is α-ionone. The ample difference in optical rotations reported for the enantiomers (+348° and –406°, respectively) leaves enough room for impurities that supposedly alter the respective original odors of the two enantiomers. Some years later, α-ionone was tested again, but with optically purer antipodes (–401° and –408°, respectively). However, the intriguing observation that the racemate smells more intensely than either of the single enantiomers could be an artifact. There is only one other example (E-α-irone) known where a racemate smells more intensely than the single enantiomers.

Another dubious report deals with 2-phenyl-4-pentenoic acid. It appears improbable that only the racemic mixture has a smell, while the single enantiomers are practically odorless. Provided that these observations are correct, Beets assumes that the two antipodes present in the racemate might interact in a synergistic way with more than one receptor at the same time.

In 1961 and 1962 compounds of high but opposite enantiomeric purity were synthesized from the same source (citronellol from (+)- and (–)-pinane, linalool from (+)- and (–)-α-pinene) for the first time.

In several examples the odours of enantiomers differ not only qualitatively, but also quantitatively. Moreover, some optically active flavor compounds exhibit differences only in threshold concentrations. Some of these show remarkable differences, such as nootkatone, the flavor impact of grapefruit (a sesquiterpenoic ketone): the threshold of the natural enantiomer is 2000 times lower. The enantiomers of a decalin derivative were found to differ at least 10,000 times in the threshold.

Table 3.1: Historical Overview of Reported Enantiospecific Odor Differences

Compound	*Odor Description*	*Year*
 Camphor	No odor differences found	1863
 Borneol	Borneocamphor oil [contains (+)-borneol] and nagicamphor oil [contains (–)-borneol] were found to smell differently. The odor of the first is weak camphor like and unpleasant peppery; the odor of the latter is camphor and turpentinelike. Possibly the first indication of odor differences of enuntiomers.	1874
 Homolinalool	Active is more intensive than racemate	1896
 Citronellal	(S)-(–) somewhat sweater than (R)-(+). According to von Braun and Kaiser, possible isopulegol traces.	1897
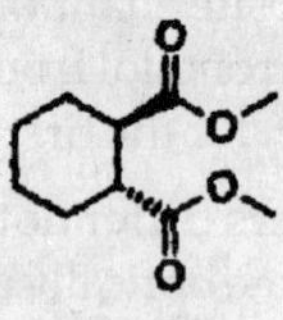 Dimethyl E-hexahydrophthalate	(–) rather strong, but (+) nearly odorless. No odor differences found by Posvic. According to von Braun and Kaiser, insufficient purification of the enantiomers.	1899

Contd...

Table 3.1–Contd...

Compound	*Odor Description*	*Year*
 Limonene	(+) isolated from caraway oil smells different than that synthesized from tetrabromide. Doubtful literature source.	1899
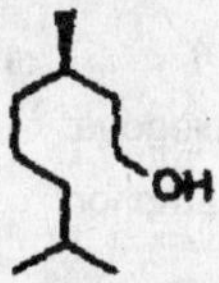 3,7-Dimethyloctanol	(+) fresher and more penetrating than racemate	1923
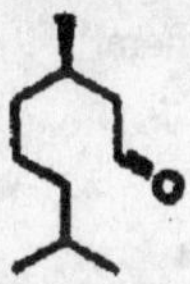 3,7-Dimethyloctanal	Racemate is similar to citronellal, with lemon note, more pleasant and more penetrating than (+). (+) is similar to citral, with lemon note.	1923
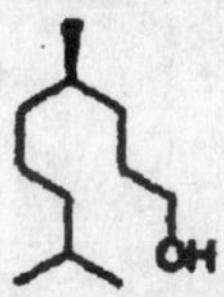 4,8-Dimenthylnonanol	Racemate is more intensive and harsher than (+).	1923
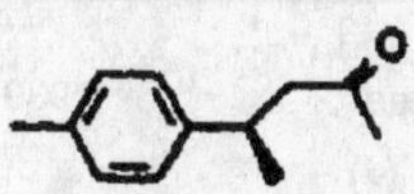 Curcumone	Racemate: strong curcuma-flavour, weaker and finer (sweeter) than active. Active: strong curcuma-flavour, more herblike and less pleasant than racemate.	1924
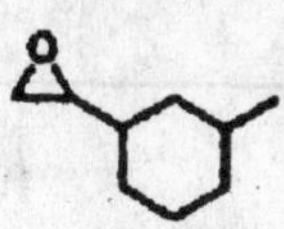 1-(1,2-Epoxyethyl)-3-methylcyclohexane	Racemate: more intensive and more pungent note than (–). (–) milder than racemate. Possible diastereomers might not be taken into account.	1925

Contd...

Table 3.1–Contd...

Compound	*Odor Description*	*Year*
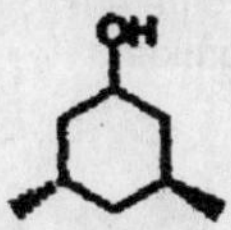 3,5-Dimethylcyclohexanol	(+) fresher, more powerful. (–) milder, heavier. Synthesized from E-3,5-dimethylcyclohexanone.	1927
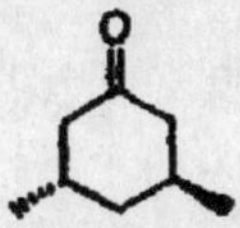 E-3,5-Dimethyl cyclohexanone	(+) minty, ester-like (amyl ester note). (–) minty, faintly reminiscent of isopulegone. Diastereomeric (Z) reminiscent of camphor and thujone.	1927
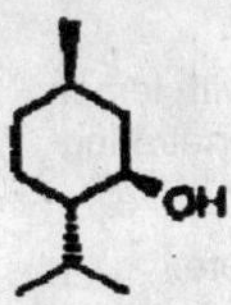 Menthol	(+) is fainter than (–), but of same general character.	1931
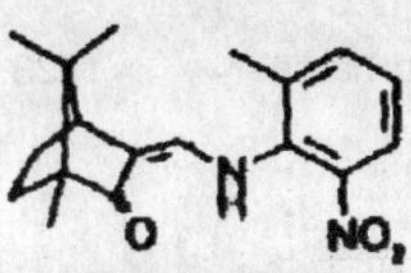 3-Nitro-o-toluidino methylenecamphor	(–) more intensive than racemate. Racemate more intensive than (+)	1939
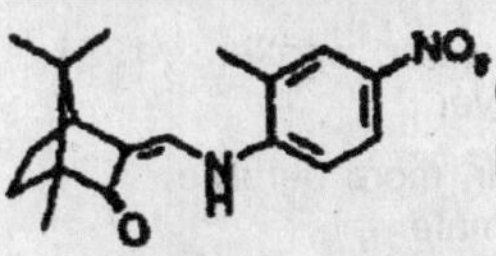 5-Nitro-o-toluidino methylenecamphor	(–) more intensive than racemate. Racemate more intensive than (+)	1939
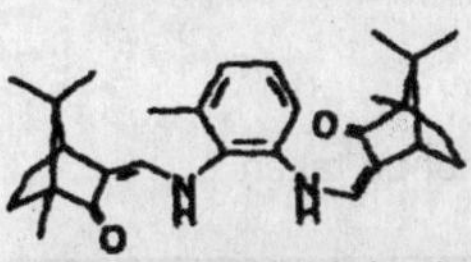 2,3-Toluylene bis(amino methylenecamphor)	(–) more intensive than racemate. Racemate more intensive than (+). Possible formation of diastereomers might not be taken into account, since two molecules of camphor were bound.	1939

Contd...

Table 3.1–Contd...

Compound	*Odor Description*	*Year*
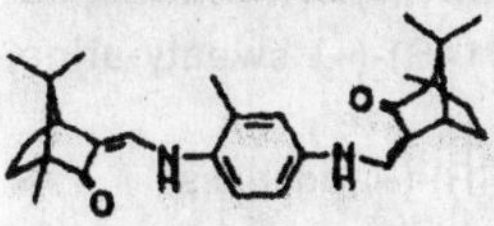 2,5-Toluylene bis(amino methylenecamphor)	(–) more intensive than racemate, racemate more intensive than (+). Possible formation of diastereomers might not be taken into account, since two molecules of camphor were bound.	1939
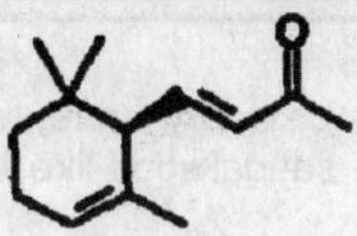 α-Ionone	Distinct odor difference between (+) and (–). Active weaker (0.002–0.008 μg/litre air) racemate more intensive (0.00025–0.0005 μg/litre air).	1943 1947
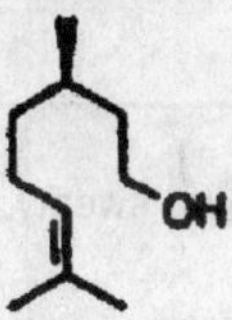 Citronellal	No odor differences found between the single enantiomers. Racemate is less pleasant and less "expensive" than the single enantiomers.	1946
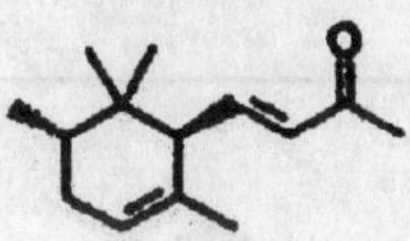 E-α-Irone	Racemate is more intensive than active.	1953
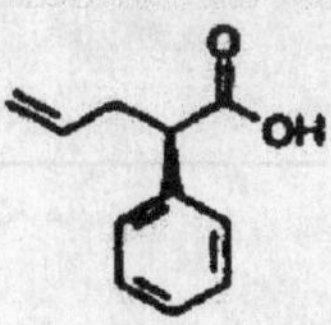 2-Phenyl-4-pentenoic acid	(+) practically odorless. (–) practically odorless. Racemate clear honey type odor. It is rather improbable that only the racemic mixture is odorous.	1961

Unfortunately, threshold values often cannot be compared due to different measurement conditions. Some researchers had reported only relative odor intensities or sniffing GC results, others used different solvents such as buffers. Therefore, standardization and harmonization of human olfactory thresholds is absolutely necessary for a better comparison of the reported data. Such

Table 3.2: Maximum Qualitative Odour Differences

Compound	*Odor Description*
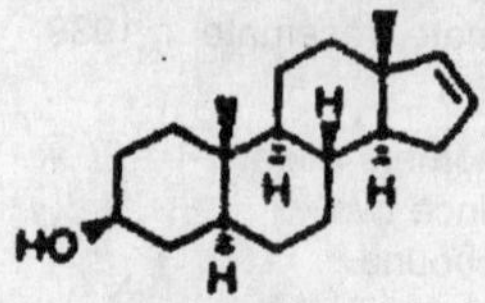 5α-Androst-16-en-3β-ol	(3S,5S,8S,9S,10R,13R,14S)-(+) sweaty-urine, very weak (3R,5R,8R,9R,10S,13S,14R)-(–) odorless
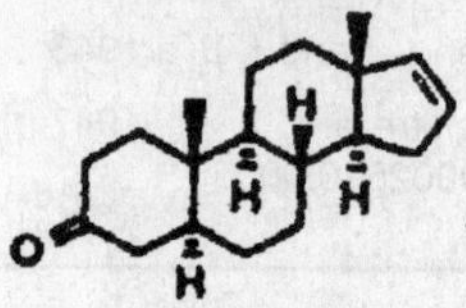 5α-Androst-16-en-3-one	(5S,8S,9S,10R,13R,14S)-(+) sweaty-urine, weak muscone-type odor with a sandalwood-like basic note (5R,8R,9R,10S,13S,14R)-(–) odorless
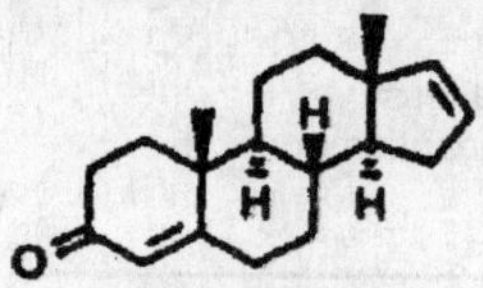 Androsta-4,16-dien-3-one	(8S,9S,10R,13R,14S)-(+) urinous, sweaty, woody, musk (8R,9R,10S,13S,14R)-(–) odorless
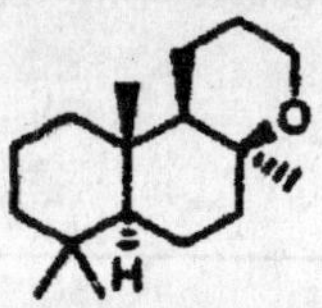 8,13-Epoxy-14,15,16-trinorlabdane	(5S,8S,9R,10S)-(+) odorless (5R,8R,9S,10R)-(–) musty menthol-like odor, woody-balsamic note, camphoraceous, fruity, odor is distinct from ambergris
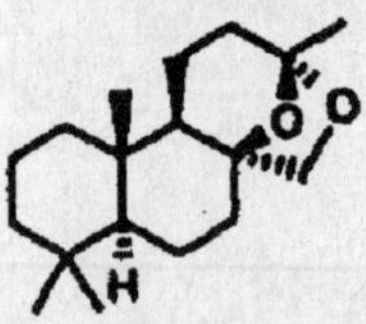 8,13:13,20-Diepoxy-14,15-dinorlabdane	(5S,8R,9R,10S,13R)-(–) odorless (5R,8S,9S,10R,13S)-(+) woody character, ambergris tonality, odor is distinct from ambergris
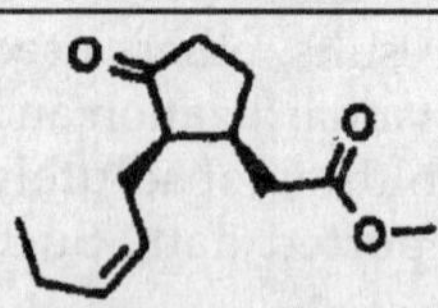 Methyl Z-epijasmonate	(IR,2S)-(+) strong jasmine odor (1S,2R)-(–) odorless

compilations already exist, but only very few chiral compounds are listed. There is still a need for systematic investigations to overcome these problems.

It is a well-known fact that the sense of smell in dogs is much more sensitive than that in humans, but one should not forget that this phenomenon is strongly dependent on the particular odorant. For instance, the dog's threshold for butyric acid is one million times lower than that of humans, but for a typical flavor compound such as α-ionone, a difference of only 2500 times was reported. This indicates that in some cases, human olfactory receptors are more specialised to specific compounds than to standard compounds such as butyric acid; in other words, some molecules interact more intensely with the receptors than others. In this context, it may be relevant that (R)-(+)-nicotine caused an unpleasant odor sensation to both smokers and nonsmokers, while only smokers perceived the (S)-(–)-enantiomer as pleasant.

Table 3.3: Quantitative Odor Differences of Enantiomers

Compound	*Threshold*
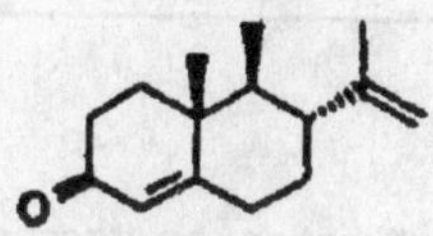 Nootkatone	(4R,5S,7R)-(+) 600–1000 ppb (4S,5R,7S)-(–) 400000–800000 ppb
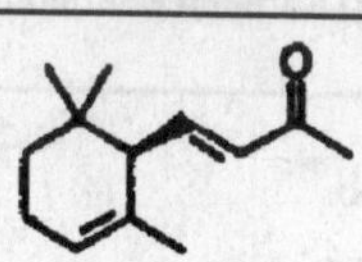 α-Ionone	(R)-(+) 0.5–5 ppb (S)-(–) 20–40 ppb
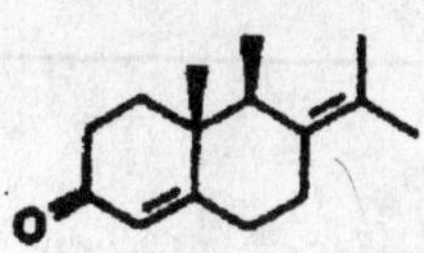 α-Vetivone	(4R,5S)-(+) 600–1000 ppb (4S,5R)-(–) 6000–15000 ppb
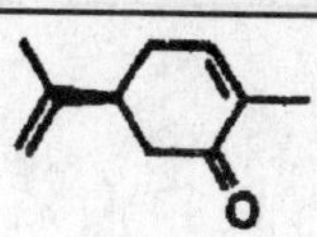 Carvone	(S)-(+) 85–130 ppb (R)-(–) 2 ppb

Contd...

Table 3.3–Contd...

Compound	*Threshold*
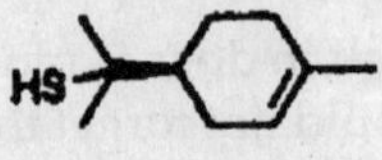 p-l-Menthene-8-thiol	(R)-(+) 0.00002 ppb (S)-(–) 0.00008 ppb
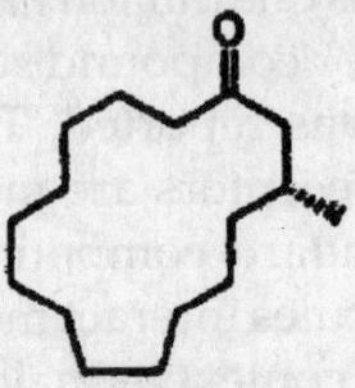 Muscone	(R)-(–) 61 ppb (S)-(+) 233 ppb
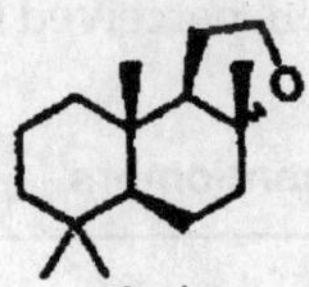 Ambrox	(3aR,5aS,9aS,9bR)-(–) 0.3 ppb (3aS,5aR,9aR,9bS)-(+) 2.4 ppb
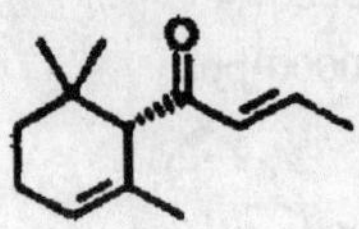 α-Damascone	(S)-(–) 1.5 ppb (R)-(+) 100 ppb In contrast to a prior publication, no threshold difference was found (1 ppb for each enantiomer).
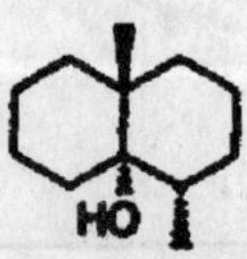 Geosmin	(4R,4aR,8aS)-(+) 0.078 ppb (4S,4aS,8aR)-(–) 0.0095 ppb Mean thresholds of 50 panelists with 6 repetitions each.
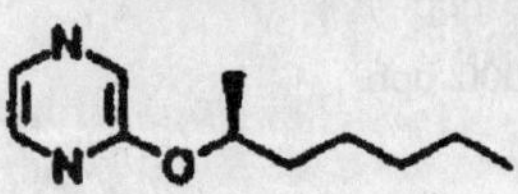 2-(2-Heptoxy)pyrazine	(R)-(+) 200 ppb (S)-(–) 70 ppb
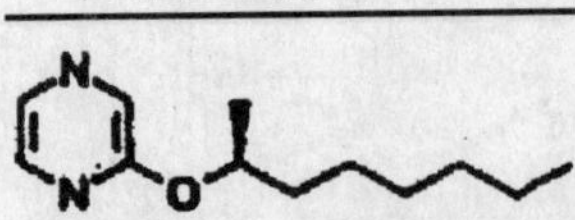 2-(2-Octoxy)pyrazine	(R)-(–) 90 ppb (S)-(+) 30 ppb

Contd...

Table 3.3–Contd...

Compound	*Threshold*
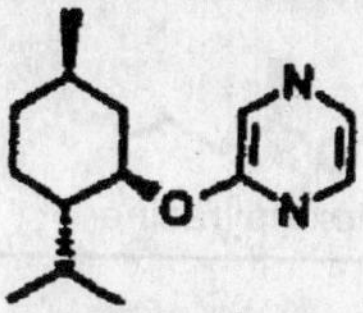 2-Menthoxypyrazine	(1'R,2'S,5'R)-(–)2 ppb (1'S,2'R,5'S)-(+) 10 ppb
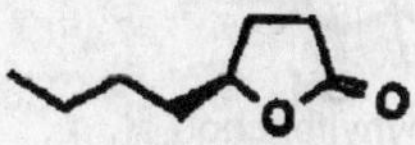 4-Octanolide	(R)-(+) 7 ppb (S)-(–) 1 ppb
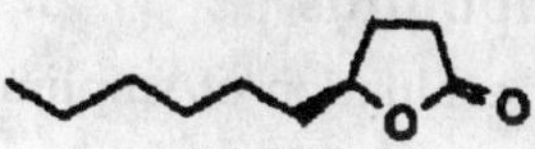 4-Decanolide	(R)-(+) 1.5 ppb (S)-(–) 5.6 ppb

Table 3.4: Compounds Exhibiting No Enantiospecific Odor Differences

Compound	*Compound*
 Camphor	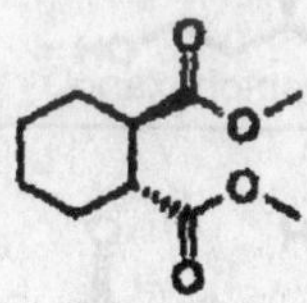 Dimethyl E-hexahydrophthalate
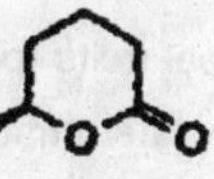 5-Hexanolide	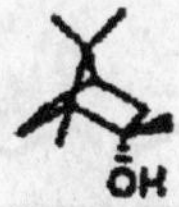 2-Methylborneol
 2-Methylisoborneol	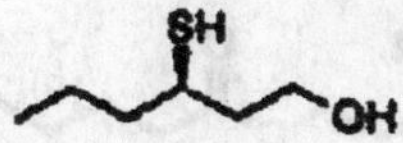 3-Mercaptohexanol

Contd...

Table 3..4–Contd...

Compound	*Compound*
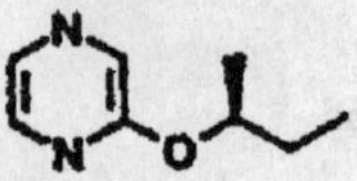 2-(2-Butoxy)pyrazine	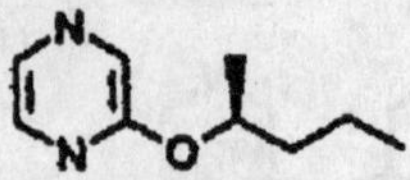 2-(2-Pentoxy)pyrazine
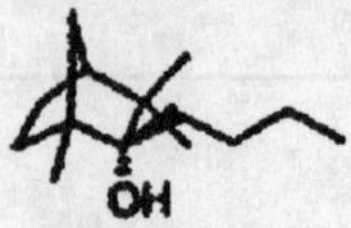 2-Butylfenchol	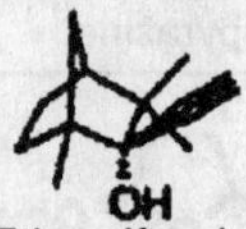 2-Ethynylfenchol

Sulphur-Containing Flavour Compounds

Table 3.5 explains about the sensory evaluation of sulphur-containing flavour compounds.

Table 3.5: Sensory Evaluation of Sulphur-Containing Flavour Compounds

Compound	*Odor Description*
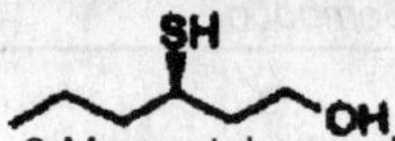 3-Mercaptohexanol	Intensive sulfur-note. No odor differences found
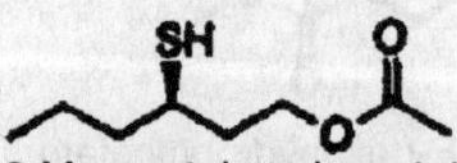 3-Mercaptohexyl acetate	(R) penetrating, reminiscent of tropical fruits (S) penetrating sulfurous, herbaceous
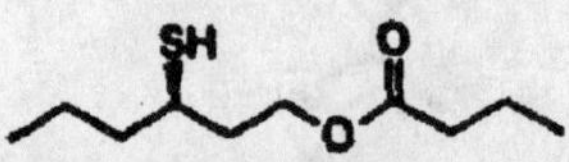 3-Mercaptohexyl butanoate	(R) intensive of tropical fruits (passion fruit) (S) sulfurous, oniony, later unspecific fruity
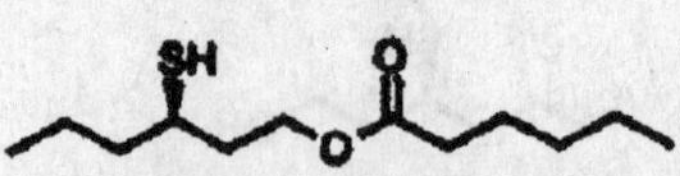 3-Mercaptohexyl hexanoate	(R) herbaceous, fresh sulfur note (S) sulfurous, burnt

Contd...

Table 3.5–Contd...

Compound	*Odor Description*
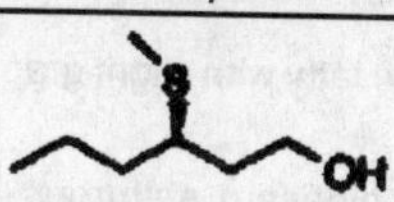 3-Methylthinohexanol	(R) herbaceous, weak (S) exotic, fruity
 3-Methylthiohexyl acetate	(R) fruity (stronger than homolog butanoate and hexanoate) (S) intensive sulfurous, herbaceous
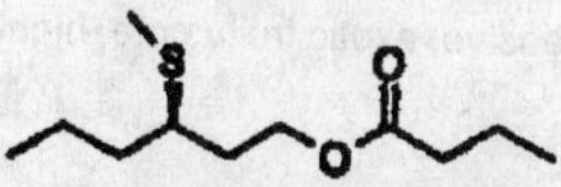 3-Methylthiohexyl butanoate	(R) very weak, unspecific fruity (S) oniony, later weak fruity
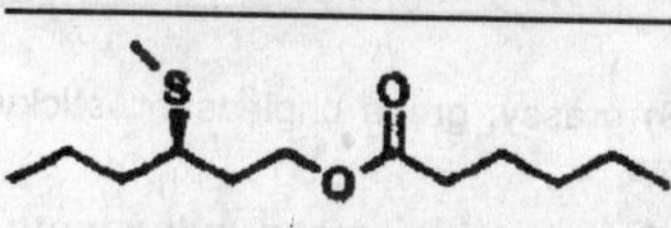 3-Methylthiohexyl hexanoate	(R) very weak, unspecific fruity (S) weak oniony, roasty
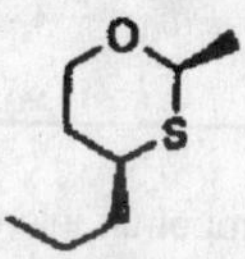 Z-2-Methyl-4-propyl-1,3-oxathiune	(2S,4R) typical sulfurous with rubbery onion note, reminiscent of grapefruit peel, mango, and passion fruit (2R,4S) weaker than the enantiomer, no pronounced sulfur character, possessing a fresh note with more iris character
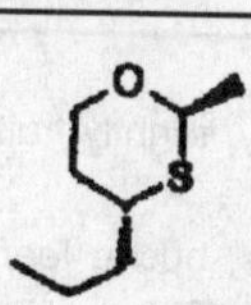 E-2-Methyl-4-propyl-1,3-oxathiane	(2R,4R) green-grass root, earthy red radish note (2S,4S) sulfurous, slightly bloomy-sweet, less intensive than enantiomer
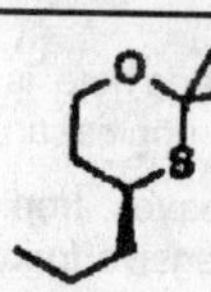 2,2-Dimethyl-4-propyl-1,3-oxathiane	(R) slight, fruity, soft lemon note (S) typical carrot note, sweet

Contd...

Table 3.5–Contd...

Compound	*Odor Description*
 4-Propyl-1,3-oxathiane	(R)-(+) artificial fruity, fatty with slight grapefruit note (S)-(–) artificial, unpleasant sulfurous note, burnt gumlike
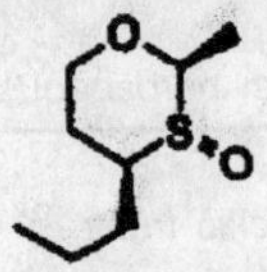 2-Methyl-4-propyl-1,3-oxathiane-S-oxide I	(2R,3R,4S) intensive, pungent green foul sulfur note (H_2S) (2S,3S,4R) intensive, exotic fruity note, highly volatile
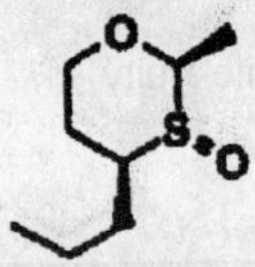 2-Methyl-4-propyl-1,3-oxathiane-5-oxide II	(2R,3S,4S) grassy, green unpleasant, sticky sulfur note (2S,3R,4R) intensive, green sulfur note, reminiscent of fresh rhubarb
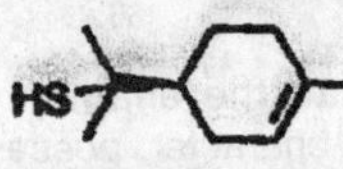 *p*-l-Menthene-8-thiol	(R) pleasant, fresh grapefruit juice (S) extremely obnoxious sulfur note
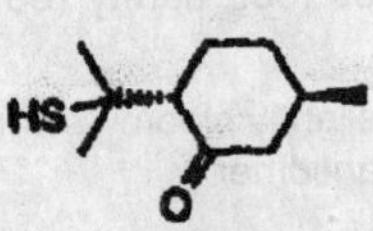 E-Thiomenthone	(1R,4R) oniony, moldy, slightly fruity, tropical fruits (1S,4S) tropical fruits, buchu leaf oil, more intensive than enantiomer
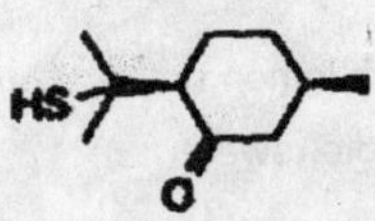 Z-Thiomenthone	(1R,4S) rubber, mercaptane note, is opulegone note, burnt, sulfurous, unpleasant (1S,4R) black currant leaves, tropical note of passion fruit, most intensive fruity note

Contd...

Table 3.5–Contd...

Compound	*Odor Description*
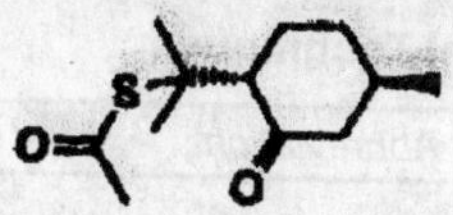 E-Thiomenthone acetate	(1R,4R) musty, sulfury note, intensive (1S,4S) green, black currant, exotic, intensive, and penetrating note
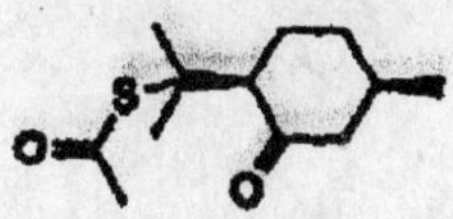 Z-Thiomenthone acetate	(1R,4S) delicate, fruity, sweet (1S,4R) strong, sweet, slightly pungent

The Chiroptical Methods Used in Analytical Chemistry

There are several chiroptical methods used in analytical chemistry, such as polarimetry, circular dichroism (CD), optical rotatory dispersion (ORD), and methods based on vibrational optical activity. In the past, polarimetry was the method of choice for flavour analysis, for single compounds, and for complex mixtures such as essential oils. Polarimetry is still part of routine analysis to determine the optical purity of flavor compounds as well as quality control of flavors and essential oils. Admittedly, polarimetry is a convenient method, but its use is restricted by relatively large sample amounts required for correct measurements. In addition, there are several factors affecting the accuracy of optical rotation determination, such as the temperature applied, the nature and the purity of the solvent used, as well as traces of optically active or inactive impurities originally present in the analyte. More recently, the chiroptical methods have increasingly been supplemented and replaced by chromatographic methods. Since the 1980s, polarimetry and circular dichroism (CD) have also been used as detectors for high-performance liquid chromatography (HPLC) and even for gas chromatography (GC).

NMR performed in an achiral solvent typically does not differentiate between enantiomers; in first order, resonances of enantiotopic nuclei are isochronous. The determination of enantiomeric composition by NMR, therefore, requires one of the three possible methodologies (CDAs, CLSRs, or CSAs). These are widely used in research, albeit less in routine analysis, of flavors.

Table 3.6: Enantioselective Analytical Techniques

Analytical Technique	*Abbreviation*
Nuclear magnetic resonance spectroscopy	NMR
High-performance liquid chromatography	HPLC
Gas chromatography	GC
Supercritical fluid chromatography	SFC
Thin-layer chromatography	TLC
Countercurrent chromatography	CCC
Capillary electrophoresis	CE

Chiral Principle	*Abbreviation*	*Analytical Technique*
Chiral derivatization agents	CDA	NMR, HPLC, GC, SFC, TLC, CCC, CE
Chiral stationary phases	CSP	HPLC, GC, SFC, TLC, CE
Chiral mobile phase additives	CMA	HPLC, TLC, CCC, CE
Chiral buffer additives	CBA	HPLC, CE
Chiral solvating agents	CSA	NMR
Chiral lanthanide shift reagents	CLSR	NMR

In the past few years, capillary electrophoresis (CE) became very popular, especially for the analysis of drugs, pharmaceutical metabolites, pesticides, and other nonvolatile compounds (*e.g.*, amino acids, carbohydrates). Unfortunately, there are several obstacles to its application to flavor compounds, such as low solubility in aqueous solvents and lack of chromophores suitable for UV detection.

The three basic chromatographic methods (GC, HPLC, and TLC) are applied to the analysis of flavors and fragrances in an uneven proportion. The use of TLC in this field is mainly restricted to achiral routine analysis. For preparative enantiomer separation, HPLC and supercritical fluid chromatography (SFC), rather than GC, offer the advantage of larger sample throughput. For analytical purposes, GC is the first choice.

The GC Separation of Enantiomers

For a long time, derivatization of enantiomers to diastereomers, originally developed by Bailey and Hass, was the only method available. Here, alcohols were derivatized with 2-acetyl action acid and acids with (–)-menthol. The volatile diastereomeric esters formed were partially separated by rectification. The first specific use of this indirect method in GC was reported by Casanova and Corey, separating racemic camphor via cyclic acetals after derivatization with (R,R)-2,3-butanediol.

In principle, this methodology is applicable to a wide range of chiral compounds, such as alcohols, aldehydes, ketones, carboxylic acids, esters, lactones, and even hydrocarbons. More than 100 different CDAs have been used so far in gas chromatography.

Most of the applications to flavor compounds were published before the advent of cyclodextrin-based CSPs. In view of the prohibitive cost of the latter method, the indirect method is still in use.

The landmark paper in enantiomer separation by GC was published by Gil-Av *et al.* in 1966, baseline separation was achieved for most derivatives of enantiomeric pairs of proteinogenic amino acids. The enantiomer separation was verified using a column coated with a mirror image stationary phase. In the early days of enantioselective GC, mainly amino acid derivatives and similar compounds were analyzed, while flavor and fragrance compounds were out of scope because of the lack of functional groups that were deemed a perquisite for the separation.

Among a great variety of CSPs developed of the amide type, the commercially available polymeric phases and D-Chirasil-Val and XE-60-(S)-Valine-(S)-(–PEA) are used frequently. These CSPs have been applied occasionally in the field of flavors and pheromones.

The separation power of these amide phases for enantiomers is sometimes higher than that of cyclodextrin phases. albeit strongly dependent on the presence of certain functional groups in the analyte structure. Even though compounds with hydrogen-bonding capability still exhibit medium polarity, the parent analytes, in particular amino acids, are often highly polar and non-volatile. Therefore, achiral derivatization is often required. On well-deactivated capillaries, however, hydroxyl groups may be left underivatized, leading to an increase in separation factors (α). While for many important flavor compounds, such as hydrocarbons, amide phases are not suitable, others like γ-lactones could be separated completely or partially.

The first attempts to use chiral metal coordination compounds as enantioselective stationary phases for GC enantiomer separation were undertaken by Schurig and Gil-Av in 1971. The first successful separation was published by Schurig in 1977 for 3-methylcyclopentene; chalcogran as the first pheromone was separated by Koppenhoefer *et al.* in 1980. Later several flavor compounds (*e.g.*, 1-octen-3-ol, menthone, linalyl acetate, oxanthianes) were separated into enantiomeric pairs. One of the most efficient CSPs of this type is nickel(II)-bis-[1R-3-heptafluorobutanoyl camphorate], either dissolved in OV-101 or, in order to overcome the drawbacks of low thermal stability, covalently bound to a dimethylpolysiloxane.

Since 1987, the field of enantiomer separation has been influenced by the ever-increasing popularity of the cyclodextrin-based CSPs. Cyclodextrins are cyclic glucans (cyclomaltooligoses) with at least 6–12 D-glucopyruanose units in α-1,4-glycosidic connection. In analytical chemistry, α-,β-, and γ-cyclodextrins are applied, containing 6, 7, and 8 glucose units, respectively. Almost all different chromatographic and electrophoretic methods (HPLC, SFC, GC, TLC, CZE, ITP, MEKC, EC) benefit from this trend.

In the early 1960s, peracetylated and perpropionylated α- and β-cyclodextrins were used above their melting points (>220°C) as stationary phases in packed GC columns for the separation of fatty acid methyl esters. In 1983, the first application of a cyclodextrin phase to the separation of enantiomers by GC was reported by Koscielski *et al.* These authors separated the enantiomers of α- and β-pinene, respectively, on celite coated with an aqueous formamide solution of α- and β-cyclodextrins in packed column gas solid chromatography (GSC).

In 1988, Schurig and Nowotny reported on permethylated β-cyclodextrin dissolved in different polysiloxanes, mainly polycyanopropyl phenyl vinyl methyl siloxane (OV-1701). Meanwhile, this CSP has been made available as a polysiloxane-anchored immobilized phase. At about the same time, several peralkylated and acylated/alkylated cyclodextrins were introduced by Konig *et al.*, forming a liquid coating at normal GC operating temperatures (40–220°C); these cyclodextrin derivatives were later diluted by the polysiloxane OV-1701.

A great variety of CSPs based on cyclodextrins, some of them very efficient for flavor analysis, were proposed during the following years by many researchers. Remarkable separations can be carried out, for instance, on heptakis(2,3-di-*O*-acetyl-6-*O*-tert-butyldimethylsilyl)-β-cyclodextrin dissolved in OV-1701. Meanwhile, nearly every chiral flavor compound has been made amenable to enantiomer separation by GC, although a researcher in this field will find it difficult to search the most suitable CSP for a given separation problem.

As compared to routine analysis of flavors and fragrances, the separation of enantiomers requires a more sophisticated instrumentation. Quality problems may arise from overlapping of the additional peaks, leading to wrong peak assignments, and from misrepresentation of enantiomer ratios (ee). In a typical flavor analysis, a single GC system equipped with an unspecific detector such as a flame ionization detector (FID) will not cope with the demand for high-precision determination of ee.

The most important chiral stationary phases used in gas chromatography can be divided into three main classes (guided by the principle separation mechanism): amide phases (hydrogen bonds, dipole, and van der Waals interactions), metal complex phases (complexation, dipole and van der Waals interactions) and cyclodextrin phases (inclusion, dipole, and van der Waals interactions). Other CSPs developed are merely of scientific interest.

Detailed knowledge of the enantiomer composition of chiral compounds is a key to answering many questions. For a better understanding of biochemical pathways and biosynthesis of flavor compounds and pheromones, such data are indispensable. From an industrial perspective, process analysis of enantiomeric purity of microbiologically produced or asymmetrically synthesized flavors are the main tasks of flavor analysts. Another major issue in quality control is the proof of authenticity and origin of flavors, fragrances, and essential oils by the above-mentioned methods. In the following, a couple of typical examples are presented to underline the importance of the methodology.

Table 3.7: Chiral Derivatization Agents Used for Enantioselective Flavor Analysis by GC

Chiral Derivatization Agent	*Analytes*
2-Butanol	Hydroxycarboxylic acids
2,3-Butanediol	Ketones, hydrocarbons (after oxidation to ketones)
1-Phenyl ethyl amine	Alkylcarboxylic acids
Trolox™ methyl ester	Sec. alcohols, 2-alkyl-1-alkanols
Acetyl lactyl chloride	Sec. alcohols, lactones (after ring opening) with or without reduction to diols
Menthylchloroformate	Sec. alcohols, hydroxycarboxylic acid esters
2-Methoxy-2-trifluoromethyl-2-phenylacetyl chloride	Sec. alcohols, ketols hydroxycarboxylic acid esters, lactones (after ring opening)
Tetrahydro-5-oxo-2-furan-carboxylic acid chloride	Sec. alcohols, hydroxycarboxylic acids, lactones (after ring opening)
Dimethyl tartrate	Aldehydes, ketones
1-Phenylethyl isocyanate	Sec. alcohols, alkylcarboxylic acids, hydroxycarboxylic acids, lactones (after opening, with or without reduction to diols)

The Odor Quality of Limonene

The odor quality of limonene being critically dependent on its enantiomer composition, a large number of separation experiments by GC are reported in the literature. Due to its abundance in a great variety of essential oils, this is one of the most widely investigated compounds.

Limonene as a typical terpene hydrocarbon is lacking functional groups, thus, it cannot be resolved into enantiomers on CSPs of the amide type. Hence, myriads of cyclodextrin CSPs have been investigated, although with varying success. Separation is due to shape selectivity brought about by numerous van der Waals interactions of the analyte with the interstitious and probably also with the cavity of the cyclodextrin molecules. On this basis, it is difficult to establish straightforward rules for the selection of a most suitable CSP for this compound.

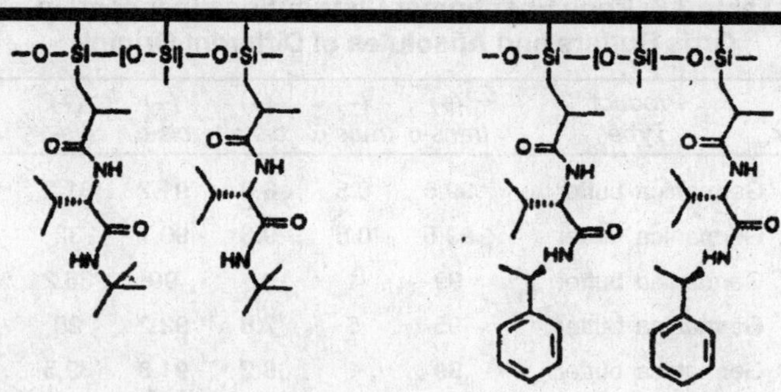

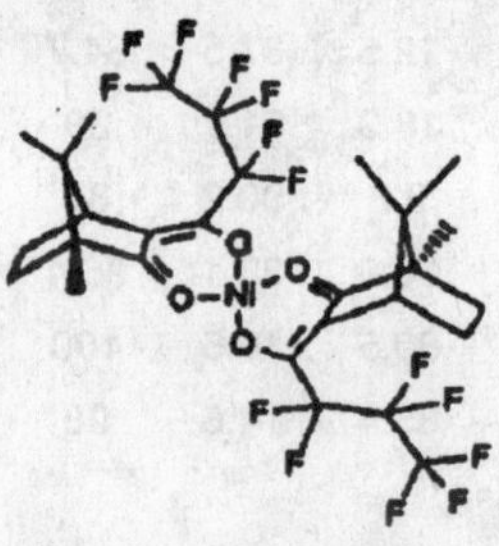

Nickel(II) bis(heptafluorobutyryl-1R-camphorate)

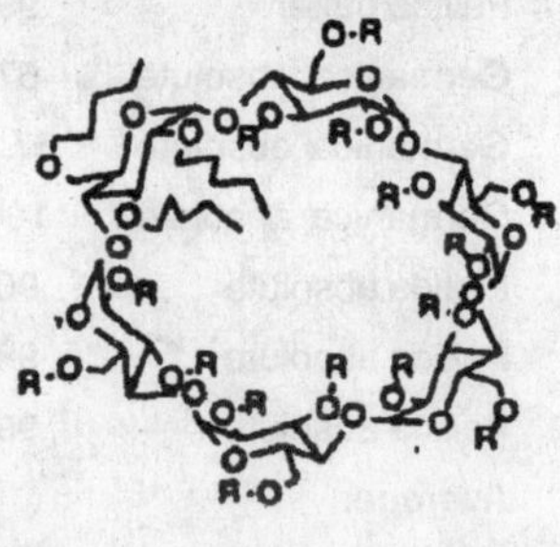

2,3,6-Tri-O-pentyl-α-cyclodextrin

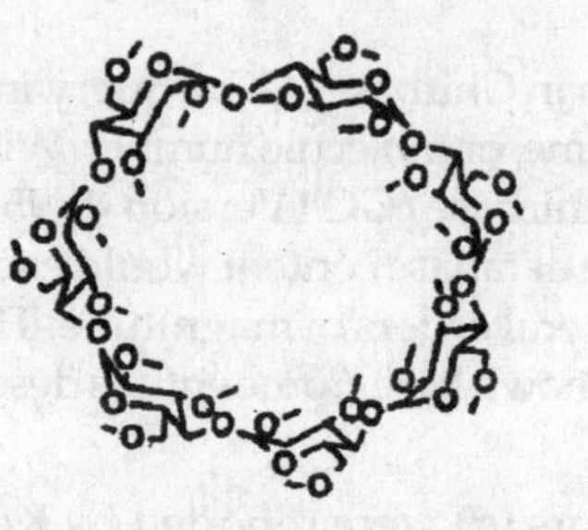

2,3,6-Tri-O-methyl-β-cyclodextrin

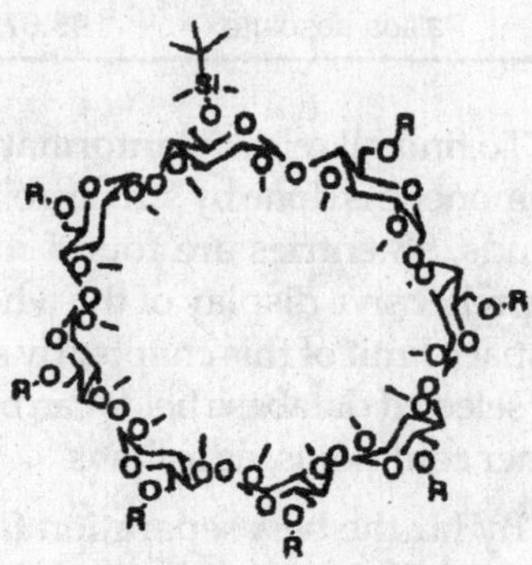

2,3-Di-O-methyl-6-O-tert.-butyldimethyl-silyl-γ-cyclodextrin

Figure 3.1: Some Typical Examples of CSPs Used in GC

Table 3.8: Irone Enantiomer Distributions (per cent) in Orris Butters and Absolutes of Different Origins

Batch Number	Product Type	(+) trans-α	(−) trans-α	(+) cis-α	(−) cis-α	(+) cis-γ	(−) cis-γ
1	Germanica butter	99.5	0.5	8.8	91.2	31.2	68.8
2	Germanica butter	99.5	0.5	9.3	90.7	32	68
3	Germanica butter	99	1	10	90	36.2	63.8
4	Germanica butter	95	5	7.8	92.2	28	72
5	Germanica butter	99	1	8.2	91.8	32.5	67.5
6	Germanica butter	95	5	9	91	27.6	72.4
7	Pallida butter	99	1	99	1	99	1
8	Pallida butter	99	1	81.6	18.4	99	1
9	Pallida butter	99	1	69	31	96	4
10	Germanica absolute	67	33	12.5	87.5	34.7	65.3
11	Germanica absolute	67.5	32.5	18.3	81.7	39	61
12	Germanica absolute	100	ca. 0	9.8	90.2	36	64
13	Pallida absolute	90	10	66.9	33.1	96.4	3.6
14	Pallida absolute	98	2	80.5	19.5	100	ca. 0
15	Pallida absolute	99	1	85.4	14.6	98	2
	Average:						
	Germanica butter	97.83	2.16	8.85	91.15	31.25	68.75
	Pallida butter	99	1	83.2	16.8	98	2
	Germanica absolute	78.16	21.83	13.53	86.46	36.56	63.43
	Pallida absolute	95.67	4.33	77.6	22.4	98.13	1.87

To find all relevant information in Chirbase/GC, a query input for limonene is done by structure, name, or molecule number. Within seconds, 98 entries are found in Chirbase/GC (Version 4/95). A comprehensive display of the whole database content would exceed the space limit of this chapter by several orders of magnitude. Thus, only selected database fields can be shown here. Some entries deserve further comments, as follows.

By far the best separation factors (α) were reported by Konig *et al.* on CSPs based on 6-O-methyl-2,3-O-pentyl-γ-cyclodextrin for slight variations in the separation conditions. In this case, the β-analogue is far less efficient in terms of the separation factor; however,

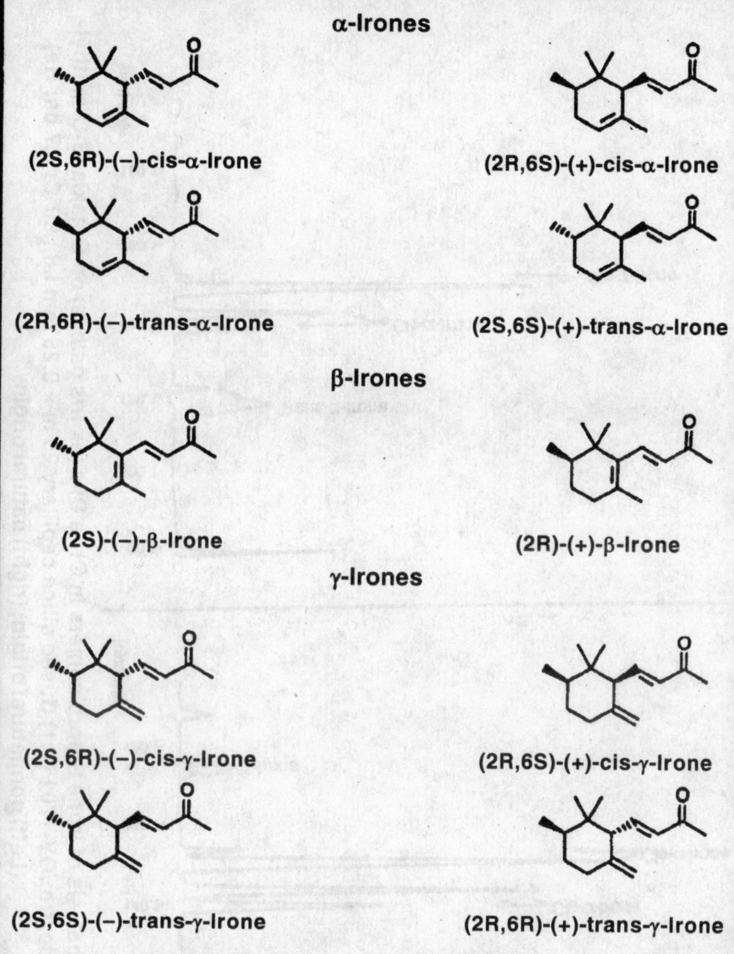

Figure 3.2: Ten Possible Stereoisomers (Five Enantiomeric Pairs) of Irone

it is still valuable for peak identification because the elution order of the two enantiomers is reversed as compared to the corresponding γ-derivative. Lindstrom *et al.* addressed the separation problem in a unique way by introducing underivatized α-cyclodextrin as a CSP for the determination of monoterpene hydrocarbons of spruce phloem.

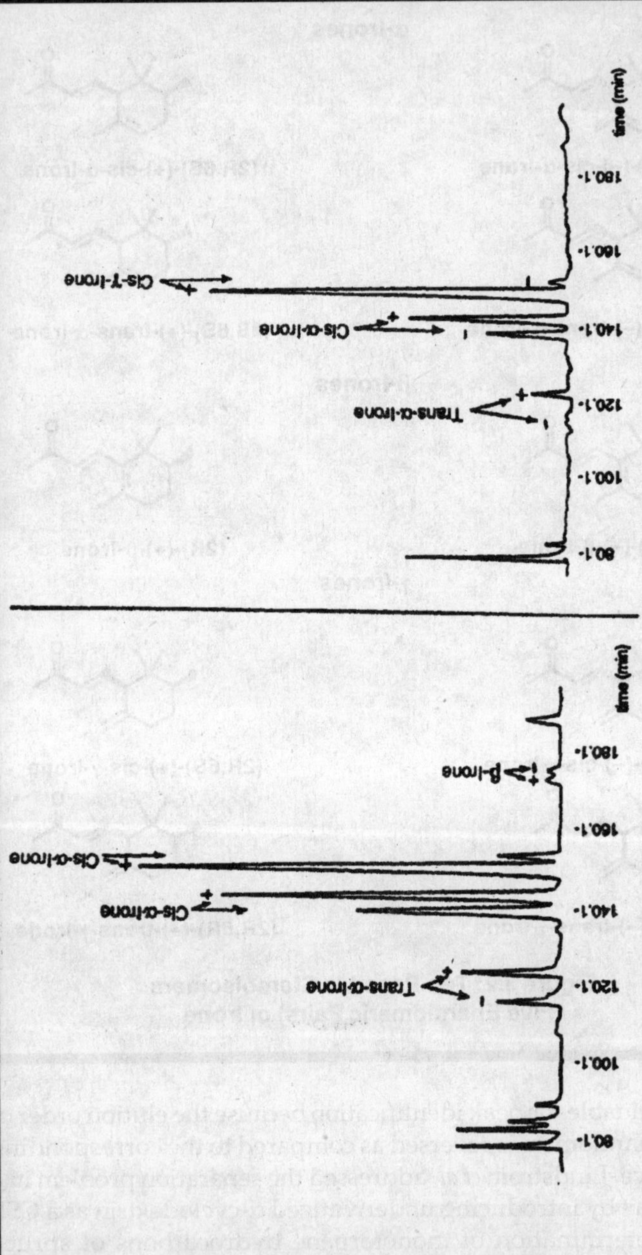

Figure 3.3: Enantiomer Analysis of Irone Stereoisomers in Orris Oils (ex *Iris pallida*) on Octakis (6-O-methyl-2,3-di-O-pentyl)-γ-cyclodextrin/OV-1701 (1:1) (fused silica capillary 25 m × 0.25 mm i.d.; 90°C; 0.7 bar He). (Left) nonnatural origin; (right) natural origin

Molecular modelling experiments on chiral recognition in GC were performed by Kobor *et al.* for 2,3-di-O-methyl-6-O-tert.butyldimethylsilyl-β-cyclodextrin and permethylated-β-cyclodextrin (both diluted in OV-1701) as selectors. They concluded that the less flexible 2,3-di-O-methyl-6-O-tertbutyldimethylsilyl-β-cyclodextrin seems advantageous for certain enantiomer separations.

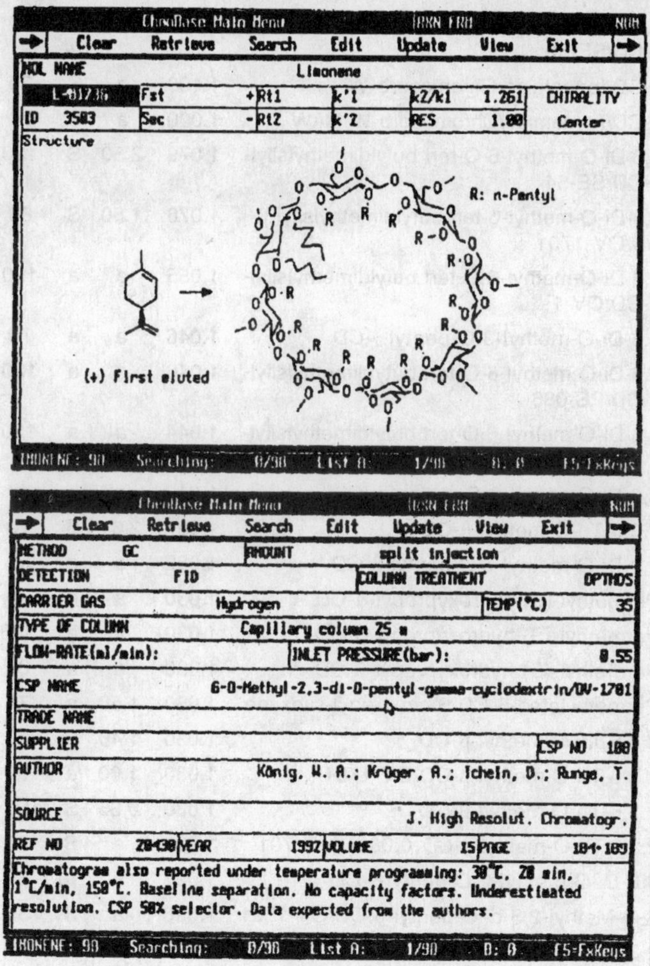

Figure 3.4: Upper and Lower Output Screen of Chirbase/GC; first hit of a search for limonene

Table 3.9: Enantiomer Separation of Limonene by GC Selected from Chirbase/GC

No.	CSP Name	α	R	First	T	Gas
1.	6-O-Methyl-2,3-di-O-pentyl-γ-CD/OV-1701	1.261	1.00	R	35	H_2
2.	6-O-Methyl-2,3-di-O-pentyl-γ-CD	1.185	5.00	a	a	H_2
3.	6-O-Methyl-2,3-di-O-pentyl-γ-CD/OV-1701	1.180	1.00	R	45	H_2
4.	α-CD	1.123	0.85	S	25	He*
5.	2,3-Di-O-methyl-6-O-tert.butyldimethylsilyl-β-CD/SE-52	1.110	5.36	a	70	H_2
6.	α-CD/formamide/Chromosorb W	1.100	a	S	30	a
7.	α-CD/formamide/Chromosorb W NAW	1.090	a	S	30	Ar
8.	2,3-Di-O-methyl-6-O-tert.butyldimethylsilyl-β-CD/SE-54	1.079	2.50	S	120	H_2
9.	2,3-Di-O-methyl-6-tert.butyldimethylsilyl-β-CD/OV-1701	1.078	1.50	S	80	H_2
10.	2,3-Di-O-methyl-6-O-tert.butyldimethylsilyl-β-CD/OV-1	1.055	a	a	120	H_2
11.	2,6-Di-O-methyl-3-O-pentyl-γ-CD	1.046	a	a	70	a
12.	2,3-Di-O-methyl-6-O-tert.butyldimethylsilyl-β-CD/PS-086	1.046	a	a	120	H_2
13.	2,3-Di-O-methyl-6-O-tert.butyldimethylsilyl-β-CD/OV-1701	1.044	a	a	120	H_2
14.	3,6-Di-O-pentyl-2-O-methyl-b-CD	1.043	a	a	40	a
15.	2,3,6-Tri-O-methyl-β-CD	1.037	2.01	S	70	H_2
16.	2,3-Di-O-methyl-6-O-pentyl-β-CD	1.032	a	a	50	a
17.	Permethyl-(S)-hydroxypropyl-α-CD	1.030	a	a	70	N_2
18.	Permethyl-(S)-hydroxypropyl-β-CD	1.030	a	a	100	N_2
19.	Permethyl-(S)-hydroxypropyl-β-CD	1.030	a	a	30	N_2
20.	Permethylated-β-CD-5-oct-1-enyl-siloxane	1.030	1.50	a	70	H_2
21.	2,3,6-Tri-O-methyl-β-CD	1.030	1.40	S	70	a
22.	2,3,6-Tri-O-methyl-β-CD/OV-1701	1.030	1.00	a	90	H_2
23.	2,3,6-Tri-O-methyl-β-CD	1.030	0.35	S	50	H_2
24.	2,3,6-Tri-O-methyl-β-CD 0.08m/OV-1701	1.029	a	S	80	a
25.	3,6-Di-O-methyl-2-O-pentyl-γ-CD	1.027	a	a	50	a
26.	6-O-Methyl-2,3-di-O-pentyl-β-CD/OV-1701	1.026	a	S	35	H_2
27.	2,3,6-Tri-O-pentyl-β-CD	1.020	a	a	90	N_2
28.	2,3,6-Tri-O-pentyl-α-CD	1.020	a	a	80	N_2
29.	2,3,6-Tri-O-pentyl-γ-CD	1.020	a	a	70	N_2

Contd...

Table 3.9–Contd...

No.	CSP Name	α	R	First	T	Gas
30.	2,3-Di-O-methyl-6-O-tert.butyldimethylsilyl-α-CD/SE-54	1.019	a	a	120	H_2
31.	2,6-Di-O-penlyl-3-O-methyl-β-CD	1.019	1.00	S	60	H_2
32.	2,3,6- Trl-O-penlyl-β-CD	1.018	a	S	70	H_2
33.	2,6-Di-tert.-butyldimethylsilyl-γ-CD 22%/ SE-52	1.015	a	a	35	H_2
34.	2,6-Di-O-tert.-butyldimethylsilyl-γ-CD 22%/ SE-52	1.013	a	a	75	H_2
35.	2,3,6-Tri-O-methyl-β-CD/OV-1701	1.010	a	a	100	N_2
36.	2,3-Di-O-methyl-6-O-pentyl-γ-CD 10%/	1.009	a	a	50	a
37.	2,6-Di-O-methyl-3-O-pentyl-β-CD 10%/ OV-225	–	2.30	a	TP	a
38.	2,6-Di-O-methyl-3[O-pentyl-β-CD 10%/ OV-1701	–	2.20	a	TP	a
39.	2,6-Di-O-methyl-3-O-pentyl-β-CD 10%/ PS-086	–	1.90	a	TP	a
40.	2,6,Di-O-methyl-3-O-pentyl-β-CD 10%/ PS-347.5	–	1.40	a	TP	a
41.	2,3,6-Tri-O-methyl-β-CD/OV-1701	a	1.00	S	50	H_2
42.	2,6-Di-O-pentyl-3-O-methyl-γ-CD	a	1.00	S	60	H_2
43.	2,3,6-Tri-O-methyl-β-CD/OV-1701	a	1.00	S	50	H_2
44.	2,3,6-Tri-O-methyl-β-CD 10%/OV-1701	a	1.00	S	50	a
45.	2,3,6-Tri-O-methyl-β-CD/DB-1701	a	1.00	S	55	a
-						
-						
-						
63.	β-CD/celite/formamide	1.000	–	a	60	He
64.	γ-CD/celite/formamide	1.000	–	a	60	He
65.	2,6-Di-O-pentyl-3-O-methyl-β-CD 30%/ OV-1701	1.000	–	a	a	a
66.	2,3,6-Tri-O-pentyl-β-CD 30%/OV-1701	1.000	–	a	a	a
67.	2,3,6-Tri-O-*n*-butylarbamate amylose/OV-61	1.000	–	a	a	H_2
68.	3,6-Di-O-pentyl-2-O-methyl-γ-CD	1.000	–	a	70	a
69.	3,6-Di-O-methyl-2-O-pentyl-β-CD	1.000	–	a	70	a
70.	2,6-Di-O-pentyl-3-O-trifluoracetyl-α-CD	1.000	–	a	110	He
71.	2,6-Di-O-pentyl-α-CD	1.000	–	a	110	He

Contd...

Table 3.9–Contd...

No.	CSP Name	α	R	First	T	Gas
72.	2,3-Di-O-methyl-6-O-tert.butyldimethylsilyl-γ-CD/SE-54	1.000	–	a	120	H_2
73.	2,6-Di-O-pentyl-3-O-butyryl-γ-CD	1.000	–	a	50	He
74.	Permethyl-(S)-2-hydroxypropyl-α-CD	1.000	–	a	100	N_2
75.	Permethyl-(S)-2-hydroxypropyl-γ-CD	1.000	–	a	100	N_2
76.	2,6-Di-O-pentyl-β-CD	1.000	–	a	100	N_2
77.	2,6-Di-O-pentyl-γ-CD	1.000	–	a	100	N_2
78.	2,6-Di-O-pentyl-3-O-trifluoroacetyl-β-CD	1.000	–	a	100	N_2
79.	2,6-Di-O-pentyl-3-O-trifluoracetyl-γ-CD	1.000	–	a	100	N_2
80.	2,3,6-Tri-O-methyl-β-CD/DB-1701	1.000	–	a	100	N_2
81.	Polydimethylsiloxane funct. with L-valine-tert.-butylamide	1.000	–	a	100	N_2
82.	Other batch of L-Chirasil-Val	1.000	–	a	100	N_2
83.	2,3,6-Tri-O-pentyl-α-CD	1.000	–	a	100	N_2
84.	2,6-Di-O-pentyl-3-O-acetyl-α-CD	1.000	–	a	100	N_2
85.	2,3,6-Tri-O-pentyl-β-CD	1.000	–	a	100	N_2
86.	2,6-Di-O-pentyl-3-O-acetyl-β-CD	1.000	–	a	100	N_2
87.	Wall-immobilized, 1:4 allylpermethyl-β-CD:PS537	1.000	–	a	100	N_2
88.	2,6-Di-O-pentyl-6-O-propylcarbamate-β-CD	1.000	–	a	80	N_2
89.	2,6-Di-O-pentyl-6-O-propylcarbamate-α-CD	1.000	–	a	80	N_2
90.	2,6-Di-O-pentyl-6-O-propylcarbamate-γ-CD	1.000	–	a	70	N_2
91.	2,6-Di-O-pentyl-6-O-isopropylcarbamute-β-CD	1.000	–	a	80	N_2
92.	2,6-Di-O-pentyl-6-O-isopropylcarbamate-α-CD	1.000	–	a	80	N_2
93.	2,6-Di-O-pentyl-6-O-isopropylcarbamate-γ-CD	1.000	–	a	80	N_2
94.	2,6-Di-O-pentyl-6-O-phenylcarbamate-β-CD	1.000	–	a	80	N_2
95.	2,6-Di-O-pentyl-6-O-phenylcarbamate-α-CD	1.000	–	a	80	N_2
96.	2,6-Di-O-pentyl-6-O-phenylcarbamate-γ-CD	1.000	–	a	80	N_2
97.	2,6-Di-O-pentyl-3-O-acetyl-γ-CD	1.000	–	a	80	N_2
98.	3,6-Di-O-ert.-butyldimethylsilyl-2-O-methyl CD 22%/SE-52	1.000	–	a	a	H_2

Quite a few publications did not allow extraction of the separation factor (α), particularly when a temperature program was applied. In these cases, the resolution factor (R) is considered a valuable measure to estimate the degree of separation under given conditions. In contrast, experiments with a clearly negative outcome are still valuable information as they prevent the reader from spending time and money on experiments that do not work. Nonetheless, we find it amazing how many researchers do spend their resources on such trials, as they are not aware of the great amount of information collected in Chirbase/GC.

Research in this field is still proliferating for several reasons. Besides the scientific challenge of driving through the sheer endless permutations of cyclodextrin substitution patterns, there is an economic need for finding columns that do an acceptable job for a many compounds as possible. In this context, a search for a given CSP or a substructure thereof will also be of great interest to many users. First of all, browsing through the CSP database will not only serve to quickly identify CSP numbers but also gives the user an unprecedented overview of the large collection of CSPs on the market. As to the separations performed on a given CSP or class of CSPs, there are several more efficient routes through Chirbase to fulfill this task, *e.g.*, search by CSP structure or a substructure, CSP name or a substring of this name, by CSP number, by author, etc. Moreover, this information may be used in a combined search, together with a given analyte or an analyte class (as defined by a substructure).

As compared to the retrieval step, the input of these data is far from being a trivial task. For Chirbase/GC, 87 journals are scrutinized page by page on a regular basis, in addition to monographs, posters, and private communications (altogether more than 400 different sources of information). Quite often the crucial information is hidden in a footnote, and most often it is incomplete. We do acknowledge a positive response from hundreds of authors to whom requests for information missing in the original paper had been sent by letter. From this rather tedious process, it turned out that enantiomer separation has matured from the early stage of development into a stage of widespread application. Therefore, the information collected in Chirbase has gained a great practical value for everyone working in this field.

Table 3.10: Selection of Flavor Compounds from the Top 75 Analytes in Chirbase/GC

Abundance	*Rank*	*Compound*	α_{max}	α_{min}
98	3	Limonene	1.261	1.030
84	5	γ-Decalactone	1.163	1.013
80	6	l-Phenylethanol	1.210	1.082
77	8	α-Pinene	2.200	1.060
73	9	Menthol	1.092	1.039
67	10	γ-Nonalactone	1.101	n.p.
61	12	γ-Octalactone	1.115	n.p.
58	13	γ-Undecalactone	1.103	n.p.
53	15	Linalool	1.080	1.056
53	16	β-Pinene	1.500	n.p.
52	17	Carvone	1.090	1.000
51	21	γ-Dodecalactone	1.050	n.p.
45	25	γ-Hexalactone	1.221	n.p.
45	26	Camphene	3.260	n.p.
44	27	γ-Heptalactone	1.186	1.030
43	29	l-Phenyl-l-propanol	1.070	1.040
43	30	γ-Valerolactone	1.439	n.p.
40	33	Methyl mandelate	1.120	1.024
40	34	2-Ethylhexanoic acid	1.037	1.036
38	36	δ-Decalactone	1.056	n.p.
37	38	Camphor	1.236	n.p.
37	39	3-Octanol	1.150	n.p.
34	44	l-Phenyl-2-propanol	1.067	1.021
34	45	Menthone	1.185	n.p.
33	49	δ-Nonalactone	1.159	n.p.
32	50	α-Terpineol	1.059	1.028
31	52	β-Butyrolactone	1.620	1.320
31	54	2-Octanol	1.109	1.020
30	55	l-Terpinen-4-ol	1.082	1.016
30	59	δ-Octalactone	1.550	n.p.
28	63	α-Ionone	2.020	1.173
27	67	Piperitone	1.123	n.p.
27	68	Pulegone	1.177	1.010
27	69	Lactic acid methyl ester	1.469	1.111
27	70	Isoborneol	1.085	1.040
27	71	2-Butanol	1.108	1.081

In the early days, some experts hoped for a standard CSP that would accomplish all relevant separation tasks. Due to its widespread commercial availability, permethyl-β-cyclodextrin derivatives were considered promising candidates. In fact, several analytes could be separated on this class of CSPs, although with limited success. With restriction to the widely used OV-1701–type cyclodextrin CSPs, satisfactory separations occur less often than expected. The selection of dedicated columns for each analyte provides a striking advantage for the separation factors achieved. A total of 38 flavor compounds made it to the top 75 analytes (selected from 5651 individual analyte structures contained in Chirbase/GC, Version 4/95); the ranking is based on the number of citations for each structure in the database. The most frequently separated flavor compound limonene, ranking at position 3 of all analytes separated into enantiomers by GC, reflects the strong attention devoted to this field. On the other hand, this raises the issue of whether re- sources for method development could have been saved by a better awareness of the possibilities offered by information retrieval in this database.

The human brain still outperforms contemporary computers when it comes to recognition and associative tasks. In the present context, unfortunately, scientists have not yet been able to establish models appropriate to predict the degree of enantiomer separation of a given analyte on any of the numerous stationary phases described in the literature. In this situation, the brute force of state-of-the-art computational equipment is required for long-term storage and fast retrieval of the growing mountain of information published in this field.

Indeed, there is an intriguing analogy between the artificial neural networks used in these studies and the biological neural networks that are trained to recognize molecular structures by odor. Merging the two scientific disciplines will certainly shed new light on the old question of how odor is brought about and how it may be predicted for a new molecular structure. As a first step in a presumably long journey, food scientists need precise qualitative and quantitative data on the odor of as many compounds as possible, determined with panels as large as necessary. Needless to say, these compounds should be of exceedingly high and well-established chemical and enantiomeric purity. At the same time, all data available must be stored in electronic form, preferentially as a graphic molecule database.

Chapter 4

Analysis of Food Volatiles

Introduction

Volatile compounds released from foods are monitored to determine composition quality and safety of the product. The very nature of food, a complex mixture of proteins, carbohydrates, and fats, results in a continuous change in the formation of the volatile compounds generated by the food over time. The application of heat during the cooking process, with variable amounts of oxygen and moisture present, greatly affects the volatile composition of a food sample. The volatile composition may become more complex with time as labile compounds react to form new compounds. The presence of some compounds at concentrations as low as the parts per billion range can have a major impact on the overall flavour and acceptability of food. Geosmum and methylisoborneol can be detected in water at the parts per trillion range. For these compounds, the human nose is more sensitive than current analytical instrumentation.

Volatile analysis of foods is used to determine various properties including quality, purity, origin, and composition. Due to the relatively low concentrations of volatile materials that can affect the acceptance or rejection of a food, a procedure is normally employed to extract and concentrate the sample sufficiently prior to instrumental analysis. The predominant method for analysing volatiles is gas chromatography (GC). Typically, compounds need to be delivered to the head of the GC column in the nanogram range in order to be detected. However, specialized detectors such as ion trap mass spectrometers (ITMS) or sulphur chemiluminescence detectors (SCD) are capable of detecting compounds in the picogram range.

The analysis of volatiles is generally accomplished by an extraction step, followed by concentration, chromatographic separation, and subsequent detection. Well-established methods of analysis include solvent extraction, static and dynamic headspace sampling, steam distillation with continuous solvent extraction, and supercritical fluid extraction. An overview of sample preparation methods is provided by Teranishi. The chromatographic profile will vary depending upon the method of sample preparation employed, and it is not uncommon to produce artifacts during this step. Thermally labile compounds may decompose in the heated zones of instruments to produce a chromatographic profile that is not truly representative of the sample.

A chromatographic "snapshot" of a food sample's volatile composition is taken at one moment in time in order to compare one sample to the next. The fewer parameters that are varied, the more likely the analysis will be reproducible. Hence, the less sample manipulation, the fewer variables in the experiment, the more likely the results can be repeated. Sample manipulation not only includes the analytical methodology, but also how the food is cooked and stored.

Direct thermal desorption (DTD) is the technique of sparging the volatiles from a sample matrix and transferring them directly onto the head of a chromatographic coloumn. The matrix is heated to facilitate the extraction of the volatile compounds from the sample. A cryofocusing unit, or cold trap, is often employed to focus the analytes at the head of the column for improved chromatographic peak shape. This technique allows for the qualitative analysis of volatile compounds with little or no sample preparation. Quantitation of volatiles may be possible, but is problematic. Variations in purging efficiency, loss of purged volatiles through split/splitless injectors, carryover, and the mechanics of the addition of an internal standards are some of the problems encountered in quantitative DTD.

In an attempt to facilitate sample preparation methods, early researchers would unscrew the top of the injection port on a gas chromatograph, remove the liner, and place a second liner filled with their sample directly into the injection port. The sample would be held in place with a plug of glass wool. The hot injection port, with its flow of carrier gas, would serve to thermally desorb the volatiles from the food sample onto a packed column held at room temperature. The volatiles from samples such as peanuts and vegetable oils have been analysed by this method. In addition to burned fingers, this method had a few drawbacks such as broad peak shapes. Liquid CO_2 was used to cool the column to subambient temperatures, focusing the desorbed volatiles onto the front end of the column, resulting in enhanced chromatographic separation.

An improvement was made in this approach by moving the sample outside of the injection port into its own heated block, Grob, Zlatkis, and Fisher/Legendre developed devices for stripping volatiles from samples and introducing them into the gas chromatograph. The external closed-loop inlet device (ECID) was developed and marketed by Scientific Instrumentation Services (SIS) of River Ridge, Louisiana. The apparatus consisted of a heating chamber, a six-port valve, heated stainless steel tubes, and an electronics unit for controlling the source block and valve temperatures. A number of these instruments were sold to researchers primarily in the food industry and are still in use.

Gas Chromatography

Gas chromatography (GC) involves the analysis of volatile organic compounds, that is, materials that exist in the vapour phase, at least at the typical GC operating temperatures between 40 and 300°C. Since aroma compounds must, by their very nature, leave the food matrix and travel through the air to be perceived, they are generally excellent candidates for analysis by GC. Although many of these compounds may be solvent extracted, distilled, or otherwise isolated from the food matrix, it is frequently preferable to take advantage of their volatility and rely instead on techniques of headspace analysis.

Headspace sampling techniques are frequently divided into three broad categories: static headspace, dynamic headspace, and purge and trap. In each case, however, the fundamental principle is the same-volatile analytes from a solid or liquid material are sampled by investigation of the atmosphere adjacent to the sample, leaving the actual sample material behind. The term "dynamic headspace" is usually used when referring to the analysis of solid materials, and the term "purge and trap" generally refers to the analysis of liquid samples by bubbling the purge gas through them.

All headspace techniques share certain advantages and considerations. Chief among these is that the analytes are removed from the sample matrix without the use of an organic solvent, so the resulting chromatogram has no solvent peak. This may be especially important when the compounds of interest are early eluters or are, in fact, solvents, and the presence of a solvent peak would both dilute and mask the analyte peaks. In addition, the effects of sample temperature, matrix solubility, and the volatility of the analyte are important considerations in optimizing a headspace assay, whether static or dynamic.

Even though the actual separation of the analytes in a gas chromatograph does take place in the vapour phase, most samples are injected as a solution of the analyte in some volatile solvent. The entire sample, solvent and analytes, vaporizes in the hot injection port, and the volatiles formed then proceed to the GC column. Many compounds, however, exist as gases at the temperature at which they are being sampled or have sufficiently high vapour pressure to evaporate and produce a gas phase solution. In these cases, the gas itself may be injected into the GC instead of a liquid solution, either by syringe or by transferring a known volume of vapour from a sample loop attached to a valve. The amount of gas that may be injected into a gas chromatograph is limited by the capacity of the injection port, the column, and consideration of the increase in pressure and flow in the injection port caused by a gas phase injection. In practical terms, injections are almost always in the low milliliter range, with sizes of 0.1–2.0 ml being typical. The utility of a headspace injection then depends on whether or not enough of the interesting analytes exist in a 1-ml gas sample to be detected reliably by GC. Many gas phase analyses are conducted by simple injection, including quality analysis of hydrocarbon products, natural gas, medical gases, and so on, and in general analytes present at about one part per million (ppm) may be assayed in a reproducible way using this technique.

The controlled analysis of vapours that have migrated into an atmosphere from some solid or liquid source forms the basis of static headspace analysis.

If a complex material, such as a piece of food, is placed into a sealed vessel and allowed to stand, some of the more volatile compounds in the sample matrix will leave the sample and pass into the headspace around it. If the concentration of such a compound reaches about 1 ppm in the headspace, then it may be assayed by a simple injection of an aliquot of the atmosphere in the vessel. How much compound enters the headspace depends on several factors, including the amount of it in the original sample, the volatility of the compound, the solubility of that compound in the sample matrix, the temperature of the vessel, and how long the sample has been inside the vessel. The concentration of the analyte in the headspace also depends, of course, on the volume of the vessel being used. At equilibrium, the amount of compound A that has escaped from the sample matrix and exists in the surrounding atmosphere is just the total amount of A minus the amount still in the matrix:

$$A_{Headspcae} = A_{Total} - A_{Matrix}$$

and the partition coefficient is just:

$$K_A = \frac{A_{Headspace}}{A_{Matrix}}$$

The amount of A that actually gets into the gas chromatograph depends on what portion of the total heads pace is injected:

$$A_{Injected} = \frac{V_S}{V_T} A_H$$

where V_S is the volume of the syringe injection, V_T is the total volume of the headspace sampling vessel, and A_H is the amount of compound A in the total headspace.

Therefore, the amount of A injected is

$$A_I = (A_T - A_M) \frac{V_S}{V_T}$$

In practice, the food sample is placed into a headspace vial, sealed and warmed to enhance vaporization of the volatiles, and then allowed to stand for a period of time to establish equilibrium at that temperature. Once the volatiles have equilibriated, an aliquot of the headspace gas is withdrawn with a syringe and injected into the gas chromatograph injection port. As an alternative, the equilibrated headspace may be allowed to pass through a sample loop of known volume, which is subsequently flushed into the injection port. Static headspace analysis has been applied to a wide variety of sample types, including herbs and fragrances.

Chief among the advantages of static headspace sampling is the ability to analyse a sample for low molecular weight volatiles without the presence of a solvent peak. This is especially important since many samples analysed by static headspace are actually being assayed for residual solvent content. Packaging, pharmaceuticals, and many other processed materials incorporate the use of solvents in some step of their production, and the amount of those solvents retained in the finished product must be determined. Since the solvents are determined as analytes in a gaseous matrix, they are not diluted by a solvent that produces a response on the GC detector, so the chromatography is simplified and more sensitive.

In addition to eliminating the solvent peak, static headspace presents a technique that is easily automated, making it attractive for sample screening applications. Commercial instruments are available from many suppliers which automatically warm the sample vials, inject the headspace, and begin the GC run. These automated systems frequently transfer a measured sample loop full of headspace to the chromatograph instead of using a syringe. The combination of careful temperature monitoring, equilibrium time, pressure control of the sample loop, and automatic injection to the chromatograph provides increased reproducibility over manual attempts at headspace analysis, as well as freeing the analyst's time for other functions.

Additional advantages of the static headspace technique include relatively low cost per analysis, simple sample preparation, and the elimination of reagents.

Any static headspace analysis can inject only a fraction of the compound of interest to the chromatograph, since the concentration in the headspace is in equilibrium with that still in the sample matrix, and only a portion of the headspace is withdrawn and transferred. Consequently, for very low levels of analyte concentration in the original sample material, static headspace techniques may lack the sensitivity required for the determination. Elevating the temperature of the sample generally increases the volatility of the analyte, but most static headspace instruments have the capability of heating samples only to about 150°C.

Analyses at fairly low temperatures also limit the usefulness of static headspace for analytes with higher boiling points. Many materials that may be extracted and solvent injected onto a GC column and that may elute well at higher column temperatures will be poorly represented in a static headspace sample produced with the sample at a cool temperature. Finally, reproducibility depends on analysing a sample after it has reached equilibration, and the time required to achieve this point may, especially for less volatile compounds, be a drawback for some analyses.

The Dynamic Headspace

The dynamic headspace involves moving the analytes away from the sample matrix in the headspace phase. Instead of allowing the sample volatiles to come to equilibrium between the sample matrix and the surrounding headspace, the atmosphere around the sample material is constantly swept away by a flow of carrier gas, taking the volatile analytes with it. This performs two functions relative to the concentration of the volatiles. First, it prevents the establishment of an equilibration state, causing more of the volatile dispersed in the sample matrix to leave the sample and pass into the headspace. Second, it increases the size of the headspace sample used beyond the limit of the actual sample vessel. It is not unusual to collect samples using a total volume of 100 ml to 1 litre of headspace, which may result in an essentially quantitative removal of the volatile analytes from the sample matrix.

To take advantage of this increased amount of volatile analyte, the entire dynamic headspace sample should be transferred to the gas chromatograph for a single analysis. This is accomplished by venting the carrier gas of the dynamic headspace through a collection trap, which retains the organic compounds while letting the carrier pass through. In this way, the analytes from a large headspace volume are concentrated in the trap, and a dynamic headspace instrument is frequently called a "sample concentrator." Since the sample is being purged with a flow of carrier and the analytes trapped for analysis, the technique is also frequently called "purge and trap." In general, the term "purge and trap" is used to refer to liquid samples analysed by bubbling the carrier through the liquid. while "dynamic headspace" is used when the sample material is a solid. In either case, however, the principle of retaining, or concentrating, the organic analytes in a trap while venting a large headspace volume is the same. The trapping step may involve adsorption onto a high-surface area sorbent material or cold trapping by condensing or freezing the analyte in the trap.

A generalised diagram of a dynamic headspace instrument is shown in Figure 4.1. The valve may be a 6-port or an 8-port one, providing for directing flow from the sample to the trap in one direction and from the trap to the GC in the other. During sample collection, the headspace gas flows from the sample vessel through the valve, to the trap and out the vent, while GC carrier flow goes directly through the transfer line to the column. When the valve is rotated, the GC carrier is diverted through the trap, which is heated

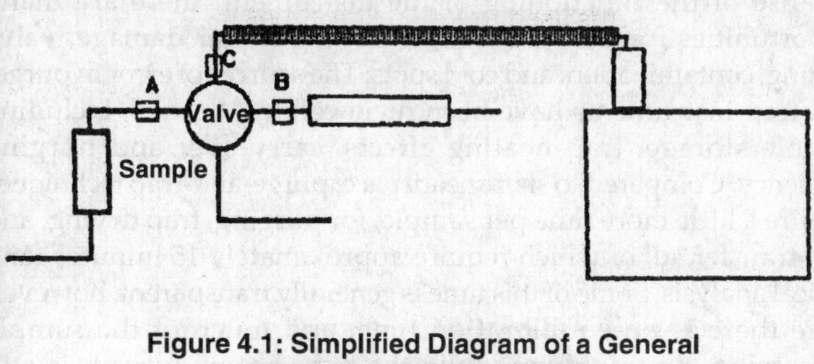

Figure 4.1: Simplified Diagram of a General Purge-and-trap/GC System

rapidly to revolatilize the collected organics, transferring them to the gas chromatograph for analysis.

Commercial instruments also provide for automatic drying of moisture from the trap, baking the trap at elevated temperatures between runs, and may include special options to handle water vapour from liquid samples, cryogenic ability for cold trapping, cryogenic refocusing on the GC column for sharper perks, an automation of multiple samples.

Dynamic headspace techniques offer many of the same advantages of static headspace, including elimination of the solvent peak, analysis of just the volatiles, automation, and easy sample preparation. In addition, the trapping stage of the analysis offers increased sensitivity, permitting the analysis of volatiles present at the parts per billion (ppb) level routinely. With careful attention to contaminants and instrument background, it has been demonstrated that purge-and-trap techniques are capable of routine application in the parts per trillion (ppt) range. Further, sorbents offer some selectivity within the range of volatiles collected, so it may be possible to select a combination of sorbent and temperature which permits the collection and concentration of specific analytes while venting others, thus simplifying the analysis.

Now let us try to learn about some disadvantages of dynamic headspace.

Because the instrumentation requires the monitoring of several steps, valving, heating zones, and so on, purge-and-trap instrumentation is more complex, and may be more expensive to purchase, than other types of sample introduction. In addition, again because of the functioning of the instrument, there are many opportunities for malfunctions, including heater damage, valve leaking, contamination, and cold spots. The sources of error in purge-and-trap instruments have been reviewed by Washall, including sample storage, trap heating effects, carry-over and purging efficiency. Compared to static headspace, purge-and-trap techniques require a little more time per sample, for purging, trap drying, and trap transfer, all of which require approximately 15 minutes for a typical analysis. Some of this time is generally transparent, however, since there is no equilibration time, and much of the sample processing may be done while the gas chromatograph is still analysing the previous sample.

Purge-and-Trap Analysis

Early applications of purge and trap were targeted at the environmental laboratory for the analysis of water samples. By purging the water with a flow of helium and trapping the purged organic pollutants, it is possible to assay analytes such as solvents at the low ppb and high ppt level routinely.

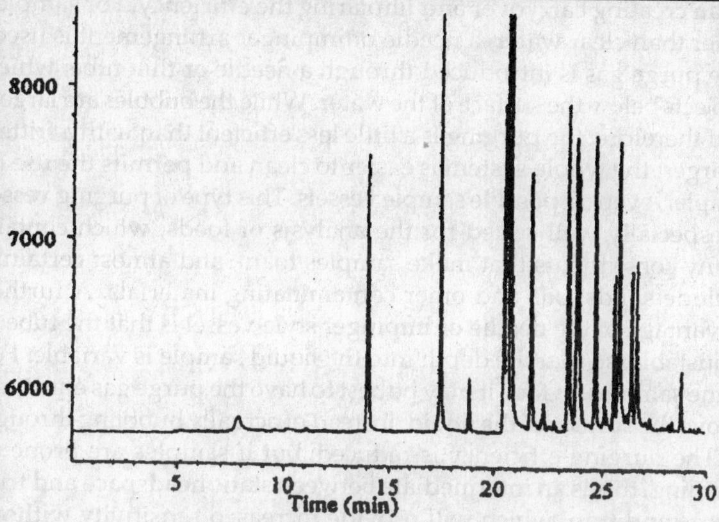

Figure 4.2: Purge-and-Trap Analysis of 5-ml Water Sample Containing Aromatics at 20 ppb each

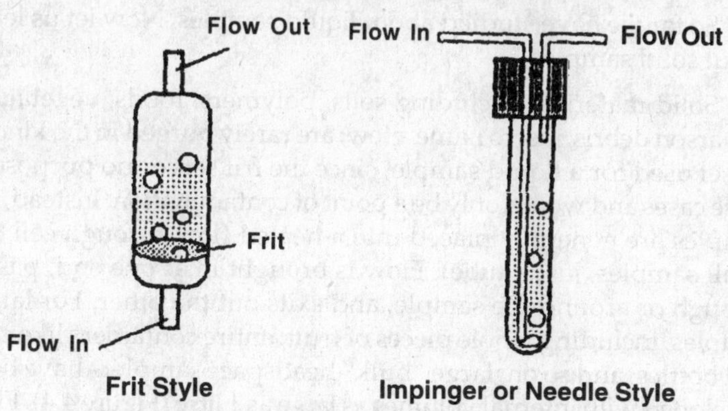

Figure 4.3: Purging Vessels for Liquid Samples

To maximise the surface area between the water and the bubbles of the purge gas, the gas is forced through a porous frit at the bottom of the vessel, making a stream of very fine bubbles, which then passes through the water, carrying away the volatile organic contaminants. These fritted vessels work well with clean samples, such as drinking water, but are not idea for all samples. If the sample contains solid particles, they may clog the frit, making it difficult to clean creating carryover and impairing the efficiency. For samples other than clear water, a needle or impinger arrangement is used. The purge gas is introduced through a needle or thin tube, which projects below the surface of the water. While the bubbles are larger, and therefore, the purging is a little less efficient than with a fritted sparger, the whole system is easier to clean and permits the use of simpler, even disposable sample vessels. This type of purging vessel is especially well suited for the analysis of foods, which contain many constituents that make samples foam, and almost certainly include solids, oils and other contaminating materials. A further advantage of the needle or impinger style vessel is that the tube is adjustable, so that the depth into the liquid sample is variable. For some samples, in fact, it may be best to have the purge gas enter just above the surface of the liquid, instead of actually bubbling through it. The purging efficiency is reduced, but if samples are prone to foaming, this is an intermediate between static headspace and true purge and trap, which will provide increased sensitivity without contaminating the valving of the instrument by having the sample foam over into the pneumatics.

So far we have studied about liquid samples. Now let us learn about solid samples.

Solid materials, including soils, polymers, foods, vegetation, and arson debris, just to name a few, are rarely purged in the kind of vessel used for a liquid sample, since the frit serves no purpose in these cases and would only be a point of contamination. Instead, the samples are generally placed into a heated flow-through cell (for small samples, just a tube). Flow is brought in at one end, passes through or around the sample, and exits out the other. For larger samples, including whole pieces of fruit, entire containers like cans and bottles, and so on, large "bulk" headspace samplers have been developed with internal volumes as large as 1 litre (Figure 4.4). Flow is usually brought in and exits through smaller tubing, rather than

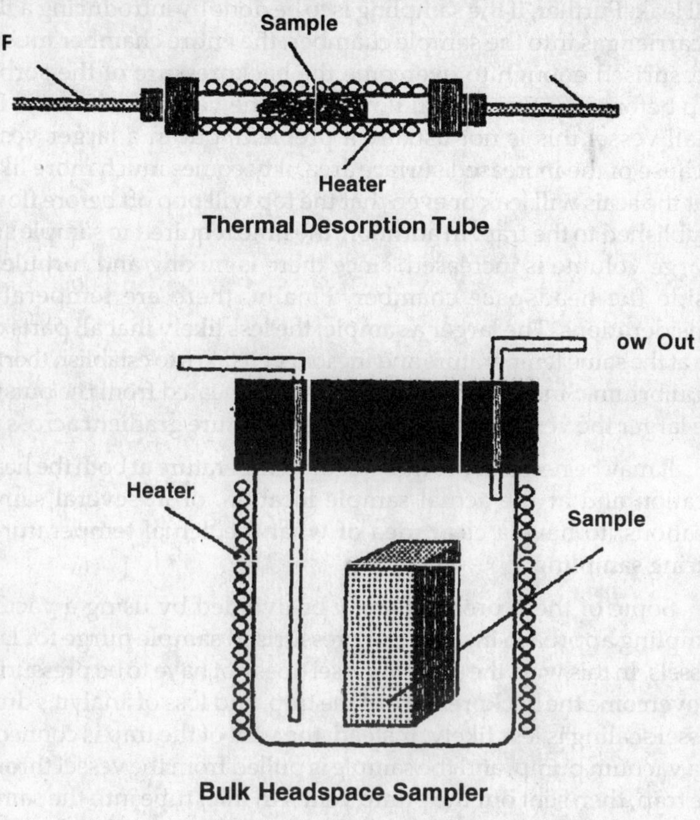

Figure 4.4: Sample Vessels for Dynamic Headspace Analysis of Solid Materials

making the large sampler a huge tube, because of sealing considerations.

In general, some additional sampling problems are introduced when using such large sample containers. These problems should be considered when choosing whether to analyse a portion of a sample in a small tube or the entire sample in a large vessel. Some analysts are concerned about the representative quality of a small piece taken from a large sample and therefore choose to an analyse the entire thing, requiring a sample vessel with considerable volume. It must be remembered, however, that the larger the fittings used, the more difficult it is to seal them, and the more likely the sample vessel will leak. Further, if the sampling is to be done by introducing a flow of carrier gas into the sample chamber, the entire chamber must be pressurised enough to overcome the backpressure of the sorbent trap before any carrier will flow out of the vessel to the trap. In a small vessel this is not usually a problem, but in a larger vessel, because of the increased surface area, it becomes much more likely that the seals will leak or even that the top will pop off before flow is established to the trap. In addition, the time required to sample such a large volume is increased, since there is mixing and turbulence inside the headspace chamber. Finally, there are temperature considerations. The larger a sample, the less likely that all parts of it are at the same temperature and the longer it takes to establish thermal equilibrium. Since most sample vessels are heated from the outside, the larger the vessel, the larger the temperature gradient across it.

It may be necessary to monitor the temperature at both the heater location and at the actual sample location, or at several sample locations, to have a clear idea of what the actual temperature is during sampling.

Some of these problems may be avoided by using a vacuum sampling approach instead of a pressurised sample purge for large vessels. In this way, the sample vessel does not have to be pressurised to overcome the backpressure of the trap, and loss of analytes due to vessel sealing is less likely. Instead, the vent of the trap is connected to a vacuum pump, and the sample is pulled from the vessel through the trap, then sent out the pump vent. An inlet tube into the sample vessel provides for replacement air or sample gas, so that the vessel stays at one atmosphere throughout the sampling.

The Setting of the Parameters

The setting of the parameters of direct thermal desorption will directly affect the desorption efficiency, collection, and quantitative analysis of the sample. Desorption temperatures must be set high enough to facilitate the stripping of the volatile compounds, yet not alter the sample or analyte. Desorption times should be sufficient to remove the majority of the volatiles. Purge/carrier gas flow rates should be sufficient to purge the analyte from the sample but not push the desorbed volatiles through the cryofocusing zone. GC

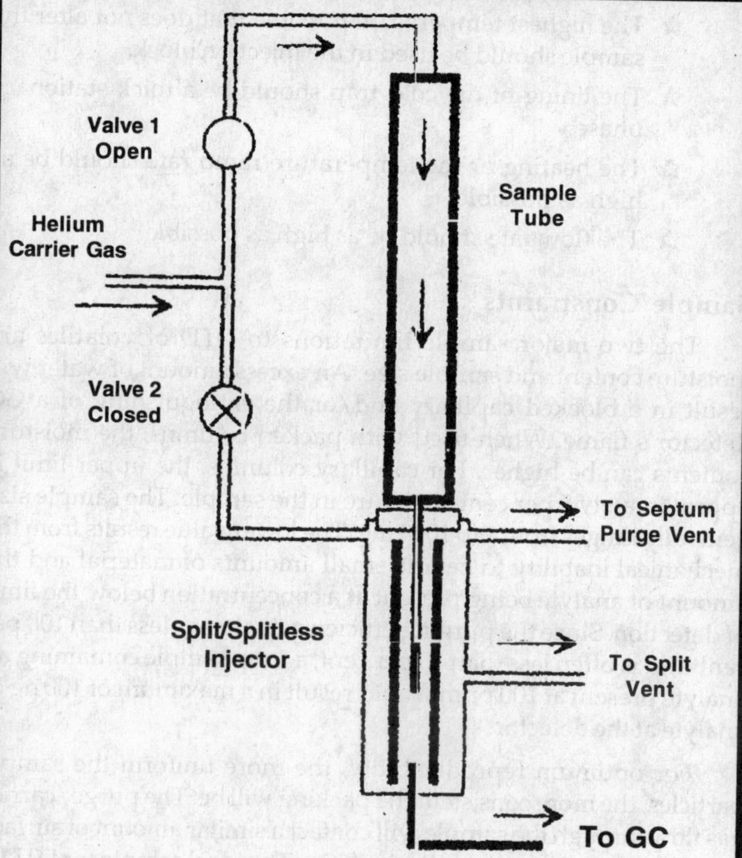

Figure 4.5: The Short-path Thermal Desorber is here shown in the Load Position. Following Desorption, Valve 1 is Closed and Valve 2 is Opened.

columns must allow sufficient flow for efficient desorption of the sample and must be suitable for analysis by direct thermal desorption.

Some researchers have performed a multivariant optimisation of parameters for the thermal desorption–cold trapping of volatiles. Their conclusions, although based on the use of a specific instrument, are generally applicable for all direct thermal desorption devices:

- Set the cold trap to its lowest setting.
- The highest temperature possible that does not alter the sample should be used in the injection block.
- The lining of the cold trap should be a thick stationary phase.
- The heating or the temperature ramp rate should be as high as possible.
- The flow rate should be as high as possible.

Sample Constraints

The two major sample limitations to DTD of volatiles are moisture content and sample size. An excess amount of water will result in a blocked capillary and/or the extinguishing of a GC detector's flame. When used with packed columns, the moisture contents can be higher. For capillary columns. the upper limit is approximately 5 per cent moisture in the sample. The sample size generally ranges from 1 to 1000 mg. The lower value results from the mechanical inability to handle small amounts of material and the amount of analyte being present at a concentration below the limit of detection. Since the purging efficiency is always less than 100 per cent and is often less than 10 per cent, a 1 mg sample containing an analyte present at 100 ppm would result in a maximum of 100 ng of analyte at the detector.

For optimum reproducibility, the more uniform the sample particles, the more consistent the packing will be. The purge/carrier gas flow through the sample will contact a similar amount of surface area if the sample particles are uniform. The ideal sample for DTD is a thermally inert low-moisture powder with the analytes present at concentrations between parts per million to parts per thousand. This description sounds like that used to describe typical adsorbent materials like Tenax, Chromosorb, and charcoal. The more the food sample resembles these adsorbent materials, the fewer problems result from the matrix.

This list contains some liquid samples, which are sparged and passed through a drying reagent and the analytes deposited directly onto the head of the column. Although not truly direct thermal desorption, these techniques are very similar.

Columns

Assuming the sample is amenable to DTD, the internal diameter (I.D.) of the chromatograph column employed is the most critical factor in determining the success of a DTD method. A trade-off must be made between sample capacity, water tolerance, and chromatographic resolution. Packed columns are superior to capillary columns for sample loading and their ability to handle moisture, but they provide poor chromatographic resolution. Their high flow rates are consistent with typical purge rates of 40 ml/min, allowing the injection ports to deliver all of the purge gas onto the head of the column. When packed columns or mega-bore glass capillary columns (0.75 mm I.D.) are employed, even samples with high moisture contents are amenable to direct thermal desorption. With capillary columns. microgram quantities of water deposited during the direct thermal desorption may result in blockage of the column during cryofocusing.

A capillary column with a 0.32 mm I.D. has an upper flow rate of approximately 2 ml/min. Sample loading can be improved and column blockage alleviated by using wide-bore and megabore capillary columns. These columns are the best for use with direct thermal desorption when analysing samples with a high degree of moisture such as meat. In going to the larger-diameter capillary columns with thicker films, a subsequent loss in chromatographic resolution should be expected. A compromise is reached between the high-capacity packed columns and the low-load high-efficiency capillary columns with the 0.75-mm-wide bore and the 0.53-mm megabore open tubular columns. These columns provide satisfactory chromatography and can handle sample loads in the microgram range. The megabore columns are made of glass, and their installation and removal can be difficult.

Even with the larger-diameter columns, water may still present a problem. High amounts of water can compromise the integrity of the column's stationary phase. As the water enters into the detector, it can quench the flames on flame ionization (FID) and flame photometric detectors (FPD). The extinguishing of the detectors can be overcome by using an increased flow rate of both hydrogen and air. This results in a slight decrease in sensitivity. This also works well with the sulphur chemiluminescence detectors, which require higher flow rates and in which hydrocarbons are converted to water and carbon dioxide, while sulphur-containing compounds produce sulphur monoxide.

Table 4.1: Substances Analysed by Direct Thermal Desorption

Sample	*Sample*
Beef	Aspirin
Candy	Carpets
Cheese	Coffee
Coriander fruit	
Glad Wrap	Marijuana
Onion	Peanuts
Pine needles	Plant material
Plywood	Polypropylene films
Rugs	Soil
Soybean oil	Spices
Sugar	
Vanillu beans	
Vegetable oil	VOCs
Wine	

Now let us learn some details about split/splitless injectors.

DTD devices are typically interfaced to the gas chromatograph via split/splitless injection ports. Split/splitless injectors have been developed to allow injected volatiles to be concentrated at the head of the capillary column, yet still provide sufficient gas flow to sweep out the injection port. This is accomplished by altering the flow through the injector. During the splitless mode, the carrier gas enters at the top of the injector and applies pressure on the volatiles to drive them into the top of the capillary column. The majority of the carrier gas exits through the septum purge line at the top of the injector. After sufficient time is allowed to void the injection volume, the flow is changed so that the majority of the carrier gas sweeps through the injection liner but exits the sweep vent. This method works well for normal injections using syringes.

Direct thermal desorption devices alter the flow through the injector. The carrier gas mixed with the analytes now enters the injection port through the sample needle. The majority of the carrier gas and volatiles exit through the septum purge, with only a fraction

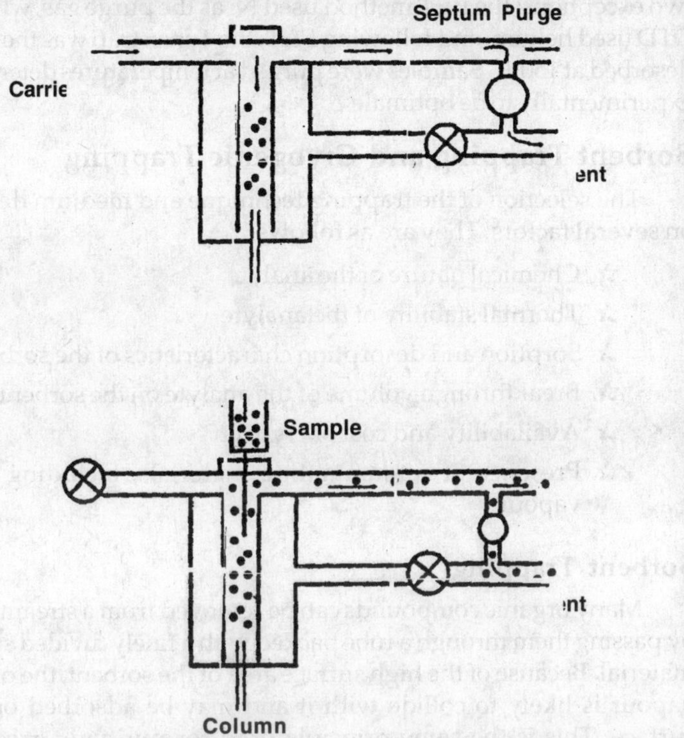

Figure 4.6: Diagram of Gas Flow of an HP Split/Splitless Injector Under Normal Operation (top) and under DTD Operation (bottom)

of the purged volatiles going onto the head of the column. For this reason, the split ratio must be decreased as much as possible, and in some cases the split vent may be capped off. However, this results in a reduced flow of carrier gas through the injection port and can lead to carryover between runs and irreproducible results. This is especially true for volatiles being desorbed from complex food samples.

A comparison of DTD was made with purge and trap (P&T) for analysing volatiles from samples of beet sugar, roasted peanuts, and grilled ground beef. Aliquots from the same sample were used for the comparison. Method parameters were kept the same with two exceptions: the P&T method used N_2 as the purge gas, while the DTD used helium, and following P&T, the Tenax trap was thermally desorbed at 150°C. Samples were purged at temperatures determined experimentally to be optimal.

Sorbent Trapping and Cryogenic Trapping

The selection of the trapping technique and medium depends on several factors. They are as follows:

- ✰ Chemical nature of the analyte
- ✰ Thermal stability of the analyte
- ✰ Sorption and desorption characteristics of the sorbent
- ✰ Breakthrough volume of the analyte on the sorbent
- ✰ Availability and cost of cryogen
- ✰ Presence of contaminating materials, including water vapour

Sorbent Trapping

Many organic compounds can be removed from a stream of gas by passing them through a tube packed with a finely divided sorbent material. Because of the high surface area of the sorbent, the organic vapour is likely to collide with it and may be adsorbed onto its surface. This is the same principle used for purifying gases and liquids by forcing them through a filter, frequently filled with activated charcoal, but in this case the fluid (carrier gas) is discarded and the trapped materials are the compounds of interest. In an ideal case, the organic volatile is held by the sorbent at room temperature while other materials pass through, and the analyte can be desorbed by heating the trap only enough to revolatilize it but not enough to cause thermal degradation. In fact, this is the case for many organic compounds, which makes the analysis of water samples for organic pollutants like solvents very straightforward by purge and trap. Other compounds are not well sorbed, or behave well only on sorbents that also collect unwanted materials. Some sorbents are quite stable thermally, whereas others produce artifacts at desorption temperatures. Some sorbents hold volatiles so efficiently that they must be heated to quite high temperatures to release them, perhaps causing thermal damage in the process. Part of the method-development stage of any dynamic headspace technique involves evaluation of the sorbent/analyte interaction and selection of the best trapping material. It is sometimes necessary to use more than one sorbent in a trap, especially if a wide range of volatiles is to be trapped, and some analysts prefer to collect the volatiles by cryogenics onto some inert surface and eliminate sorbents altogether.

Most sorbent materials are porous polymers similar to (or identical to) the kinds of materials used to fill packed GC columns for gas analyses. Tenax® (poly-2, 6-diphenyl-*p*-phenylene oxide) is perhaps the most widely used, general purpose sorbent for dynamic headspace techniques. It is capable of sorbing a fairly wide range of organic volatiles, is especially good with aromatics, may be heated to relatively high temperatures for desorption, and is long lasting. It is not suitable for very volatile hydrocarbons (pentane and below) or for small alcohols, which is frequently an advantage. Because it has been used for dynamic headspace–type analyses for such a long time, there is much information available in the literature regarding its suitability for particular analysis.

Although it is sometimes regarded as a "universal sorbent," Tenax® is not suitable for every application, and many analysts choose to augment or replace it with other sorbent materials. In an effort to extend the purge-and-trap technique, the U.S. Environmental Protection Agency (EPA) has devised additional traps, which use Tenax® as the primary sorbent backed by other, more retentive sorbents. To concentrate on a wide range of volatiles, such as in EPA method 502.2, which includes compounds as light as vinyl chloride and as heavy as trichlorobenzene, the trap specifies Tenax®, silica gel, and activated charcoal. As a general rule, the more retentive the sorbent or the smaller the molecules it is capable of retaining, the more heat is required to desorb the analytes and regenerate the trap. A particular problem with activated charcoal, and especially silica gel, is their tendency to adsorb water, which must be dealt with if it is not to be transferred to the gas chromatograph.

For the analysis of small molecules by trapping and thermal desorption, several new sobent materials have been introduced that provide the retentive ability of activated charcoal, but collect less water. Graphitized carbon sorbents (Carbotrap, Carbopack) can collect hydrocarbons larger than propane and release them thermally. Very small molecules, such as chloromethane, may be trapped using carbon molecular sieves, which differ from standard, inorganic molecular sieves in that they are prepared by charring polymers at high temperatures. These include the various Carbosieves™, Carboxen™, and Ambersorb™ materials, with Carboxen™-569 in particular reported as having a very low water affinity, increasing the ability to collect small organics without transferring too much water to the analytical instrument. Various combinations of these sorbents, with and without Tenax®, have been demonstrated to provide both good trapping efficiency and may be desorbed at relatively high temperatures, producing a tighter analyte plug transferred to the gas chromatograph. This results in better chromatographic resolution, particularly for the early eluting peaks in the chromatogram.

When a volatile organic compound enters a bed of trapping material in a carrier gas stream, it may be adsorbed by the packing, but not irreversibly, since it is important to desorb it later for analysis. Some materials are quite firmly adsorbed and will remain on the surface of the sorbent for a considerable time, requiring fairly high temperatures (150–250°C) to remove them. Other compounds are not as well adsorbed, even at room temperature, and will eventually work their way through the sorbent bed, just as a retained compound works its way through a GC column. The volume of carrier gas that may be passed through a trap before a particular analyte leaves the other end of the sorbent bed is called the breakthrough volume. The breakthrough volume depends on the nature of the compound, its volatility, the interaction between the compound and the sorbent, the amount of sorbent used, and the temperature of the trap. In practice, a safe sampling volume is used to develop a sampling technique, which is a smaller volume than the actual breakthrough volume and is reported per gram or sorbent material.

Now let us learn about cryogenic trapping.

Even well-conditioned solid sorbents exhibit out-gassing at the temperatures required for thermal desorption of adsorbed compounds. Tenax®, for example, produces aromatic volatiles at temperatures above 180°C. For many applications, the amount of organic material produced from the polymer sorbent may be negligible, but for trace-level applications the presence of background peaks from the sorbent may be a problem. This is accentuated in the analysis of heavier organics, since they require a higher desorption temperature to transfer from the trap to the gas chromatograph.

Frequently the desorption parameters become a compromise between temperatures high enough to desorb the analytes efficiently but low enough to minimise artifacts. One solution is to eliminate the sorbent altogether and collect the analytes cryogenically.

Liquid nitrogen (boiling point–196°C) and solid carbon dioxide (boiling point–79°C) have both been used to chill traps for cryogenic sample concentration. Whether one uses liquid nitrogen or carbon dioxide depends on availability, cost, and the temperature range desired. Although it may seem that CO_2 would suffice for many purposes, the fact is that many analysts find they need temperatures of –100°C or colder to collect their analytes efficiently. The pneumatics involved in delivering liquid nitrogen and CO_2 as cryogens are significantly different and generally not interchangeable. Liquid nitrogen is usually used at about 20 psi, while CO_2 is supplied at about 900 psi. Further, nitrogen stays as a liquid when delivered, while CO_2 becomes a solid, so the cryogenic wells used as reservoirs to cool the trap must be designed differently.

By replacing the trap packing with glass beads, glass wool, or some other inert material, surface area is provided for the analytes to condense upon during trapping. When the collection step is complete, the trap need only be heated enough to volatilize the analyte, since it is not necessary to desorb the compounds from the surface of a sorbent. This has additional advantages for the collection of thermally unstable materials, which could decompose at temperatures required for desorption from a porous polymer or charcoal.

Perhaps the greatest advantage of cryogenic trapping is the ability to tune the trap to the analytes of interest. By chilling the trap just enough to condense a particular analyte, other, more volatile compounds may be allowed to pass through and vent from the system, simplifying the analysis. On the other hand, since traps may be cooled to temperatures below –180°C using liquid nitrogen, verious volatile analytes (with the exception of methane) may be collected, which would break through ordinary sorbent traps. Some analysts use a combination of sorbent and cryogenics to extend the range of the sorbent, for example, using a cryotrap filled with Tenax. For applications needing only sorption, the Tenax is used at room temperature. When light hydrocarbons or small alcohols are needed, the collection temperature is dropped and the sorbent becomes a cold surface for condensation, just like glass beads in a standard cryotrap.

Although in theory one can tune the trap temperature to collect only the desired compounds, in practice there may well be compounds that behave similarly to the analytes of interest and are collected anyway. In general, any compound with a boiling point higher than that for which the trap collection temperature was designed will also be trapped. Perhaps the most troublesome is water, since it is present in many samples and creates significant chromatographic problems. Since the point of using cryogenics is to collect at subambient temperatures, it should be assumed that if water is present in the sample, it will be condensed or frozen in the cryotrap.

A second drawback to cryogenic collection is the cost of the additional instrumentation needed to handle the cryogen, including solenoids capable of functioning at 180°C below zero, control electronics, and the cost of the cryogen itself. If the trap is filled with glass beads for a clean background, cryogen must be used for every run. In addition, there is a finite time–a few minutes each run-needed to bring the trap from a rest temperature to the cryogenic temperature for collection. A final caution involves cold spots. It is important to consider the effects on the system as a whole of cooling a portion of it to –100°C. Even if the cryogenic trap has its own heater, adjacent portions of the pneumatic path, especially unheated fittings, will also be cooled, and may warm slowly if not specifically heated. The longer the trapping time, the more pronounced this effect becomes, and the more important it is to investigate portions of the flow path that may be inadvertently cooled, creating a source for subsequent poor chromatography, bleed, inefficient transfer of heavier materials, etc.

Managing Water Vapour in Dynamic Headspace Analysis

There are several approaches to managing water vapour in dynamic headspace analysis, including selection of a trapping medium that is hydrophobic, trapping the water independently of the analytes, venting the water independently, and combinations of these.

One reason for the popularity of Tenax as a sorbent is its low affinity for water, even if the sample being purged is aqueous, so the purge gas is essentially saturated. A trapping tube filled with 100–150 mg of Tenax will still retain about 1 µl of water for each of 40 ml of purge gas used in the process, so a 10-minute purge cycle at 40 ml/min would deliver about 10 µl of water to the trap. Since Tenax does not adsorb water, however, it is usually enough to pass a source of dry carrier gas through the trap for a minute or two to vent the water from the trap without disturbing the organics, which are actually adsorbed onto the surface of the Tenax. The carbon molecular sieve Carboxe-569 is reported also to be highly hydrophobic and useful in collection of smaller molecules or in conjunction with Tenax for a wider-range sorbent trap.

Two types of devices are in current use to help remove water vapour from the analytical stream of a purge-and-trap instrument. namely, condensation and permeation. The condensation units produce an intentional cold spot in the pneumatics of the system, providing an area for water to condense out of the carrier. There is always the concern that less volatile organics will drop out as well, at least partially, reducing recovery and contaminating subsequent runs. In general, most of the water present in a purge stream can be removed by passing the carrier through a zone at about 25°C, while many organics, even substituted aromatics and naphthalene, stay vaporised and pass through to the trap. Some instruments use a plain piece of stainless steel or nickel tubing at positions A or B to accomplish this, whereas some fill the tubing with glass beads to increase the surface area. These zones should have independent heaters permitting the collected water to be vaporised and vented from the water trap before the next run, or eventually the water trap will become saturated and stop functioning. Some instruments actively cool these zones, using either a cryogen or a Peltier device to increase the efficiency of the water collection. Care must be taken to control the temperature, since the colder the trap, the more likely that compounds other than water will be condensed in the zone.

Permeation or diffusion devices eliminate water by having it pass through the wall of the drying tube while the analyte molecules stay in the carrier stream, Nafion® tubing is quite efficient in its ability to remove water vapour from a gas stream, partly because its polymer structure includes sulfonic acid groups. A drying tube made with Nafion® is usually a double-walled device, with the analytical stream passing through the center of the Nafion® tube in one direction and a flow of dry air passing the outside of the Nafion® in the other direction. Water is removed from the inside gas stream by the sulfonic acid groups in the polymer and transferred through the polymer tube to the dry countercurrent air flow, where it is removed from the system.

Whichever water-elimination device is used, its effect on the organic analytes in the carrier stream is increasingly pronounced the more similar the analyte is to water. Polar compounds, especially small alcohols, are likely to be affected by diffusion-type dryers, while the higher the boiling point of an organic, the more likely it is to be slowed in its transfer though a condensation trap.

Volatiles from Peanuts, Beet Sugar and Grilled Beef

Figure 4.7 shows the chromatographic traces of a crushed peanut sample analysed by the two different techniques. The upper chromatogram was obtained using the P&T method, while the bottom chromatogram was run using the DTD method. Again, the conditions were optimised for DTD and not for P&T.

The volatile composition of roasted peanuts consists of aldehydes, alkylpyrazines, furanones, and alcohols. For the peanuts, the total volatile concentration is greater for the DTD method than for the P&T method. The relatively larger chunks of the peanut sample prevent close packing and result in enhanced desorption efficiency from the sample in the DTD method.

Beet sugars are prone to adsorb off-odours as a result of contact of sugar beets with soil microorganisms that produce potent off-flavours. Odour is a major factor in quality control of the acceptability of the sugar. The volatile compounds previously reported in beet sugar are primarily mixtures of short-chain fatty acids, furanones, aldehydes, and alcohols. The sample chosen possessed an exceptionally offensive odour and does not represent a typical chromatographic profile of beet sugars. The volatile composition of the sample is dominated by short-chain fatty acids and straight-chain aldehyes. Figure 4.8 shows a comparison of the beet sugar analysed by the purge-and-trap method and by direct thermal desorption. The total amount of volatiles loaded onto the column is greater when using the purge-and-trap method. A likely explanation

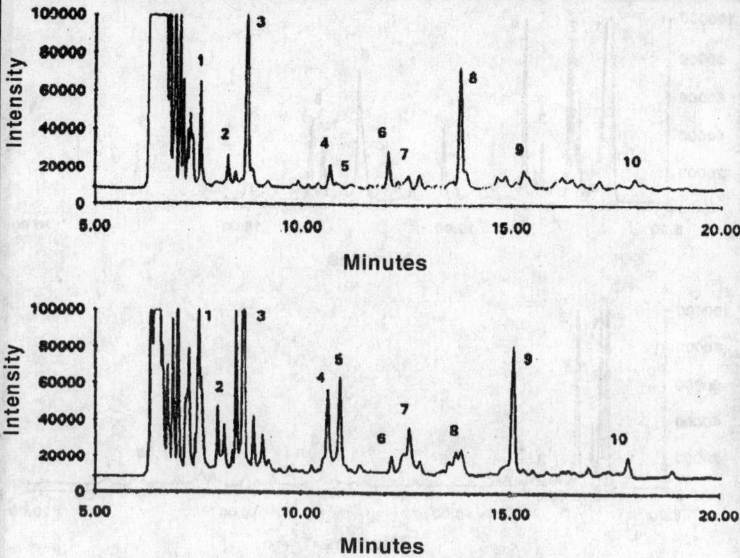

Figure 4.7 : GC-FID Trace of Roasted Peanuts

(Top) Volatiles desorbed by purge and trap: 1: Pentanal; 2: N-methylpyrrole; 3: Hexanal; 4: Hepatanal; 5: 2,5 and 2,6-dimentylpyrazine; 6: 1-octen-3-ol; 7: Methylethylpyrazine; 8: 2-pentylfuran; 9: Phenylacetaldehyde; 10: Vinylphenol. (Bottom) Volatiles directly desorbed onto the column.

is that the dense packing of the sugar in the tube for DTD does not allow the purge/carrier gas to efficiently desorb the volatiles from the sugar.

Acetic acid is one of the first components to elute with a retention time of 6.37 minutes. Propionic, butyric, isovaleric, and hexanoic acids are observed in both methods. These short-chain fatty acids are the primary causes of the offensive odour of this sugar. The concentrations of these compounds are much greater using the P&T method relative to DTD. In the P&T trace, the straight-chain aldehydes heptanal, octanal, and nonanal are also observed, while only trace levels are observed in the DTD chromatogram.

Figure 4.9 shows the chromatographic traces volatiles from grilled ground beef.

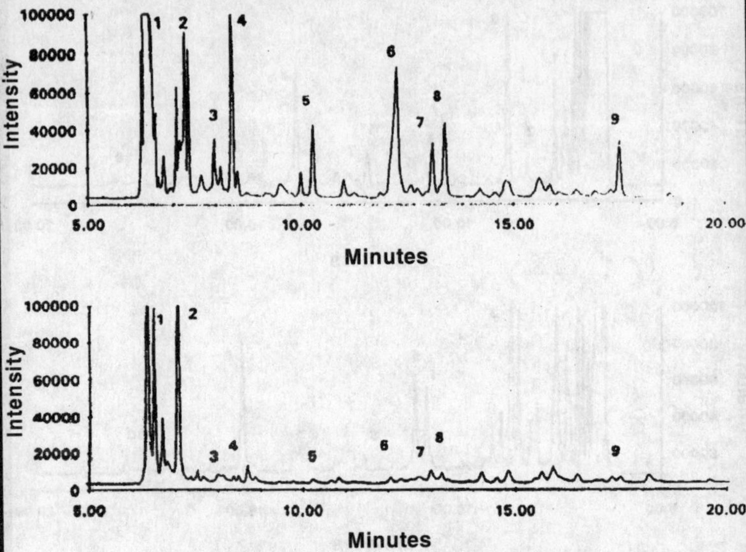

Figure 4.8: GC-FID Trace of Beet Sugar

(Top) Volatiles desorbed by purge and trap: 1: Acetic acid; 2: Propionic acid; 3: Butyric acid; 4: Hexanal; 5: Heptanal; 6: Methylbutyric acid; 7: 2-octenal; 8: Octanal; 9: Nonanal. (Bottom) Volatiles directly desorbed onto the column.

The volatile profile has been shown to vary with purge temperature. A purge temperature of 70°C was selected because protein denaturation has been shown to occur at higher temperatures. The sample was taken from a 4-day-old refrigerated sample and is typical of samples having undergone meat flavour deterioration. The large peak at 8.5 minutes is hexanal, which overloads the capillary column in both the P&T trace and the DTD trace. As observed with the sugar sample, the total volatile concentration is greater in the P&T method.

Pentanal and hexanal are observed in higher concentrations using the DTD method, while heptanal, 2-octenal, and nonanal are present in relatively greater concentrations in the P&T method.

These three examples show that for low-boiling compounds, DTD can be more efficient for desorbing samples, but that the

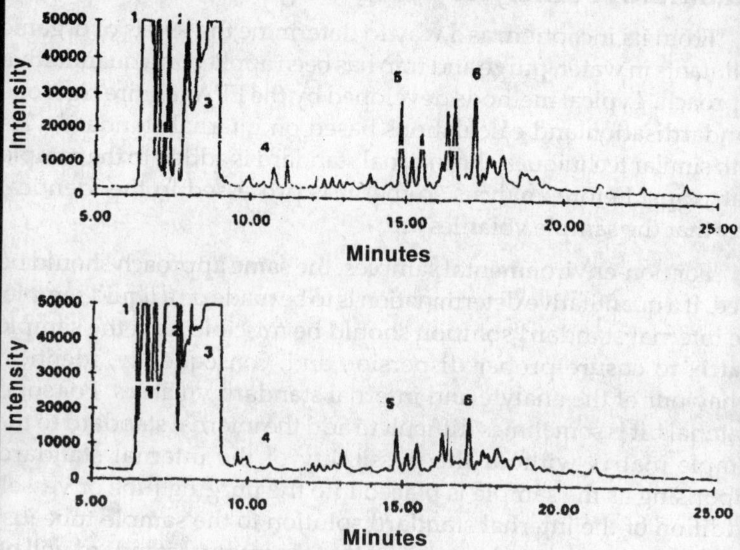

Figure 4.9: GC-FID Trace of Grilled Beef

(Top) Volatiles Desorbed by Purge and Trap: 1: Acetaldehyde; 2: Pentanal; 3: Hexanal; 4: Heptanal; 5: 2-octenal; 6: Nonanal. (Bottom) Volatiles directly desorbed onto the column.

concentrating power of P&T is needed for higher boiling compounds. The relative purging efficiency of P&T versus the desorbing efficiency of DTD is sample dependent.

Table 4.2: Repeatability of Three Runs of a 100 ppm Mixture of Hydrocarbons by DTD

	Direct Thermal Desorption		
	Average	*Std. Dev.*	*%*
Pentanal	32923	1831	5.6
Hexanal	41436	2145	5.2
Heptanal	33072	1395	4.2
Octanal	62003	1507	2.4
Nonanal	59425	1513	2.5

Quantitative Analysis Using Purge and Trap

From its inception, as a way to determine the levels of organic pollutants in water, purge and trap has been applied in a quantitative approach. Typical methods developed by the EPA require rigorous standardisation and calculations based on internal standards. As with similar techniques, the internal standard is added to the sample matrix just before analysis so that it is processed in the identical way that the sample volatiles are.

For non-environmental samples, the same approach should be used. If a quantitative determination is to be made on a liquid sample, the internal standard solution should be miscible with the sample matrix to ensure proper dispersion and, consequently, identical behaviour of the analyte and internal standard volatiles. For solid materials, it is sometimes difficult to add the internal standard to the sample matrix without the possibility of the internal standard vaporising as the sample is placed into the purging tube or vessel. Addition of the internal standard solution to the sample tube just before purging reduced the chance that the internal standard will be preferentially volatilized, as does the selection of an internal standard of similar volatility to the analyte materials. If the solid material is a powder, the syringe may be inserted into the center of the sample plug in the tube and the solution expelled directly into the sample. This approach has been used successfully for the determination of residual solvents in pharmaceuticals by dynamic headspace. If the sample is a solid piece, such as citrus peel or peppercorns, the sample may be placed in the tube and held in place with a generous quantity of glass wool. The internal standard may then be injected into the glass wool before thermal desorption. Quantitative procedures have been developed for a variety of food and packaging analyses, including the determination of ethylene dibromide in prepared foods and the use of multiple runs to quantitate N-nitrosodimethylamine in baby bottle nipples.

Some purge-and-trap instruments have trap injection ports that permit the injection of the internal standard solution onto the trap directly while the sample is being purged, which ensures that the whole injection is trapped but does not compensate for any loss due to purging efficiency, vessel leaking, and so on. With attention to sampling parameters and the selection of a compatible internal

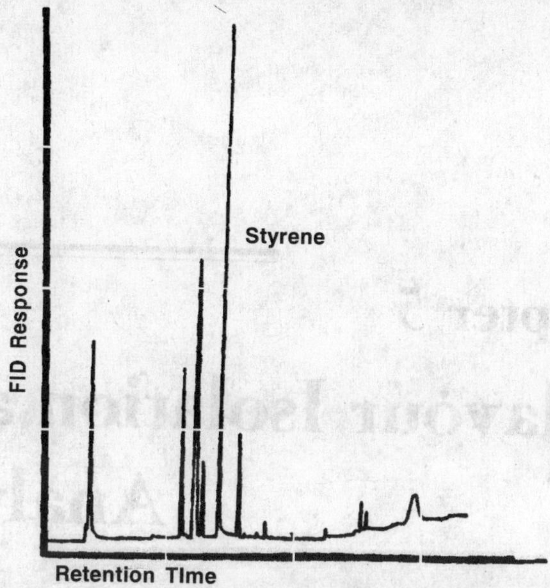

Figure 4.10: Purge-and-Trap Analysis of Soup Made in Foam Cup in Microwave Showing Styrene from Packaging

standard, purge-and-trap analysis can easily provide quantitative results with relative standard deviations for replicates below 5 per cent.

Chapter 5

Flavour Isolation and Analysis

Solid-phase Microextraction

Solid-phase microextraction (SPME) is a relatively new technique for the rapid, solventless extraction or preconcentration of volatile and semi-volatile organic compounds. It utilises the partitioning of organic components between a bulk aqueous or vapour phase and the thin polymeric films coated onto fused silica fibers in the SPME apparatus. The technique was first described by Berlardi and Pawliszyn for the analysis of environmental chemicals in water. Since that time, environmental studies and theoretical treatments and practical applications have continued to account for most of the publications. The areas of food, beverage, and related analyses have generated only a few references.

Solid-phase microextraction techniques are independent of the form of the matrix; liquids, solids, and gases all can be sampled readily. SPME is an equilibrium technique, and accurate quantitation requires that the extractions be carefully controlled. Each component will behave differently depending on its polarity, volatility, organic/ water partition coefficient, the volume of the sample or the volume of the headspace, the rate of agitation, the pH of the solu ion, and the temperature. The incorporation of an internal standard into the matrix and adherence to specific sampling times will usually result in excellent quantitative correlations. Since the SPME technique requires no solvents and can be performed without heating the sample, the formation of chemical artifacts is greatly reduced, if not completely eliminated.

The manual device is essentially a modified syringe having a spring-loaded plunger and a barrel with a detent to allow the plunger to be held in an extended position during the extraction phase and during the injection period.

Also contained within the barrel is a modified 24 gauge stainless steel needle, which encloses another length of stainless steel tubing fitted tightly to a short piece of solid-core fused silica fiber. The bottom centimeter of the fused silica fiber is coated with a relatively thin film of any of several stationary phases. This film serves as the organic "solvent" during the absorption of the volatile compounds from the analytical matrix. The needle functions to puncture the septa sealing both the sample container and the GC injection port and to protect the fragile fused silica fiber during storage and use.

Fibers coated with nonpolar polydimethylsiloxane (similar to SE-30 or OV-101) and the more polar polycarylate are commercially available at the present time. The development of several other fiber types is actively underway, including Carbowax, Carboxen (a porous activated carbon support), and divinylbenzene copolymers. For most analyses, especially of volatile flavour compounds, a fiber having a 100-µm coating of polydimethylsiloxane is preferred. If a more rapid equilibration is needed, a fiber with a 30-µm coating of polydimethylsiloxane might be more appropriate. Fibers with a 7-µm thickness of polydimethylsiloxane will work well with samples having high boiling components, *e.g.*, polyaromatic hydrocarbons, or where higher temperatures might be required to desorb them in the injection port of the gas chromatograph. In general, the fibers coated with thicker films will require a somewhat longer time to achieve equilibrium but might provide higher sensitivity due to the greater mass of the analytes that can be absorbed. A fiber coated with an 85-µm film of polyacrylate is available for the extraction of more polar compounds, especially those possessing phenolic structures.

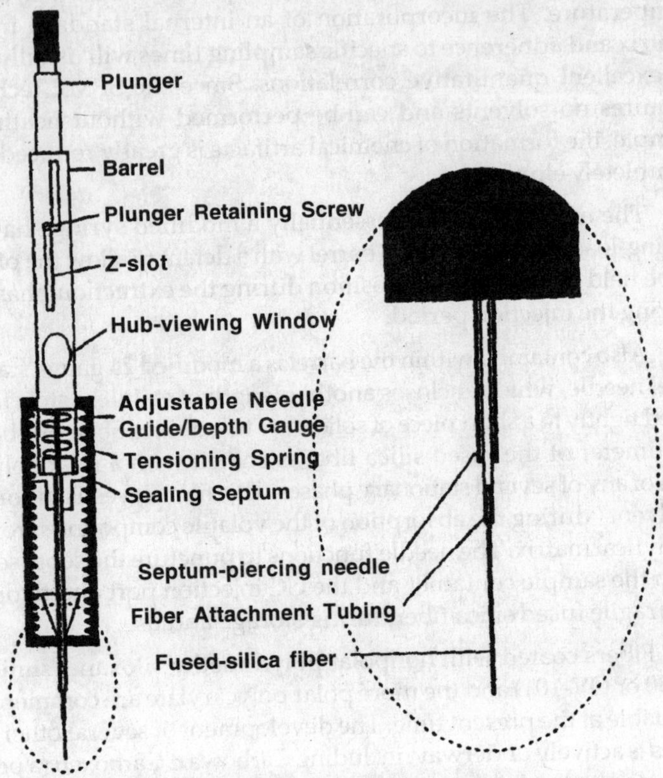

Figure 5.1: Graphical Representation of a Solid-Phase Microextraction (SPME) Device

A sample is placed into a vial or other suitable container, which is sealed with a septum-type cap. The fiber should be cleaned before analysing any sample because the polymer phase can absorb aroma chemicals from the air and produce a high background in the chromatogram. Cleaning can be done in a few minutes by inserting the fiber into an auxiliary injection port or using a syringe cleaner. For liquid sampling the SPME needle pierces the septum and the fiber is extended through the needle and into the solution. During headspace sampling the fiber is extended into the vapour phase above a liquid or solid sample. The SPME apparatus and sample vial can be supported during the equilibration period by placing them inside a test tube (18 × 150 mm or larger). Both direct liquid sampling and headspace techniques often benefit from the addition of sodium chloride to the solution, which enhances the equilibrium toward the organic phase of the SPME fiber. Some care must be exercised when penetrating the septa because the needle point on the SPME device is flat. It might be appropriate to use prepunched septa both for sealing the sample vials and in the injection port of the gas chromatograph.

After a suitable sampling time (1–20 minutes), the fiber is withdrawn into the needle; the needle is removed from the septum and is then inserted directly into the injection port of a gas chromatograph for 1–2 minutes. The absorbed chemicals are thermally desorbed by the heat of the injection port and are transferred directly to the column for analysis.

Any manner of injection is suitable for SPME as long as the needle can be introduced through the septum nut and can be extended into the heated zone of any injection system. Since this

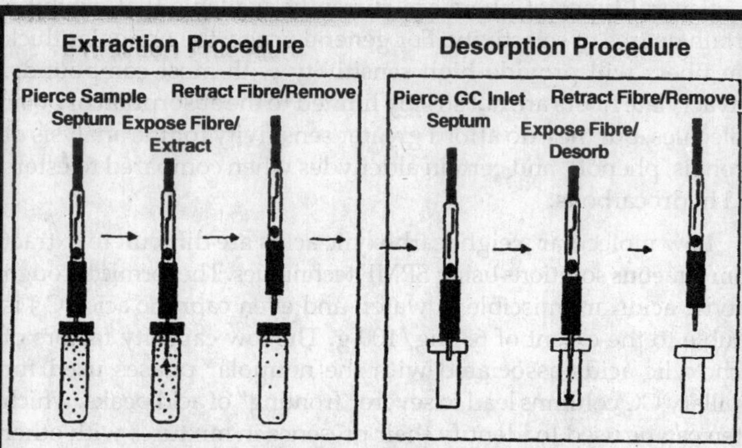

Figure 5.2: Sequence of Events Showing Extraction Steps and Desorption (injection) Steps Followed to Perform an Analysis Using SPME.

The fiber is inserted directly into a liquid sample with the subsequent absorption of most of the analyte molecules (small circles) from the solution.

technique often involves the preconcentration of very dilute substances, the split ratio of a split/splitless capillary injection port should be set to a low value (around 10:1) so that the benefit of the preconcentration step is not wasted. For some applications where the components are not at trace levels, higher split flow will work as well. The use of an injection port liner with an internal diameter of 1 mm or less usually provides somewhat sharper peaks for highly volatile compounds, although completely satisfactory chromatographic separations and peak shapes can be achieved using a standard split liner packed with glass wool.

Cryogenic cooling of the column is not necessary for most applications, although some sharpening of early eluting peaks will result if that capability is available. Care should be taken to ensure that the upper surface of the glass wool or other packing material used in the injection liner is below the level of the tip of the SPME fiber when it is inserted into the injection port. The penalty for extending the fiber into glass wool is often a broken or damaged fiber.

Several types of fibers are currently available that exhibit a certain degree of selectivity. For general usage, the nonpolar thick film fibers will provide high sensitivity with most compounds. Polyacrylate fibers are not strictly limited to the absorption of polar molecules, but they do afford greater sensitivity for the analysis of alcohols, phenols, and certain aldehydes when compared to esters and hydrocarbons.

Low molecular weight carboxylic acids are difficult to extract from aqueous solutions using SPME techniques. The formic through butyric acids are miscible in water, and even caprylic acid (C_8) is soluble to the extent of 68 mg/100 g. The low capacity factors of carboxylic acids associated with the nonpolar phases used for capillary GC columns lead to severe "fronting" of acid peaks, which often can be used to identify their presence in mixtures with other flavour compounds. The same phenomenon also has an effect on the absorption of acids by SPME phases. It is possible to enhance their extraction with SPME techniques, however, Figure 5.2 shows the relative extraction efficiencies for several carboxylic acids, each at a concentration of 10 ppm in water. The results show the effectiveness of headspace extractions for both the 85-μm polyacrylate and 100-μm polydimethylsiloxane fibers and of the addition of 25 per cent NaCl to the solutions. With the exception of caprylic acid, the polyacrylate fiber is more efficient for headspace extractions. The salting out effect is dramatic for carboxylic acids more than four carbons in length.

Table 5.1: Relative GC Peak Areas of a Flavour Mixture Obtained by Direct Split Injection and by Different SPME Sampling Methods

Compound	*Relative Peak Area (%)*		
	Direct Injection	*SPME Liquid Sampling*	*SPME Headspace Sampling*
Ethyl acetate	4.4	0.2	1.2
Ethyl butyrate	5.0	2.6	11.5
Limonene	6.4	1.2	2.6
Ethyl caproate	4.3	6.9	8.4
3-Hexenyl acetale	4.3	7.8	12.0
cis-3-Hexenol	4.9	0.3	2.1
Benzaldehyde	5.5	1.1	6.0
Linalool	4.5	1.1	6.0
Diethyl succinate	3.4	<0.1	<0.1
Neral	2.9	7.0	5.9
2-Methylbutyric acid	2.9	0.1	<0.1
γ-Hexalactone	3.4	0.l	0.3
l-Carvone	4.7	9.6	7.9
Geranial	5.0	13.6	9.7
Anethole	4.8	14.1	5.0
Caproic acid	3.2	0.1	<0.1
Phenylethanol	4.9	0.2	0.4
β-Ionone	4.3	14.9	8.9
Cinnamic aldehyde	4.6	2.5	0.2
Triacetin	2.1	0.2	0.2
γ-Decalactone	3.7	8.0	1.5
Heliotropin	2.4	0.5	0.2
Triethyl citrate	2.2	0.1	<0.1
Ethyl vanillin	3.3	<0.1	<0.1
Vanillin	3.0	<0.1	<0.1

The Theoretical Aspects of Solid-phase Micro-extraction

The theoretical aspects of solid-phase microextraction have been well documented, and the reader should refer to these references for a complete discussion. Essentially, the principles affecting extraction of organic compounds from solutions using SPME are the same ones that control their partitioning between phases of immiscible liquids in a separatory funnel, a countercurrent extraction system, a Likens-Nickerson distillation head, or any other liquid-liquid extraction device. Therefore, the factors affecting efficient extraction by these methods (contact time, efficiency of mixing, pH, salt concentration, temperature, phase ratios etc.) also affect the partitioning in SPME extractions. This is not an unreasonable concept if the SPME fiber is regarded simply as an immobilised liquid phase in contact with an aqueous solution.

The volume of the fiber coating is small relative to the bulk of the aqueous phase being extracted, and the mass of analyte absorbed by the coating at equilibrium is directly related to its initial concentration in the solution and the distribution coefficients controlling the equilibria. The principle behind the partitioning process is the equilibrium established for the analyte(s) between the fiber organic phase and the solution phase. If you consider the equilibrium expression in effect for the placement of the fiber in the solution

$$[X]_l \Leftrightarrow [X]_f$$

then

$$K_{lf} = \frac{[X]_f}{[X]_l}$$

where, [X] is the concentration of the flavour chemical in solution (l) and in the organic phase of the SPME fiber (f). K_{lf} is the distribution coefficient for X between the liquid phase and the fiber. The amount of material absorbed from the solution by the fiber can be described by the relationship.

$$n = \frac{C_0 V_1 V_f K_{lf}}{K_{lf} V_f + V_1}$$

where, n is the amount of compound X absorbed by the fiber, C_0 is the initial concentration of X in the solution, and V_l and V_f are the respective volumes of the solution and the organic phase of the fiber. In order to obtain a quantitative extraction (>90 per cent of the analyte absorbed by the fiber), the distribution coefficient of X needs to be about an order of magnitude greater than the volume ratio V_l/V_f of the system. Complete extractions are usually not necessary to obtain quantitative information, since the amounts of the analytes in the SPME phase are controlled by the various distribution constants in effect under the experimental conditions. As long as the conditions are carefully repeated from run to run, the equilibrium concentrations in the phases also will remain constant.

In the case of headspace SPME extraction, the equilibrium partitioning occurs between the liquid organic phase of the fiber and the vapour phase above a liquid or solid sample. The diffusion of analytes to the fiber in the vapour phase is about four orders of magnitude greater than in solution. The speed of analysis by headspace sampling should reflect this greater diffusion. In fact,

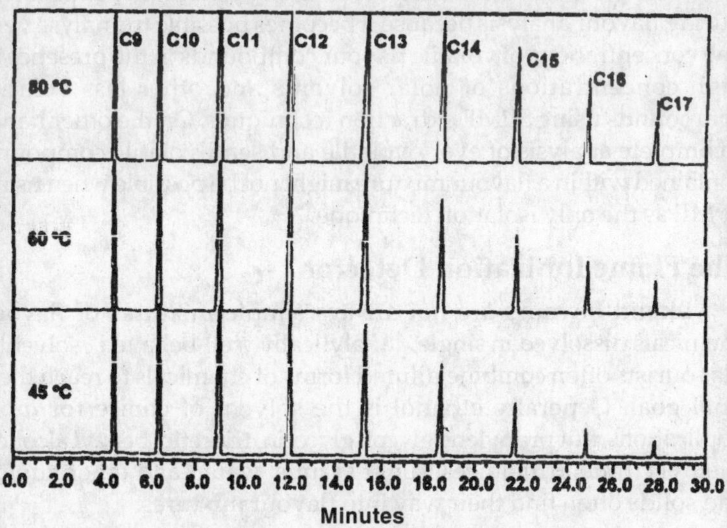

Figure 5.3: Stacked Chromatogrames Showing the Gas Chromatographic Analysis of a Series of *n*-hydrocarbons Isolated by Headspace SPME at Various Temperatures

headspace SPME can reduce the extraction time from 5 minutes to 1 minute or less and still maintain high sensitivities for most analytes. Heating the sample greatly increases the diffusion of analytes into the vapour phase. Zhang and Pawliszyn have taken advantage of this to effect quantitative recoveries of BTEX compounds from difficult matrices by simultaneously heating the sample and cooling the fiber.

Considering the mild temperatures utilised, the recovery of *n*-heptadecane (boiling point 302°C) is remarkable. In fact, a room temperature extraction also provided a significant peak for each of the nine components. It is not surprising, then, that headspace extractions of food samples can provide considerable detail about the composition of spices, herbs, and flavours. According to Zhang and Pawllszyn, compounds with Henry's constants greater than 90 $atm.cm^3.mol^{-1}$ can be isolated using headspace SPME at ambient temperature. This would include three-ring polyaromatic hydrocarbons with boiling points around 340°C, for example.

For compounds that have appreciable water solubility, both the transfer to the vapour phase and the corresponding decrease in the magnitude of K_{lf} can prevent observing them in chromatograms obtained by SPME extraction. This is not necessarily a problem during flavour analysis because it becomes possible to analyse very low concentrations of volatile flavour compounds in the presence of high concentrations of polar solvents and other less volatile compounds using SPME extraction techniques. On the other hand, a complete analysis of every volatile and semi-volatile compound contained within a flavour mixture might not be possible when using SPME as the only isolation technique.

The Flame Ionization Detector

Liquid flavours are not always simple mixtures of flavour chemicals dissolved in single, "analytically well-behaved" solvents. Flavourists often combine diluted forms of chemicals to reach their final goal. Generally ethanol is the solvent of choice for most applications, but propylene glycol, glycerin, triacetin, benzyl alcohol, triethyl citrate, fruit juices, sugar syrups, water, and other liquids and solids often find their way into flavour mixtures.

Figure 5.4 shows a capillary gas chromatogram of the result of a direct split injection of a fruit punch flavour using flame ionisation

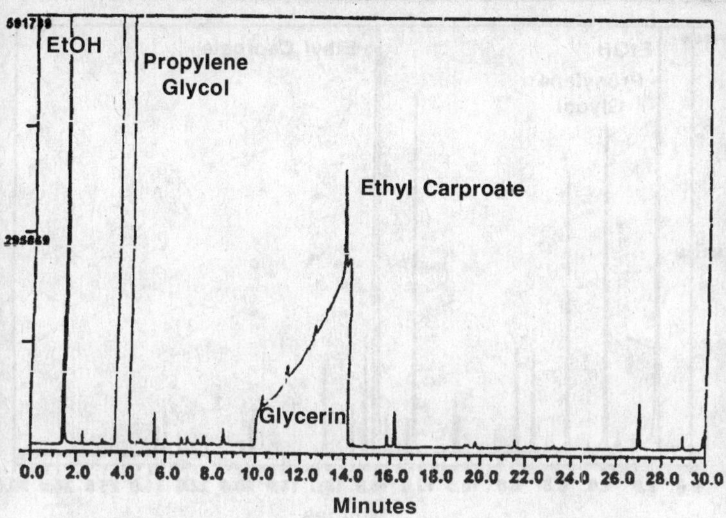

Figure 5.4: Chromatogram Showing the Flame Ionization Detector Response After a Direct Split Injection of a Punch Flavour onto a Capillary GC Column

detection. Three solvents were used in the flavour, all in large proportion, along with a lesser amount of a fruit juice. Only ethyl caproate could be identified by GC/MS as a primary flavour chemical among the ethanol, propylene glycol, and glycerin components. The other, smaller peaks in the chromatogram were primarily associated with dimeric and polymeric ethers arising from the solvents. In addition, several artifacts associated with sugar decomposition were observed.

Clearly, the two methods provide different results. One should first compare the contributions of the various solvents to the chromatograms. Headspace SPME sampling has completely eliminated the glycerin peak, which revealed 13 additional flavour components that had coeluted with that solvent as a result of direct split injection. Glycerin could not be detected even with a selected ion chromatogram. The propylene glycol peak has been reduced to a well-resolved minor component by the headspace extraction, but ethanol remains as a major solvent peak. These differences are due both to the lower volatilities of propylene glycol and glycerin and to

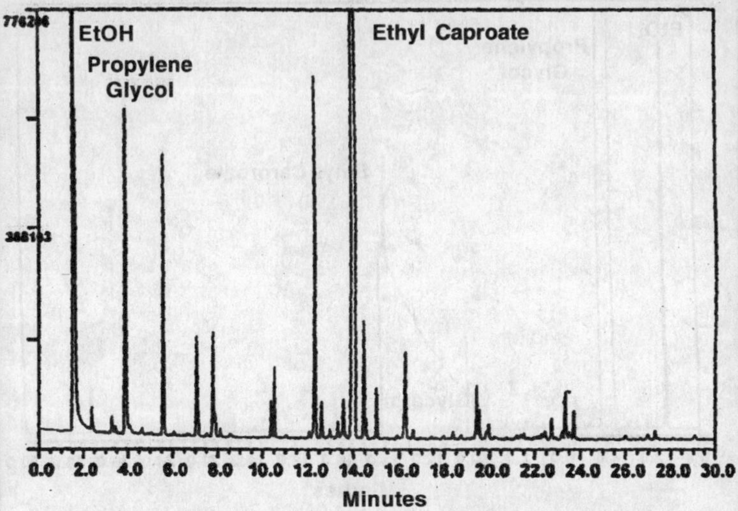

Figure 5.5: Chromatogram Showing the Flame Ionization Detector Response to the Headspace SPME Extract Obtained from Six Drops of a Punch Flavour using a 100-μm Polydimethylsiloxane Fiber for 10 Minutes at 45°C

their hydrophilic nature. The affinity of the hydroxylic solvents for the polydimethylsiloxane fiber used in this analysis is much less than the affinities of less polar, more hydrophobic flavour chemicals. Although a chromatogram has not been included to show it, a Likens-Nickerson extraction of this flavour also did not provide a satisfactory analysis due to the formation of numerous artifacts from the thermal decomposition of sugars during the steam distillation.

The natural chemicals comprising the aroma of fresh fruits are usually complex mixtures of alcohols, aldehydes, esters, and terpenoids that may transform markedly during the ripening cycle. These chemicals are generally recovered from the fruit pulp or their juices by vacuum or steam distillation before separation and analysis using capillary GC or GC/MS. Such isolation techniques require relatively large amounts of fruit, sometimes on the order of several kilograms, to obtain a suitable analytical sample, which then is diluted and contaminated with the organic solvents used during the isolation. Additionally, traditional isolation methods require from 4 to 24 hours before the identification phase can begin. Purge-and-trap techniques will reduce both the amount of sample required and the time needed to prepare a suitable isolate, but the equipment is expensive and requires time to establish the operating interface to a GC or a GC/MS system. Headspace SPME can be utilised with small samples of fruit, the extract can be prepared in a few minutes with little sample preparation, and it is readily transported to any number of gas chromatographic systems.

Yang and Peppard have shown that direct liquid immersion SPME of a sample of fruit juice beverage was comparable or higher in sensitivity to a conventional solvent extraction using dichloromethane for most of the recovered flavour chemicals. Although they did not compare the sensitivity of headspace SPME extraction in the same study, it would have provided a similar result. For studies in our laboratories, fresh fruits have been sampled by simply removing three or four small "cores" of fruit pulp using the blunt end of a disposable Pasteur pipet and depositing the pieces into a 15-ml headspace vial. After fitting the vial with a Teflon-lined seal, the fruit is immediately extracted using headspace SPME at room temperature for 10 minutes before injection and analysis by GC/MS.

Cantaloupe is the orange, delicately flavoured fruit of *Cucumis melo* L., which becomes progressively stronger in flavour and aroma with increasing ripeness. The primary aroma compounds have been identified in the Figure 5.6. These compounds were not determined in a quantitative experiment, but it has been reported that isobutyl acetate, butyl acetate, and ethyl butyrate are present in cantaloupe at a level of 0.1 ppm and that hexyl acetate is present at 0.04 ppm. Obviously, these amounts will vary from sample to sample, but if these levels are indicative of the concentrations in this melon, the headspace SPME technique is able to detect very low levels of nonpolar volatile chemicals.

A ripe banana (*Musa sapientum* L.) was also examined in the same manner. After transferring about 2 g of banana "cores" to a vial, the headspace SPME extract provided the GC/MS chromatogram. This chromatogram is considerably more complex than a "typical" banana flavour, which usually is highly concentrated in isoamyl acetate. Quantitative values have been reported for several of the compounds from banana extracts, among

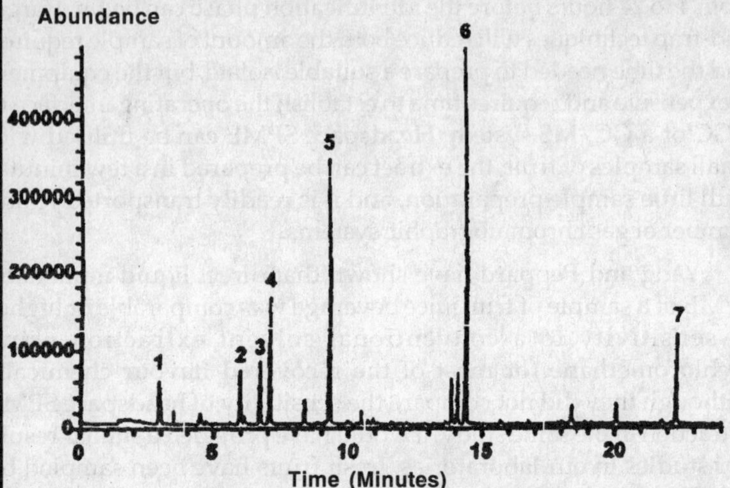

Figure 5.6: Total Ion Chromatogram of a Portion of the Volatile Components Obtained from a Sample of Ripe Cantaloupe by Headspace SPME Using a 100 μm Polydimethylsiloxane Fiber

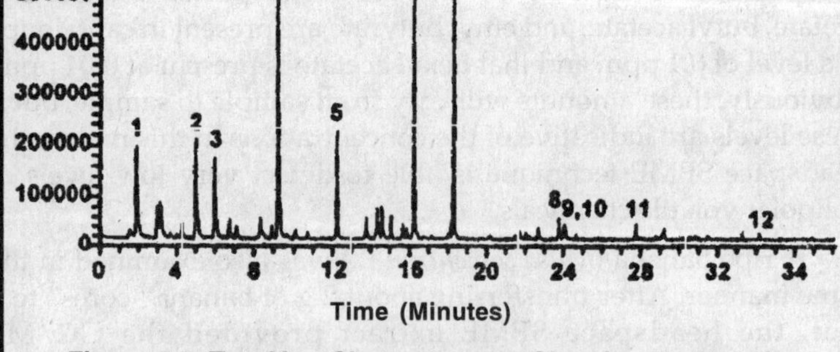

Figure 5.7: Total Ion Chromatogram Showing the Volatile Components Obtained from a Ripe Banana by Headspace SPME Using a 100 μm Polydimethylsiloxane Fiber

them isoamyl alcohol (2–12 ppm), isobutyl acetate (47 ppm), isoamyl acetate (12–75 ppm), isoamyl isobutyrate (0.7 ppm), isoamyl butyrate (6 ppm), isoamyl caproate (0.07 ppm), eugenol (1.2 ppm), and elemicin (7.5 ppm). The relative peak areas shown in this chromatogram suggest a different quantitative profile, but this might have been affected by the different ripeness of the samples and the relative extraction efficiency of the SPME fiber. 3-Hexenyl caproate was found in the SPME extract but was not listed among the banana flavour compounds in that reference.

The Flavour and Aroma of Herbs and Spices

For many spices and herbs, the aroma and flavour will vary depending upon its country of origin, processing conditions, the age of the sample, the type of packaging, the ratio of essential oil volatiles to heat-producing principles, and many other factors. Black pepper is one of the most widely consumed spices in the world. It might be of benefit to be able to evaluate the chemical composition of the volatile oil of single peppercorns to correlate with sensory attributes. This chromatogram was the result of a 5-minute room temperature headspace SPME extraction of a single black peppercorn (42 mg) that had been crushed with pliers and rapidly transferred to a 4-ml vial. The chromatogram has been expanded along the vertical axis to show the smaller components in the mixture. The composition is somewhat atypical of a "normal" chromatogram obtained by steam distillation, but the general appearance is readily identified. Considering that the whole sample could have provided no more than 1.5 mg of volatile oil, the sensitivity of the extraction is remarkable.

Since the spice was known to contain a unique aroma chemical, it was an easy matter to transfer a small amount of the curry to a vial, perform a headspace extraction, and determine whether the spice had been added. The complete analysis required less than one hour from the time the sample was received. As a quality control measure, SPME can have a significant impact on the analysis of raw materials and finished products.

Beverage manufacturers often compete with one another for customer approval of their flavours. Typical among these were the "cola wars" conducted a few years ago. SPME would have provided a rapid technique to compare various brands of cola volatiles to

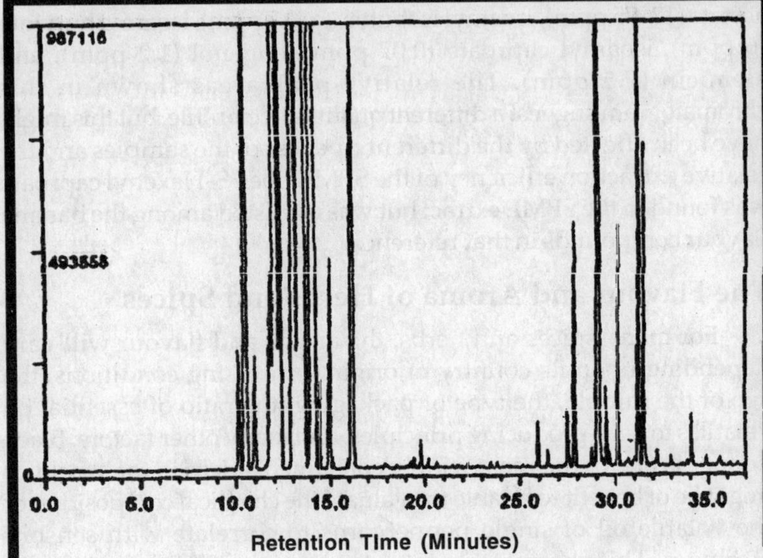

Figure 5.8: Chromatogram Showing the Volatile Compounds Isolated from a Single Black Peppercorn Using Headspace SPME

determine whether they really were different. The chromatograms shown in Figure 5.11 offer a comparison between two cola products. Obviously, these two products are very similar in their aroma profiles, and they have probably been formulated using similar ingredients. Unfortunately, nothing can be determined regarding the more subtle volatile compounds or the non-volatile and more polar portions of the beverages using headspace SPME.

Few people would confuse the flavour of root beer with a typical cola. Even fewer would find it difficult to discriminate between their chromatograms.

Solid-phase microextraction is still in its infancy. As research continues toward the development of different fiber materials and techniques, the resulting greater specificity and enhanced performance can only benefit the analytical flavour chemist. Even now the applications for SPME in flavour analysis appear to be

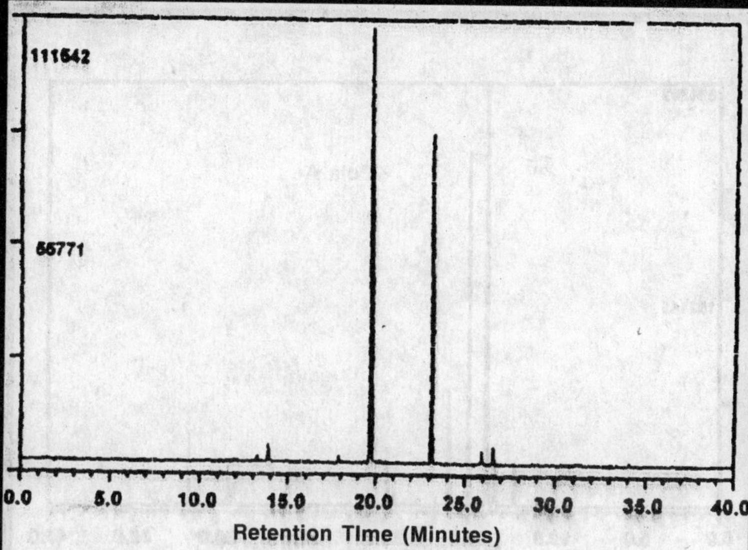

Figure 5.9: Chromatogram Showing the Volatile Compounds Isolated from a Sample of Root Beer-flavoured Beverage

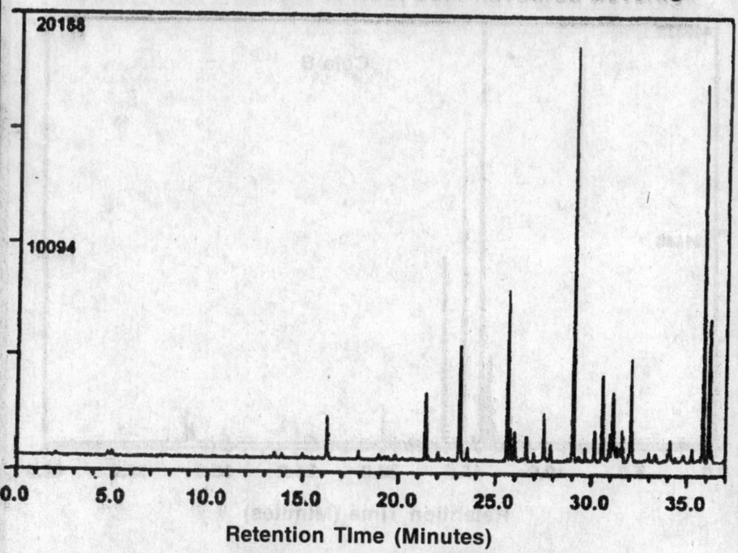

Figure 5.10: Chromatogram of a Portion of the Volatile Components Obtained by Headspace SPME of a Sample of Curry Powder

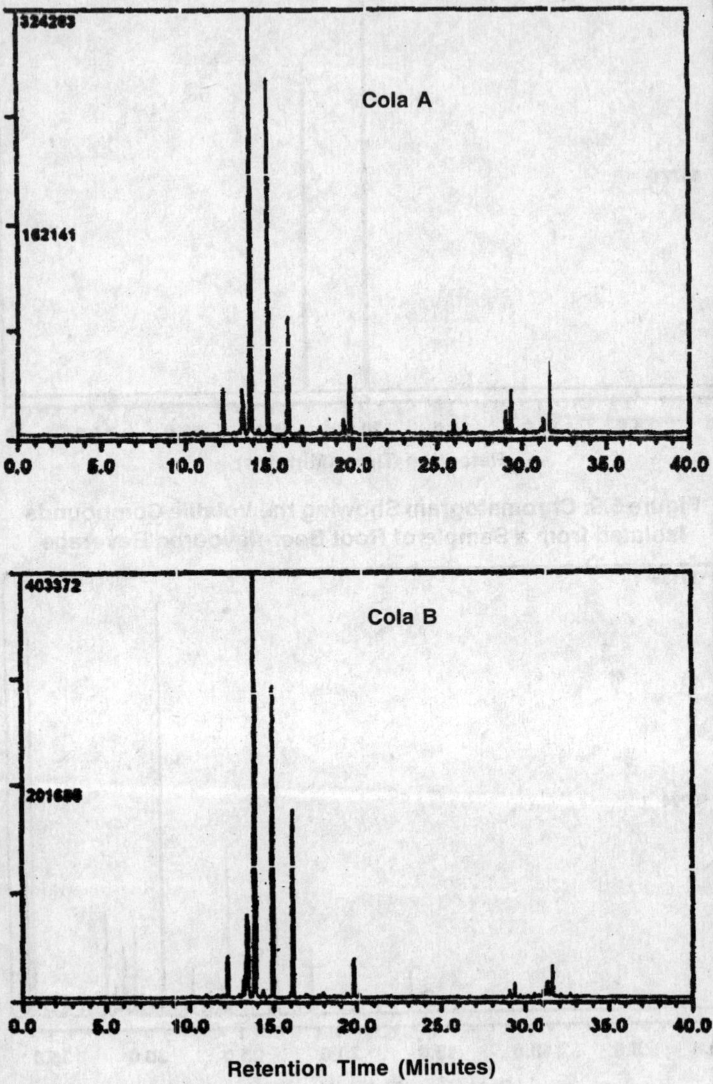

Figure 5.11: Chromatograms Showing the Similarities Between Two Popular Brands of Cola Beverages

limited only by the imagination. Automation will move the techniques into quality control applications and will greatly improve the quantitative aspects of analyses. SPME will result in a need for smaller samples and will decrease the likelihood of the identification of artifacts as flavour components.

SPME has become the method of choice for the initial isolation and analysis of aroma chemicals in the laboratory. For many applications it is the only technique required to solve the problem.

Chapter 6

Fluorescence Techniques

Introduction

Fluorescence is undeniably a powerful diagnostic tool, a1though in plant science–in contrast to the medical, animal and food sciences–its use has been relatively neglected. However, at the level of the plant cell and protoplast, fluorescence techniques are today being used increasingly in a wide range of applications, examples of which are estimation of cell viability correlation of the onset of DNA synthesis with that of protein and cell wall synthesis, determination of the cell cycle phase, flow-cytometric protoplast sorting, immunocytological localization of cyto-skeletal components and the monitoring of microinjection immobilization, substrate delivery, organelle exchange and somatic fusion.

By taking advantage of the three genomic components of plant cells, namely the nucleus, chloroplast and mitochondrion, somatic protoplast fusion makes possible the creation of novel hybrid and cybrid plants and is therefore, an important tool in the improvement of food crops. However, one of the limitations in modern breeding biotechnology is the paucity of methods for discriminating between fusion products. Fluorescent dyes are potentially useful selective markers.

Fluorescence in plant tissues emanates either from compounds such as chlorophyll, lignin and cuticular waxes inherent to the plant cell or from added fluorochromes. Under natural light, chlorophyll containing cells appear green, but upon irradiation with near-ultravlolet (320–400 nm) or violet-blue (*ca* 400–470 nm) light they will appear red provided that a cut-off filter is used to isolate the emission light over the range of wavelengths 600–700 nm. This type of luminescence, which ceases immediately upon termination of the excitation, is fluorescence. The autofluorescence displayed by chlorophyll may interfere with other fluorochromes having overlapping emission spectra. However, where double-labelling of either homologous or heterologous populations of protoplasts is desirable, effective use can be made of autofluorescence in combination with particular fluorochromes.

When estimating cell viability it is important to distinguish clearly between live cells and dead cells. In homologous labelling, two fluorochromes are simultaneously introduced into the same cell or protoplast population, one for the identification of viable cells and the other for the non-viable, *i.e.*, injured and/or dead cells. Alternatively, when determining viability of chloroplast-containing cells, chlorophyll autofluorescence can be used in conjunction with a fluorogenic ester that exhibits fluorochromasia in living cells. The relative emission intensity of the chlorophyll autofluorescence in the presence of the introduced dye, made fluorochromic as a result of intracellular enzymatic hydrolysis, is then taken as a measure of the degree of viability: the greater the intensity of the autofluorescence, the lower the viability, and vice-versa.

In contrast, heterologous labelling involves the separate staining of two different populations of plant protoplasts, each with a specific fluorochrome. This procedure is useful for monitoring the sequence of the fusion process and identifying the fusion products. The simultaneous presence of two fluorochromes is indicative of a reconstituted hybrid cell. Again, where protoplasts of green tissues are used, the residual chlorophyll autofluorescence of one fusion partner may be substituted for an exogenously introduced fluorochrome.

Some fluorochromes such as Acridine Orange and ethidium bromide are mutagenic and some are toxic to living cells, whereas others such as fluorescein diacetate, fluorescein isothiocyanate, and cellufluor, are non-toxic in low concentrations. However, toxicity becomes irrelevant when fluorescent probes are carried out on a sample of protoplasts for the purpose of acquiring information that may be extrapolated to the population. A number of fluorochromes that have been shown to be non-toxic at low concentrations, but still effective as markers, can be incorporated into plant tissues before or during the protoplast isolation procedure without any apparent deleterious effects on subsequent cytological events such as cell wall resynthesis and sustained mitosis.

Fluorescence Induction Kinetics

Fluorescence induction kinetics reveal information about the activity of the photosynthetic apparatus. In the case of non-chlorophyllous protoplasts, the time-course of cell impairment based on FDA vital staining should preferably be matched to a suitable metabolic parameter, for example membrane potential, heat effects, or oxygen uptake. Membrane potential gives an indication of the integrity of the plasmalemma and the physiological condition of the protoplast. Deterioration in the physiology of the cell results in a reduction of the membrane potential as the system approaches the equilibrium state. Electrochromic fluorescent probes can be used to monitor membrane potential. Since heat effects accompany all life processes, the quantity of heat evolved from a biological system can be taken as an indication of its viability. For complex biological systems, colorimetric methods are non-specific as they do not discriminate against different compartments of the cell, but few studies have been carried out on plant protoplasts in this regard. The immediate responses of fluorescence induction and oxygen uptake derive from chloroplasts and mitochondria, respectively, *i.e.*, the responses are compartmentalized. Nevertheless the physiological state of these organelles is intimately integrated with and inseparable from that of the cell as a whole. Combining subjective with objective measurements would minimize the variation in estimates of viability often found between workers even in the same laboratory. Unfortunately, with few exceptions, plant biologists are not making any meaningful comparisons of fluorochrome fluorescence spectra using micro-spectrofluorometry.

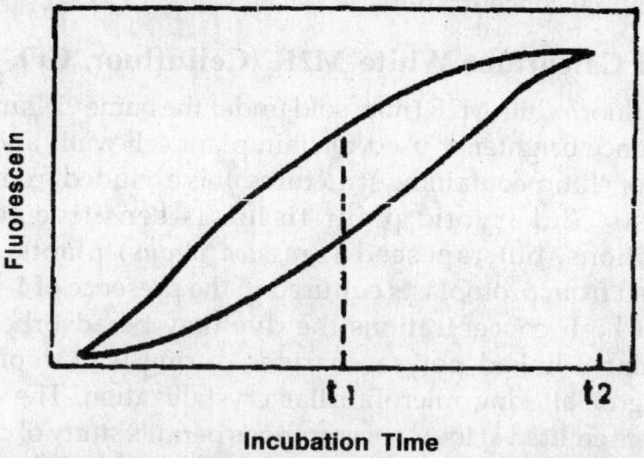

Figure 6.1: Hypothetical Kinetics of FDA Hydrolysis by Two Cell Populations with Different Esterase Activities

Few investigators indicate the length of the time interval between the introduction of FDA and observation of the fluorescence response. In cases where this is done, a rationale for selecting a particular time interval is not explained.

Now let us try to understand about dyes which are applied to the same population of isolated protoplasts.

The phenanthridinium dye, propidium iodide, does not enter intact cells and therefore, only damaged protoplasts are counterstained. This dye is specific for double-stranded DNA and upon intercalation results in a manifold increase in fluorescence emission at 610 nm. A stock solution is made up in an iso-osmotic protoplast rinse or culture medium and used at a final concentration of 10-50 µg/ml. Huang *et al.* found that by using a double-exposure method, the FDA-PI combination could effectively distinguish dead from living barley aleurone protoplasts. Both green (FDA) and red (PI) fluorescing cells can also be visualized simultaneously using a 100 W halogen lamp, blue excitation and a 520 nm barrier filter.

FDA and Ethidium Bromide (EB)

Ethidium bromide, an analogue of PI, also intercalates into DNA. Although reported to stain nuclei in fresh plant material, EB does not pass through membranes of viable protoplasts within the timeframe of staining using FDA (10 min). Ethidium bromide is used at 1 μg/ml final concentration.

FDA and Calcofluor White M2R (Cellufluor, CF)

Calcofluor White M2R (now sold under the name Cellufluor) is a fluorescence brightener used to stain plant cell walls and other cellulose- or chitin-containing structures. It is excluded from living protoplasts. Eukaryotic plant tissue is sensitive to high concentrations, but rapeseed (*Brassica napus*) plants can be regenerated from protoplasts cultured in the presence of 1–10 μg/ml CF. At high concentrations the dye may be adsorbed onto extracellular β-linked polysaccharides during wall deposition, preventing or altering microfibrillar crystallization. The intense fluorescence emitted at low concentrations permits study of cell wall resynthesis by viable protoplasts. Conversely, incomplete removal of the cell wall during protoplast isolation is easily detected.

FDA and Tinopal CBS-X (T-CBS)

Tinopal CBS-X, like CF, is an optical brightener that stains cell wall material and, like CF, it is also excluded from living protoplasts. Because of this dye's high extinction coefficient, Huang *et al.* used T-CBS at a concentration of 300 μg/ml to distinguish living (yellow-brown) from dead (blue) barley aleurone protoplasts under combined bright-field and epifluorescent illumination.

Acridine Orange (AO) and Ethidium Bromide

Both dyes intercalate into DNA, AO including fluorochromasia in living protoplasts and EB likewise in dead protoplasts. However, the difference in fluorochromasia is not as distinct as that produced between FDA and PI or FDA and EB. Both AO and EB are used at a final concentration of 1 μg/ml.

The Fluorescence Intensity

More recently, a highly specific method has been reported for measuring germ that utilizes the fluorescence emission of germ extracts in the presence of boron compounds. There is no direct evidence to explain why some boron compounds cause fluorescence emission in germ extracts. Possibly the formation of boron-flavonoid complexes is involved. Using boron trifluoride-methanol complex (BF_3-MeOH) as the extractant, a yellow solution is obtained from ether-defatted wheat germ, whereas methanol alone yields a colourless solution. Absorption spectra confirm that the presence of boron trifluoride shifts the absorption band from 330 nm in the methanol extract to 395 nm. The absorption band in the spectrum of germ glycoflavones in alcohol is known to show a similar shift in the presence of aluminium chloride, an effect of the formation of an aluminium-flavonoid complex. Boron trifluoride has many

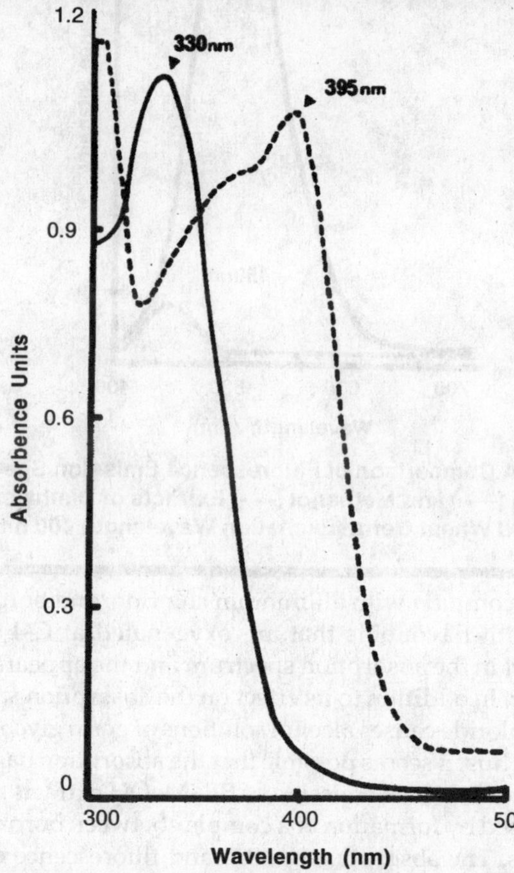

Figure 6.2: A Comparison of the Absorption Spectra of BF_3-MeOH (- - -) and Methanol (——) Extracts of Diethylether-defatted Wheat Germ. Arrows Indicate the Absorption Maxima.

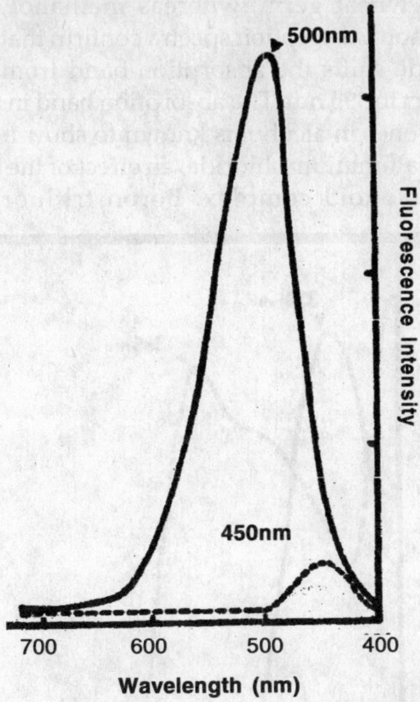

Figure 6.3: A Comparison of Fluorescence Emission Spectra of BF_3-MeOH (—) and Methanol (- - -) Extracts of Diethylether-defatted Wheat Germ (Excitation Wavelength 400 nm)

properties in common with aluminium chloride, and boron forms complexes with flavonoids that are oxygenated at C-4 and C-5 causing a shift in the absorption spectrum and the appearance of a yellow colour. In addition to its effect on the absorption spectrum, aluminium chloride causes alcohol solutions of germ glycoflavones to fluoresce. Thus, it seems possible that the absorption band at 395 nm and the fluorescence emission of BF_3-MeOH extracts of wheat germ are caused by formation of a complex between boron and the glycoflavones. The absorption spectra and fluorescence emission spectra of ferulic acid and methyl ferulate in BF_3-MeOH are not significantly different from those found using methanol, confirming that the ferulic acid and esters found in grain tissues should not interfere with measurement of germ glycoflavone fluorescence.

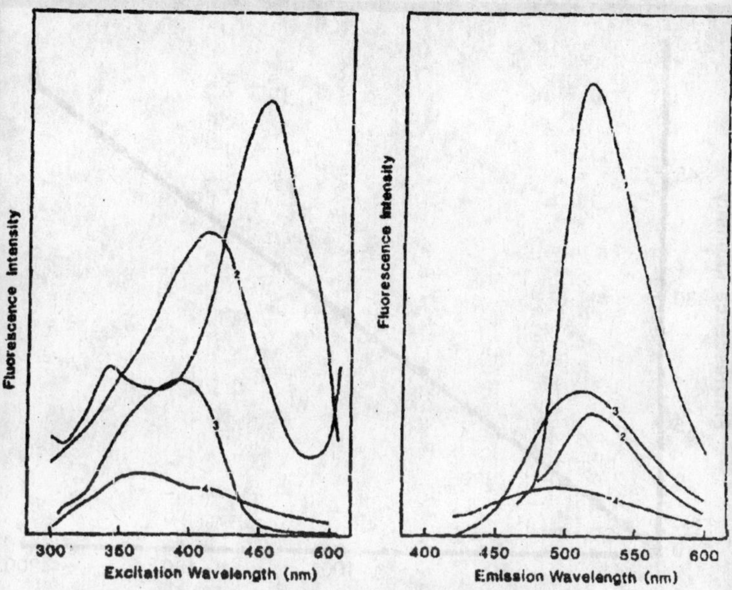

Figure 6.4: Excitation and Emission Spectra of BF_3-MeOH and Sodium Tetraborate Extracts of Wheat Germ and Bran-plus-endosperm Fractions

Using a 400 nm excitation filter, a BF_3-MeOH extract of germ shows an emission maximum at 500 nm wavelength. By comparison a methanol extract of germ has only negligible emission at 500 nm and instead shows an emission maximum at 450 nm, which is probably due to ferulic acid. BF_3-MeOH extracts of bran or white flour also have emission maxima at 450 nm, as do solutions of ferulic acid and methyl ferulate in BF_3-MeOH.

Although BF3-MeOH is an effective reagent for germ extract fluorescence measurements, aqueous sodium tetraborate is preferred because it is much safer. The fact that both reagents cause similar fluorescence emission is further evidence that chelation of boron by the glycoflavones is responsible for this fluorescence.

Using BF_3-MeOH or aqueous sodium tetraborate ('borate') with continuous mixing at room temperature, fluorescence is almost at a maximum after 15 min but 30 min provides the most reliable results.

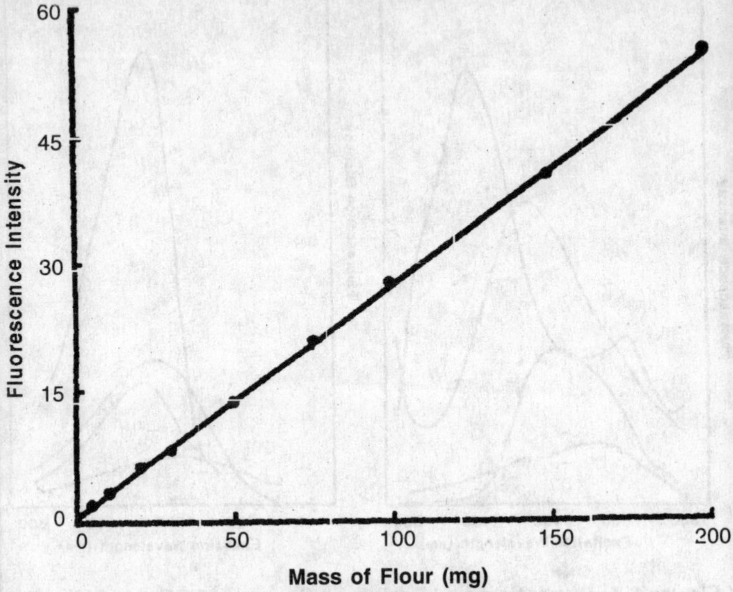

Figure 6.5: Relationship Between Fluorescence Intensity at 520 nm of Borate Extracts and the Mass of Flour Extracted (r = 0.9999)

The assay is very sensitive and the extracts must be diluted (with BF_3-MeOH or borate solution, as appropriate) to obtain a linear response.

Nevertheless, this sensitivity is valuable when measuring the germ content of white flour. The concentration of borate used in the extractant is not critical at 2 per cent (w/v) or above (although it should be consistent in order to obtain maximum precision) but the fluorescence falls dramatically when the concentration is below 1 per cent. A concentration of 2 per cent has been chosen as a satisfactory compromise between fluorescence response and solubility; 3 per cent sodium tetraborate remains dissolved in water at 20°C but crystallizes out of solution if the ambient temperature falls much below this at night.

The Fluorescence of Fish Bone and Fish Muscle

The fishbones exhibit a specific blue-violet light emission of 390 nm at an excitation wavelength of 340 nm.

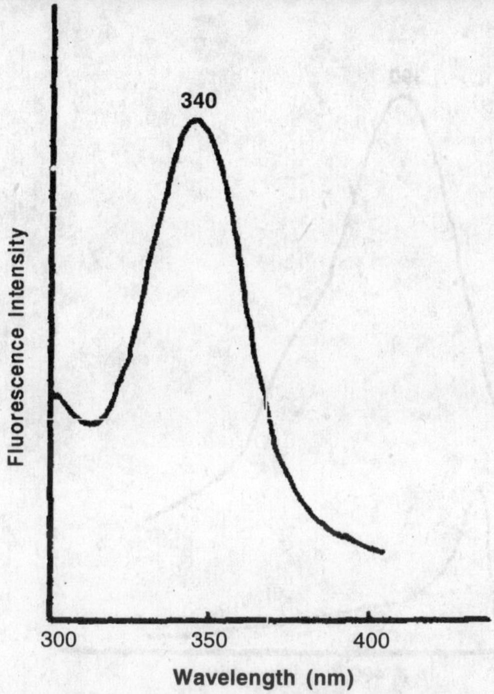

Figure 6.6: Excitation Spectrum for Fishbone at Emission 390 nm

The penetration capacity of the UV radiation through fish meat was investigated. The relative fluorescence intensity decreased by one-half when the bones were covered with 1.0 mm of meat. Therefore, the present technique is directed to surface or near-surface detection which is not a serious limitation for the fish-filleting industry because the sensitivity of the technique and the anatomy of the fish fillet assures that the bony areas are precisely detected for removal with high precision and with a minimum loss in the product–the fish meat.

The first commercial available instrument for the fish industry-the Lumetech fishbone detector-uses autofluorescence detection techniques. It can automatically evaluate deboned fish fillets and reject those containing an unacceptable number of bones. The row of transversely cut pin bones which has to be removed is clearly

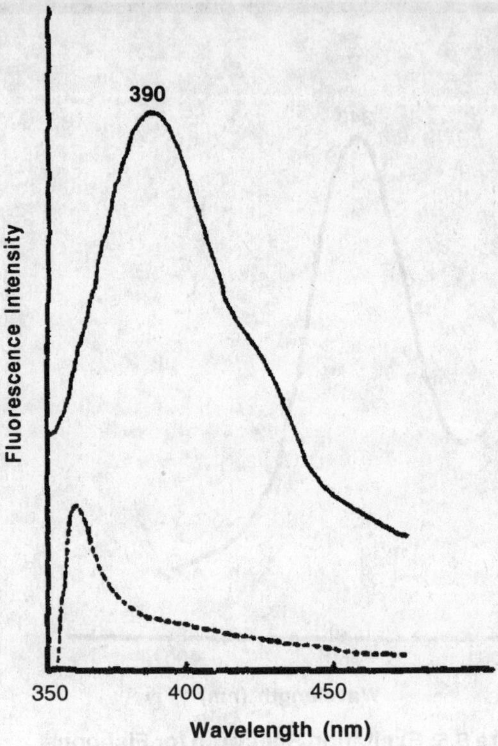

Figure 6.7: Emission Spectra for Fish Bone (—) and Fish Meat (- - -) at Excitation at 340 nm

seen. The detector can register cross-sections of bone fragments in the magnitude of a few square millimetres and by automatic sorting reduce the bone and fin frequency in manually processed cod fillets by a factor of 10. In a trial with cod fillets, a frequency of 41 bones/ 100 kg fillets was reduced to only three bone defects in the accepted products while a total of 38 bone defects were found in the rejected products.

The strong autofluorescence of fishbones at 390 nm was observed to be constant for all species examined including cod, whiting, haddock, place, flounder, and sole.

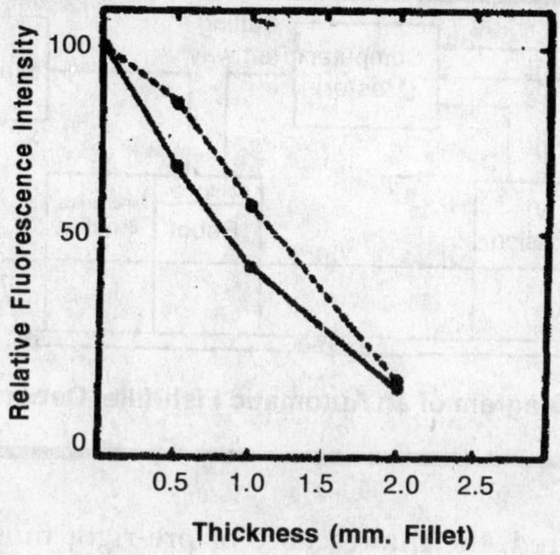

Figure 6.8: The Penetration Effect as Visualized by Covering Bones from Cod (——) and Plaice (- - -) with Meat Slices of Various Thickness of Cod and Plaice, respectively

The next step in this development is to utilize the detection system to control a water jet integrated with a robot. Representatives from the robot industry predict that, within the present decade, developments in sensing capabilities would allow the meat industry to begin full-scale integration of robotics in about 5 per cent of the fabrication tasks. With regards to the fish industry, this goal seems to be well within reach.

The automatic techniques now available do not only diminish personnel costs but improve the working environment for the operators and strengthen the economy by improving the yield of the premium product by reducing waste.

The fluorescence of fish-fillet muscle tissue is very low in samples stored on ice for 2–3 days. However, Wittfogel and Manohar demonstrated that fresh muscle tissue from various species of fish displays significant fluorescence at 460 nm with 366 nm excitation. It was found that this fluorescence was at least partly caused by the respiratory co-enzyme NADH which is known to be fluorescent.

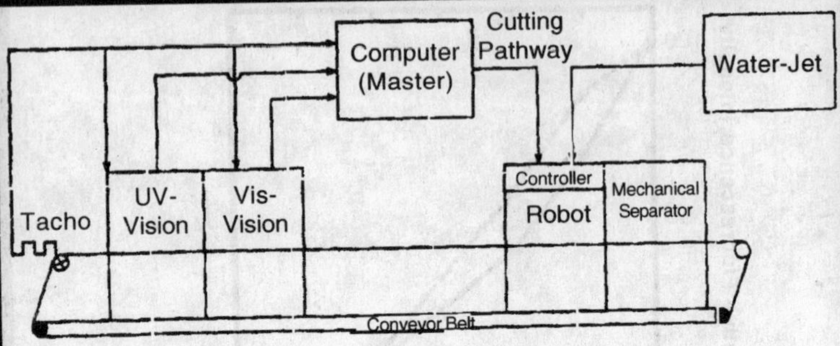

Figure 6.9: Diagram of an Automatic Fish-fillet Deboner

When frozen stored, the fluorescence of pre-rigor muscle was maintained for a long time and the fluorescence remained also after freeze-drying. There was very little fluorescence of muscle in full rigor and in post-rigor conditions also after deep-freezing. The fluorescence intensity of the fish muscle rapidly decreases after two days of storage in crushed ice.

Fluorescence Methods for the Detection of Lipid Oxidation

The observation of fluorescent products from lipid peroxidation has primarily been reported for 'biological' systems; the few examples reported of the occurrence of fluorescence in frozen herring and other fish, pork, chicken, and beef, indicate that this technique can also be applied for the objective assessment of lipid oxidation in muscle foods.

The formation of lipid-oxidation-generated fluorescent compounds involves malonaldehyde, a carbonyl compound product from the decomposition of hydroperoxides, the latter result from the peroxidation of unsaturated fatty acid. Malonaldehyde, a water-soluble compound, exists primarily in the storage occurs as a consequence of the reaction of peroxidizing lipids and proteins. The conjugated Schiff bases are converted into brown macromolecular products by aldolization reactions. The rate of browning is affected by the degree of unsaturation, available free amino groups, and by the extent of lipid oxidation. A method to detect and measure the fluorescence from lipid oxidation uses the formation of polymer-bound amino-imino-propene compounds from the reaction of malonaldehyde and known amine end groups of the polyamide powder (polymerized ε-caprolactam)-coated plates. This method is rapid, dry, and non-destructive. Plate fluorescence is measured by solid-sample fluorescence spectrophotometry and shows excitation and emission maxima at 356 and 422 nm, respectively. The method can also measure the fluorescence produced from the reaction of carbohydrate-derived carbonyl groups with polyamide plate (sugar-amine browning). This shows excitation and emission maxima at 362 and 430 nm, respectively.

Most of the investigators have attributed the formation of oxidation-produced fluorescence to the 'conjugated Schiff base structure'. However, Kikugawa and his co-workers suggested malonaldehyde-produced fluorescent compounds to be 'dihydropyridine derivatives,' such as, 1,4-dihydropyridine-3,5-dicarbaldehyde from the malonaldehyde reactions with primary amines under neutral conditions, haemoglobin, lipofuscin fluorescent compounds, and polylysine products. They also suggested that upon reaction of malonaldehyde and amino acids, three types of compounds are formed: the amorphous conjugated Schiff bases, crystalline 1,4-dihydropyridine-3,5-dicarbaldehyde, and aminopropenals (RNH-CH=CH-CHO). These compounds can be characterized by their fluorescence, UV and visible absorption spectra, and TBA-reactivity. The dihydropyridine derivatives have excitation and emission maxima at 400 and 465 nm and absorption maxima at 235, 265, and 400 nm. They do not produce malonaldehyde as measured by the TBA-reaction. The aminopropenals are unstable, non-fluorescent, have an absorption maximum at 280 nm and liberate malonaldehyde in the TBA-reaction. It is important to notice that the fluorophores derived from the reaction of polylysine with hydroperoxides and monofunctional aldehydes are formed by different mechanisms from those involved in the case of malonaldehyde. The former compounds exhibit a much weaker fluorescence with excitation and emission maxima at 340–360 and 410– 430 nm, respectively.

The Measurement of Oxidation in Muscle Food

The following factors must be considered in the measurement of oxidation in muscle food.

- ✰ The pre-treatment and storage history of meat.
- ✰ Lipid content and degree of unstauration of fatty acids of the muscle.
- ✰ The species of origin.

There are very few reports in this area and, of those, the following examples deal directly with quality control of muscle foods: the degree of oxidation of pork samples treated with salt, sodium nitrite, butylated hydroxytoluene (BHT) and citric acid, by means of TBA values, formation of fluorescent products, hexanal and 2,4-decadienal, and sensory analysis. During the first week of storage, the off-odour/flavour formation correlated significantly with both TBA values and the formation of fluorescent products. The relationship between fluorescent products and off-odour/flavours became not significant after two week's storage. The levels of hexanal and 2,4-decadienal were drastically lower in meat treated with nitrite, BHT, or citric acid as compared with pork samples containing only salt. Studies on the effects of frozen storage and subsequent cooking (microwave and convection) on the lipid oxidation of chicken meats showed an increase (as measured by a modified TBA assay) in malonaldehyde; the fluorescence excitation (360 nm) and emission (400 nm) increased by an average of 34 per cent after a six-month storage. On average, there was an 83 per cent increase in malonaldehyde concentration and a 21 per cent increase in fluorescence after cooking in a convection oven.

Some researchers have used fluorescence techniques to assess the effectiveness of the antioxidant TBHQ (mono-*t*-butylhydroquinone), reduction of headspace oxygen and compression on the storage stability of freeze-dried meats. These consisted of freeze-dried restructured beef patties (15±1 per cent fat containing 0.5 per cent sodium chloride and 0.2 per cent sodium tripolyphosphate (TPP), with and without (control) antioxidant. They were stored at 37°C for up to 30 days in the presence (normal atmospheric conditions) or absence of air (vacuum). Fluorescence spectra of 'oxidized' beef showed maximum excitation (λ_{ex}) and emission (λ_{em}) at 350 and 440 nm, respectively. In contrast, 'unoxidized' beef showed three peaks in excitation spectrum at λ_{ex1} = 308, λ_{ex2} = 318 (with maximum intensity), and λ_{ex3} = 350 nm. The intensity of these excitation peaks varied with the extent of oxidation.

For unoxidized samples, λ_{ex2} and λ_{ex3} had the highest and lowest intensities, respectively. As the oxidation proceeded, intensity of λ_{ex2} decreased (progressively appeared as a shoulder) while that of λ_{ex3} increased. In the emission spectra, there was only one broad single peak; its intensity increased gradually upon oxidation while its maximum wavelength shifted from 476±2 nm to 400±2 nm. The intensity ratio of λ_{ex3} or λ_{em} over λ_{ex2} served as a sensitive and reliable 'internal standard' for determination of the extent of lipid oxidation in freeze-dried meats.

Chapter 7

Fluorescence and Scanning Electron Microscopy

The Phenomenon of Fluorescence

The phenomenon of fluorescence has been described in considerable detail by Guilbault. Microscopy in any context is not an easy art to learn, but perseverance and due attention to chemical, biological and optical detail will reward the practitioner many times over. Fluorescence microscopy will reward the practitioner more so.

Every fluorescent compound has a specific *excitation spectrum*, and a specific *emission spectrum*. In most laboratory instruments, an *exciter* filter, which closely matches the excitation peak of the substance under examination, is inserted between the illuminator and specimen (thus maximising excitation and limiting the amount of non-specific illumination). For the resulting fluorescence wavelengths to be detected selectively (and without interference from the exciting wavelengths) it follows that an additional filter the barrier filter, must be inserted between the fluorescing specimen and the detector (observer) to remove unwanted illumination from the light source which might reach the detector. Note that the specimen should be thin enough to allow transmitted light through. Thus, in its most elementary form, the instrument is no more than a conventional light microscope to which a high-intensity light source and a few simple filters have been added. This arrangement, in ideal circumstances, results in a bright, self-luminous (fluorescent) object on a dark background. The high contrast of such specimens affords spectacular sensitivity and ease of detection. With these few additions, it is claimed that the instrument is capable of detecting as little as 10^{-18} mol of fluorescent substance *in situ*.

Surprisingly, the long history of the fluorescence microscope has not been paralleled by an equally lengthy popularity. O'Brien and McCully have provided a brief history of the instrument, and point out that commercial instruments were available from two well-known manufacturers (Zeiss and Reichert) as early as 1913. No doubt some of the difficulty which earlier proponents encountered related to the low intensity of fluorescent emissions from naturally occurring biological specimens, the lack of suitable fluorescent stains or probes (fluorochromes) with specificities matching those of the older, common bright-field stains (diachromes), and the general unavailability of filter and mirror systems suitable for fluorescence applications. Most of these limitations have been overcome and an accelerated interest in fluorescence microscopy in all branches of biological and medical sciences has sparked several improvements in instrument design and fluorochrome chemistry.

One of the critical improvements in the past 10 to 20 years is the introduction of epi-illumination (reflectance) systems as standard modules on current fluorescence microscopes. Today it is rare to encounter instruments utilising the traditional transmission mode of illumination (dia-illumination), yet only a few years ago the latter was the norm. Indeed, it was the most common type of fluorescence microscope for many of us during our earliest exposure to fluorescence, and that particular configuration was almost enough to prompt a change in research interests-photographic exposure times were extraordinarily long, film quality was poor and suitable fluorescence filters were hard to obtain.

Illuminators have become lighter, more efficient, and less expensive, microscope objectives have been designed specifically for fluorescence, and most microscope manufacturers now list a wide range of exciter/barrier filter sets for many diverse applications.

The basic construction of the fluorescence microscope is similar in many ways to that of a conventional, bright-field research microscope. With the exception of epi-illumination option there are few significant optical differences between the two instruments, and details of the lightpaths are outlined by Rost and O'Brien and McCully. Briefly, the design of the instrument can be discussed in terms of three main components: the illuminating system (including light sources); filters; and optical components specific to fluorescence analysis (primarily objectives).

Generation of a detectable fluorescence emission spectrum requires intense illumination of the object. This is accomplished by providing a suitable high-intensity light source, such as mercury or xenon lamps, in combination with other optical modifications such as epi-illuminators.

The advantages over substage illumination are many, and have been discussed by Fulcher and Wong, O'Brien and McCully, Rost and Fulcher. Briefly, the broad spectrum illumination normally generated by the light source first passes through the exciter filter as in the dia-illuminations system (Figure 7.1A) limiting the range of incident illumination to those wavelengths which maximally excite the specimen. The exciting beam is then reflected by a dichroic beam splitter and focused by the objective onto the upper surface of the specimen (dia-illumination systems found in conventional bright-field microscopes and older fluorescence microscopes illuminate the lower surface of the specimen). The advantages of this configuration are several:

1. Because the epi-illuminator excites the top surface of the specimen, the loss of resolution and intensity due to absorption and scattering within the specimen is minimised.
2. Because the objective acts as the condenser, excitation occurs only in the field of view, and fading of fluorochromes as a result of prolonged exposure to high-energy illumination is restricted to the field of view (substage condensers illuminate relatively large areas of the specimen).

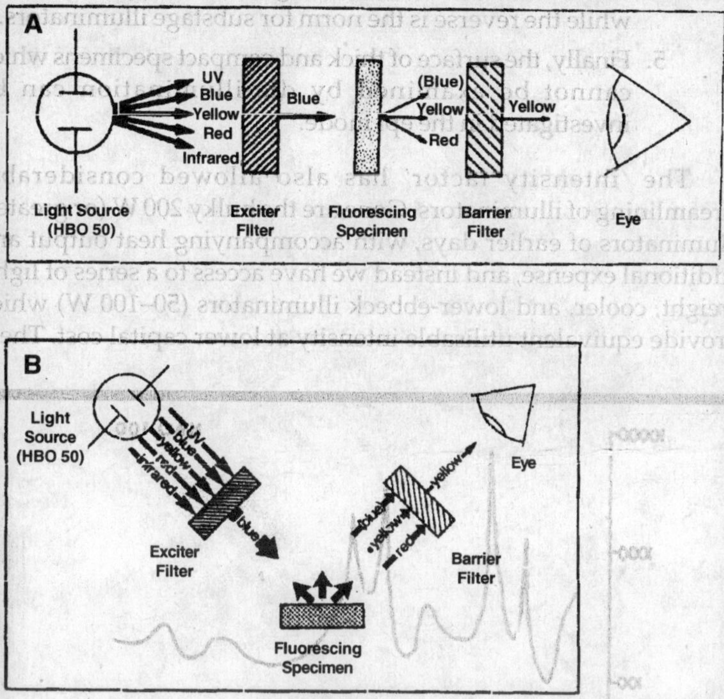

Figure 7.1: Diagrammatic Representation of a Simple (A) Transmitted-light and (B) Incident Light Fluorescence System

3. Again, because the objective is the condenser, it does not need to be centered, which increases the ease of use.
4. Perhaps most important is the fact that excitation energy and fluorescence intensity, increase dramatically as objective power increases. This latter advantage is perhaps the single most important feature of modern epi-illuminating fluorescence microscopes–with substage dia-illuminators there is generally a reduction in fluorescence intensity as one selects higher-power objectives, while epi-illuminators produce a spectacular increase in relative fluorescence 'brightness' of several thousand times over the same magnification increment (cf. 4 × vs 100 × objectives). Consequently, with epi-illuminators, higher

resolution is coincident with higher sensitivity of detection, while the reverse is the norm for substage illuminators.

5. Finally, the surface of thick and compact specimens which cannot be examined by dia-illumination can be investigated in the epi mode.

The 'intensity factor' has also allowed considerable streamlining of illuminators. Gone are the bulky 200 W (or greater) illuminators of earlier days, with accompanying heat output and additional expense, and instead we have access to a series of lightweight, cooler, and lower-ebbeck illuminators (50–100 W) which provide equivalent utilisable intensity at lower capital cost. These

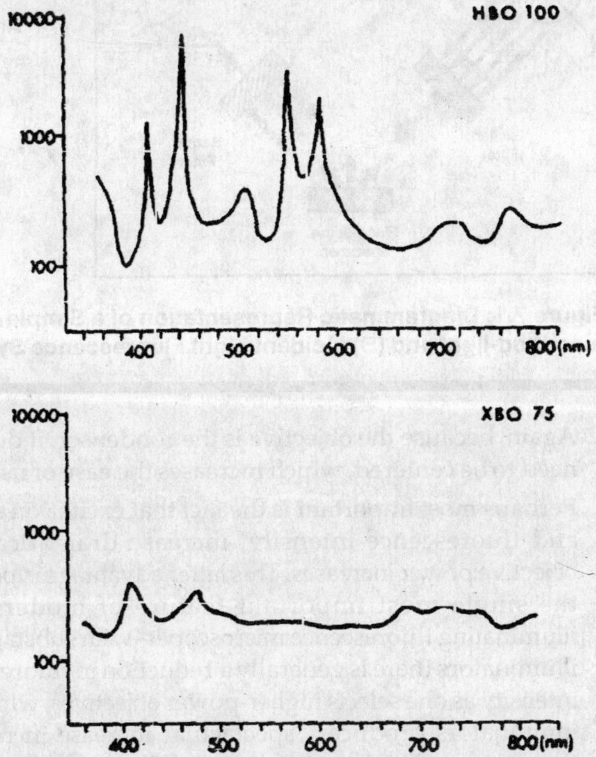

Figure 7.2: Examples of Spectral Outputs Typical of Common Illuminators Used in Fluorescence Microscopy

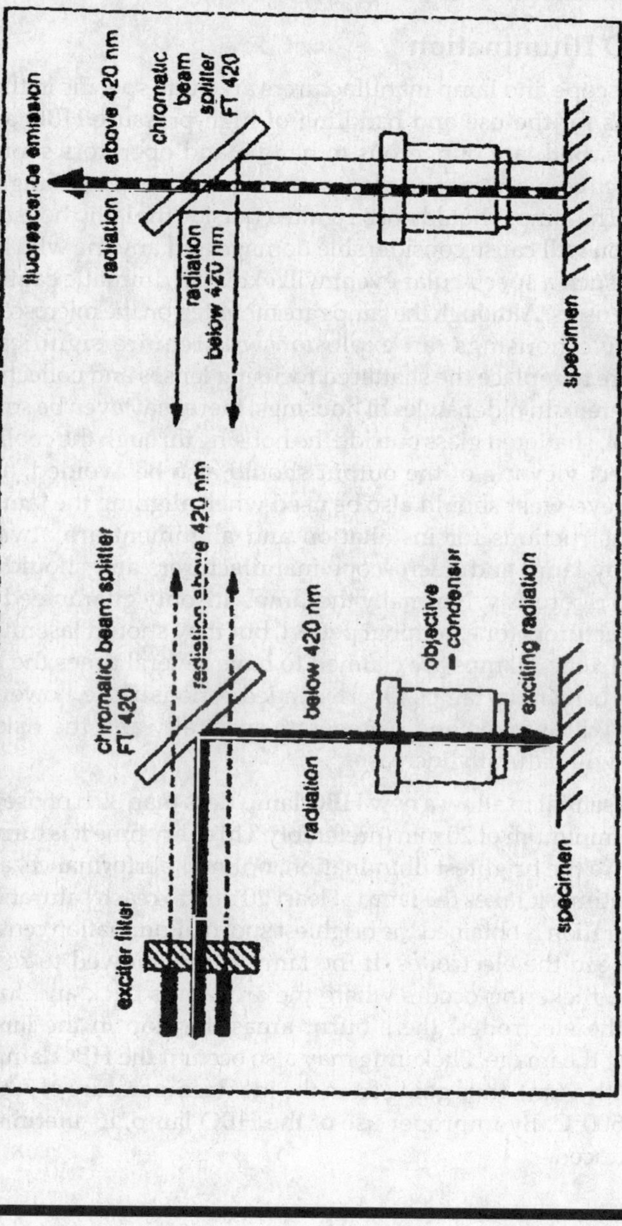

Figure 7.3: Diagrammatic Representation of a Typical Epi-illumination System

low-power illuminators are particularly suited to the new generation of 'infinity-corrected' microscopes, which also provide remarkably uniform illumination over the entire field of view.

The HBO Illumination

Microscope and lamp manufacturers are quite specific in their instructions for the use and handling of high-pressure HBO and XBO lamps. Both are dangerous to handle and operators should wear protective eye-wear and gloves when installing or exchanging the lamps. The lamps should not be ignited outside the lamp housing: an explosion will cause considerable damage and anyone who has witnessed such a spectacular event will extend a dramatic caution to potential users. Although the lamps are mounted on the microscope in protective housings, an explosion will require significant expenditure to replace the shattered focusing lenses and collecting mirrors therein. In older styles of housings, there may even be some spray of hot, shattered glass outside the housing through the cooling vents. Direct viewing of the output should also be avoided, and protective eye-wear should also be used when aligning the lamps. Specific instructions for installation and alignment are always provided by lamp and microscope manufacturers and should be adhered to rigorously. Normally the lamps are only guaranteed by the manufacturers for a nominal period, but they should last much longer and xenon lamps are claimed to have several times the life expectancy of mercury lamps. Over extended periods of use, however, the lamps will weaken and degenerate spectrally and the risk of explosion will naturally increase.

It is essential to allow a new HBO lamp (less than 30 h of use) to burn for a minimum of 20 min (preferably 2 h) every time it is turned on, to assure the brightest illumination, optimal performance, and longest lifetime. It takes the lamp at least 20 min to reach saturation. When saturation is obtained the brightest spot of illumination centers itself between the electrodes. If the lamp is not allowed to reach saturation, flickering occurs where the arc jumps back and forth between the electrodes; then, burnt areas develop in the lamp, shadowing the image. Flickering may also occur if the HBO lamp is cooled (with a fan), thus going from the ideal temperature of 700°C to below 500°C. By improper use of the HBO lamp, its lifetime is greatly reduced.

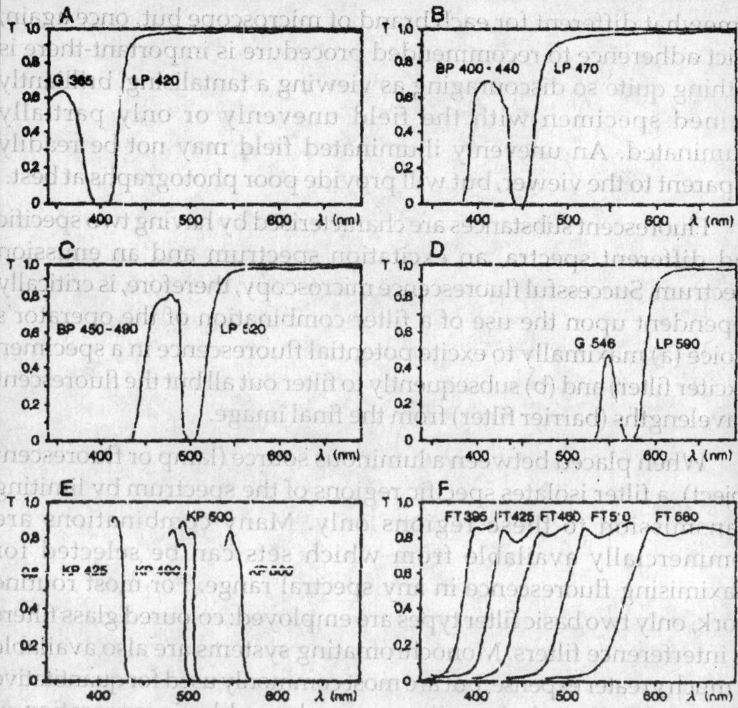

Figure 7.4: (A–D) Typical spectral transmission curves of paired exciter and barrier filters designed to optimise fluorescence generated by an HBO illumination. Spectral transmission curves of common chromatic beam splitters are shown below. Many different filters are available from commercial suppliers to allow quite selective definition of fluorescence. (E, F) Typical spectral transmission curves of band-pass filters. Short-pass filters (E) can be used as exciting filters. Long-pass filters (F) can be used as barrier filters.

Improper alignment can also cause uneven heating of the lamp, further raising the risk of explosion. Alignment of the lamps is a process requiring some experience. Although manufacturers usually provide adequate details of the procedure, in our experience the process can be tedious and time-consuming, involving sequential re-adjustment of one to several alignment screws. The process is somewhat different for each brand of microscope but, once again, strict adherence to recommended procedure is important-there is nothing quite so discouraging as viewing a tantalising, brilliantly stained specimen with the field unevenly or only partially illuminated. An unevenly illuminated field may not be readily apparent to the viewer, but will provide poor photographs at best.

Fluorescent substances are characterised by having two specific and different spectra, an excitation spectrum and an emission spectrum. Successful fluorescence microscopy, therefore, is critically dependent upon the use of a filter combination of the operator's choice (a) maximally to excite potential fluorescence in a specimen (exciter filter) and (b) subsequently to filter out all but the fluorescent wavelengths (barrier filter) from the final image.

When placed between a luminous source (lamp or fluorescent object), a filter isolates specific regions of the spectrum by limiting transmission to these regions only. Many combinations are commercially available from which sets can be selected for maximising fluorescence in any spectral range. For most routine work, only two basic filter types are employed: coloured glass filters or interference filters. Monochromating systems are also available at much greater expense, but are most commonly used for quantitative analyses. Coloured glass filters are coloured by incorporation of dyeing oxide stains of heavy metals into the molten glass or by annealing colloidal particles of sulphides, selenides or metals to the clear glass. They have been in use for many years and offer a comparatively inexpensive way of generating relatively narrow excitation spectra. These particular filters are commonly used to isolate the 365 and 546 nm peaks of the HBO lamps and other peaks can be isolated similarly (*e.g.* at 405 and 436 nm) although the range of available glass filters is rather limited. Interference filters are also usually made of glass, where thin coatings of metallic salts are vacuum-deposited on the surface of a glass disc to produce filtering layers. The optical properties of the coatings can be selected so that interference effects at the filter surface result in enhancement or suppression of transmittance at very specific wavelengths. Using this approach, manufacturers can provide filtering capability at almost any wavelength which might be required to detect specific fluorescent substances, and these filters have the added advantage of being more resistant to heat than coloured glass filters. Where the transmittance curves show sharp cut-offs on each side of the curve, they are called 'band-pass' (BP) filters and identified by the cut-off wavelengths. These can be short- or long-pass filters. The short-pass (KP) type suppresses long-wavelength light and shows a steep cut-off at the high limit of transmittance. Short-pass filters can be used as exciting filters. They show steep cut-offs at the lower limit of transmittance and relatively uniform transmittance through the rest of the visible range. With this type of filter, a range of emission spectra can be detected using only one barrier filter, an advantage where multiple stains might be contemplated for simultaneous detection of more than one cellular constituent. Regardless of the application, however, it should be obvious that filter combinations (of which there are many) can be arranged to provide maximum detection of one or more fluorescent compounds, with minimal interference from other emissions.

The Microscope Objective Characteristics

Microscope objective characteristics are almost as variable as the number of manufacturers providing them. We have stated that the fluorescence microscope is little more than a conventional light microscope with a few very specific modifications. It is often a simple matter to modify most bright-field microscopes with these additions (epi-illuminator, filters) in modular form, and in many circumstances objectives normally suited to bright-field analysis will serve. There are some very notable exceptions, however, in which high-quality fluorescent images are produced only with appropriate objectives. In earlier discussions, it was pointed out that some of the best high-numerical-aperture (*e.g.* planapochromatic) objectives used for bright-field work were quite inadequate for high-quality fluorescence microscopy; these objectives may have many components that decrease light intensity as the light beam goes through them. They may also absorb some or all of certain wavelengths (particularly short wavelengths such as the HBO 365 nm peak which is on the low limit of transmission for normal non-quartz optics) and many chromatically corrected objectives will exhibit some of the same defects. Although a few objectives (*e.g.* fluorite) with adequate transmission characteristics were on the market at that time, they often did not possess the high numerical apertures required for obtaining the best images. Microscope manufacturers are now devoting considerable energies to improving the quality of objectives specifically designed for fluorescence analysis and some of these are becoming quite popular. These include the UVFL series from Olympus and the Plan-Neofluars from Carl Zeiss. There are dramatic differences between the two lines, but both offer considerable improvements over their predecessors; other manufacturers such as Leitz and Reichert also provide fluorescence objectives with excellent transmission properties. Quartz objectives are not required for most fluorescence microscopy. They are extremely expensive, have low numerical apertures, and are generally reserved for quantitative applications which require true ultraviolet irradiation.

Regardless of the source of the objective, however, it is essential for a beginner to explore many different objective options to obtain the best image with his or her particular application. The user should experiment widely with different objective powers and numerical apertures, with and without oil-immersion techniques, and it is likely that a limited number of objectives (three or four) will be found which satisfy routine requirements. Objective manufacture is a sophisticated technology but fluorescence microscopy remains something of an art, and the best objective for any new application is the one which works best.

For the practising food microscopist, these combined modifications (epi-illumination, specific interference filters, small high-intensity lamps and efficient fluorescence objectives) mean that (a) fluorescent compounds (either applied fluorochromes or naturally occurring substances) can be detected at very low concentrations, and (b) relatively crude preparations (thick sections or powdered materials) can be examined quickly and easily with a minimum of sample processing. In the frequent rush to scan specimens in food processing control situations, the latter advantage can be a significant one: it is not, however, without difficulties and requires considerable experimentation to optimise suitable conditions for routine use.

O'Brien and McCully have described several guidelines for optimising the quality of fluorescence microscopic images, and all potential (and experienced!) users are encouraged to review their recommendations.

Although microchemistry (*i.e.* the localisation of specific substances in tissues using microscopy) is not a new science, preparative techniques for localisation of structures were often difficult and time-consuming. Microchemistry using fluorescence microscopy combined with improved sample preparation and specific fluorochromes, however, is simple, rapid, and highly accurate. In the following paragraphs, we provide collection of methods which have been found especially useful for preparing mainly seed and other food materials (*e.g.* cereals) for fluorescence microscopy. These methods are presented here as guidelines only. Most of the food scientists have quite diverse basic research interests and we must emphasise that many of the methods which are being described are specialised and provide only a basis for further development. Each new specimen must be evaluated on its own merits. Therefore, new methods should be developed and old ones considerably be modified to optimise the final microscopic results. The methods here described are thus merely example, several of which could be extended to many other less-investigated food areas and could even serve as a source of inspiration in other fields of research.

Methods for sample preparation are as varied as the morphological and chemical constituents under examination. Most foods, whether raw or processed, are biological materials and must be sectioned prior to microscopic examination. Furthermore, careful consideration must be given to selecting methods (fixation, dehydration, embedding) which will allow retention of whatever molecular species are of interest. In some cases (*e.g.* detection of lipids) certain solvent systems must be avoided if extraction of the target molecules is to be minimised. In others (detection of aromatic amines, flavonoids), all embedding materials normally used for high-resolution microscopy must be avoided, and only hand-cut or cryo-cut sectioning methods will suffice. In view of these requirements, we have adopted a few relatively simple preparative techniques for routine use such that most major seed components may be localised with a minimum of manipulation. The methods are complementary and involve: hand sectioning for optimising constituent retention, low resolution, and rapid scanning; cryosectioning for similar results but to provide more uniform and thinner sections; and glycol methacrylate (GMA) embedment and thin (glass-knife) sectioning to provide maximum resolution. In some cases, materials may be fixed while others are left unfixed; the choice is dictated by the molecular species under investigation, and by other considerations such as resolution required, time available for the analysis etc. Once prepared, samples may be examined for primary (or auto-)

fluorescence characteristics, or they may be selectively stained to generate secondary fluorescence in specific structures.

If there can be a guiding principle in this type of work, it is that one should not be locked into any particular set of procedures. The fluorescence microscope is a powerful chemical instrument but it can only be used to maximum potential if the procedures are suitably flexible and appropriate to the research requirements. In the following paragraphs some consideration is given to the fundamentals of many of these procedures. The descriptions are not exhaustive and further details are available from the included references.

Ideally a minimum amount of preparation should be used for the microscopic examination of plant material in its most natural state. However, it is quite often necessary to compromise this value in order to achieve a higher image resolution. It is of paramount importance then to use a combination of methods to assess plant specimens objectively. If an elaborate procedure such as plastic embedding is needed for high resolution, it should concur with parallel techniques such as hand-cut sectioning of fresh (untreated) material, half-seed observation or even cryosectioning of an untreated sample to identify artifacts caused by the preparation method itself.

One of the most overlooked procedures for obtaining specimens is the use of hand-sectioning techniques. The procedures require some practice, but sections can be made quickly and easily of most fresh biological materials. Relatively thin (10–20 μm) sections can be cut with a little practice using an ethanol- or acetone-cleaned double-edged razor blade. The material should be held in one hand, a clamp, or a hand-held microtome, and sliced repeatedly with a razor blade. In some cases, it may be useful to control the cut by first slotting thin specimens between, say, two halves of a supporting medium such as a carrot.

The food microscopist is often asked to evaluate the composition of granular, powdered or otherwise ground material. This is done readily by simply mixing the sample in a minimal amount of a suitable high-refractive-index material such as immersion oil or fluorescence-free glycerol, placing a cover glass over it and viewing directly with no further manipulation. Care must be taken to ensure that the material of interest is not soluble in the medium.

Cryotomy, sectioning at freezing temperatures on a freezing microtome or cryostat, also allows the observation of samples after minimal preparation and, therefore, minimal disruption of cellular components. Cryotomy is often used in other forms of microscopy (*e.g.* transmission electron microscopy, TEM) and can be applied readily to fluorescence microscopy. A number of developments have been made for obtaining samples free of apparent ice crystal damage. Ice crystals cannot be prevented but the size can and should be minimised to below the required resolution. Methods include cold block and plunge freezing. Material may be fixed or unfixed prior to freezing. Tissue may require a cryoprotectant such as DMSO (dimethyl sulphoxide) to minimise freezing damage due to ice crystal growth. Fresh samples can be quick-frozen by one of the TEM methods. Because of the tremendous differences in resolution between TEM and light microscopy, it usually will not be necessary to resort to such complicated procedures. For example, some samples may be frozen directly in the cryostat chamber and others may be frozen in liquid propane or liquid nitrogen. Liquid nitrogen is generally not a good cryogen alone because it boils at room temperature and therefore, does not freeze the sample immediately (liquid propane, or nitrogen slush prepared by putting liquid nitrogen under vacuum, are more suitable for initial freezing, with subsequent transfer to liquid nitrogen). Freon is not recommended for ecological reasons. Initial freezing of the sample is the most critical step in preserving structures.

The cryostat is cooled to –20°C and specimens no larger than 0.5 cm^3 affixed to precooled specimen mounting stubs with mounting medium (Tissue Tek II O.C.T. Compound, Lab-Tek Products, Naperville, IL, USA) or medium by Reichert–Jung, NuBlock, Heidelberg, FRG). The sample is prefrozen in a small amount of mounting medium. Extra mounting medium is applied to the sample on the mounting stub to affix the sample firmly and provide rigidity during sectioning. Sections 4–10 µm thick are cut and picked up on a warm (room temperature), albumin fixative-coated slide (Fisher Scientific Co., Fairlawn, NJ, USA) or on a 1 per cent gelatine-coated slide ('home-made'). Brushing with water the spot where the section will be placed, allows the section to be stretched with a fine paint brush to remove any wrinkles. The slide can then be held by hand or by a wooden stick with a suction device attached to it (*e.g.* a child's toy arrow from a bow and arrow set). Several sections may be collected on one slide using this technique. Serial-sectioning is difficult using a cryostat but sections will ribbon two to three at a time. Sections may also be picked up on a coverglass.

The Study of GMA Embedding

GMA embedding media can be purchased in kit from along with instructions and formulae for specific uses.

Basically, the embedding media consist of four components, three of which are absolutely necessary. The kits consist of a monomer (glycol methacrylate to which butoxyethanol, a plasticizer, has been added), a catalyst (benzoyl peroxide), and an initiator of polymerization (*N*, N-dimethylaniline). The latter may be included if rapid polymerization is required, otherwise it may be omitted and polymerization initiated by heat or ultraviolet light. Suppliers of GMA kits include Polysciences (JB-4 medium, Warrington, PA, USA), Sorvall (Sorvall Embedding Medium, New Town, CT, USA), and LKB Products (GMA Kit, Bromma, Sweden). Although the JB-4 medium does not appear to be as pure as the Sorvall kit, it is less expensive and can be used for routine work. This medium is best suited for embedding of dense tissues where the initiator is left out. Addition of the initiator causes undesirable discoloration (deep amber) in the polymerized blocks. The Sorvall kit as well as LKB are very high-quality GMA embedding media and can be used for many specialised purposes.

GMA is easy to handle, can be used at room temperature, and needs not (and cannot) be removed from tissues prior to staining. GMA fluoresces minimally or not at all depending on the purity, and excellent high-quality sections can be cut from GMA-embedded material with only a minimum of practice. Staining procedures may need modification when adapted from older paraffin procedures but, for the most part, may be used without modification. Modifications are usually simple and involve shortening the exposure time of sections to dye or the elimination of steps. For example, tissue sections do not require hydration or dehydration prior to staining and simple air-drying following staining is sufficient. Rinsing following staining is usually less involved. GMA monomer (the unpolymerized infiltration liquid) has a low viscosity at room temperature which allows faster infiltration into tissues. The final polymerized block is much harder than paraffin and thus, can be sectioned more thinly. Preservation of structures, especially when combined with proper fixation regimes, is far superior to paraffin.

Now let us try to understand about infiltration technique with GMA. Infiltration involves getting the embedding medium into the tissue in an unpolymerized (*i.e.* monomeric) form so that the embedment will subsequently polymerize evenly both inside and outside the tissues. Several exchanges of the monomer must be made to replace completely the final traces of dehydrant as this will interfere with polymerization.

To begin infiltration with GMA, the last dehydrant is first removed using a Pasteur pipette and enough GMA monomer mixture (GMA, catalyst, and plasticizer) is added to cover the tissues completely. They are left to infiltrate for an appropriate time, from a few hours to overnight, either at room temperature (best for dense tissues) or refrigerated. Infiltration is a critical step and the time is tissue-dependent. A few hours would probably suffice for soft tissues such as meat whilst plant vegetative tissues generally require longer infiltration, and cereal grains and other seeds may require a considerable time, three to five days.

Regardless of tissue type, GMA monomer mixture should be exchanged at least twice over the infiltration time. Fresh medium should be used to embed the tissue as the catalyst deteriorates with time, and is temperature-dependent.

Excess GMA monomer mixture may be stored in a refrigerator in a closed container for up to two weeks. The container should have a little free space at the top to avoid premature polymerization of GMA, although this is generally not a problem. The monomer should be used as rapidly as possible and be relatively fresh for embedding. Disposable plastic containers with a tight-fitting lid for mixing and storing of GMA are advisable.

Used GMA may be saved and re-used for the first infiltration step following dehydration. Before it is discarded, GMA should be polymerized in a disposable cup. It should not be poured down the drain as it can polymerize in the pipes. GMA can cause contact dermatitis.

Embedding with GMA

Once the tissue has been infiltrated with a suitable plastic such as GMA in liquid form, it must be transferred to appropriate containers and polymerized to form a solid, sectionable block. There are a number of moulds in the market for embedding including some for GMA embedding (Sorvall, New Town, CT, USA). Any container may be used for GMA embedding as long as it has a cap or some mechanism is available (*i.e.* a vacuum oven) for eliminating oxygen (which inhibits polymerization) from GMA during polymerization. Gelatine (size 0 or 00) or Beem capsules are ideal for small tissues or particles such as bran. Aluminium weigh-boats are recommended for flat embedding of larger tissues.

There are two methods of preparing GMA for embedding, either using the initiator for rapid polymerization, or omitting it to allow slow polymerization. For the former, the GMA kits may be used according to the manufacturer's instructions and will produce blocks which are ready to section within a few hours. Care must be taken not to prepare an excess of this solution as it polymerizes very rapidly; large volumes also polymerize faster than small volumes. The polymerization process can be slowed by handling reagents on ice. If rapid polymerization is used, the Sorvall GMA kit is recommended because it is purer. The Polysciences kit produces blocks which are dark amber in colour; this interferes somewhat with fluorescence. It is not recommended to use the rapid polymerization kit for hard or fibrous tissues, such as cereal grains or celery, although satisfactory results have been achieved with wheat when reagents were kept at 0°C. Some experimentation will be necessary (purification procedures may be needed, and correct amounts of plasticizer and catalyst must be evaluated experimentally for any new tissue).

Regardless of the choice of polymerization protocol, samples are handled in much the same manner for both procedures. The GMA is placed first into the embedment container, then the tissues are gently picked up with fine forceps and placed in the container. If possible, the tissues are transferred with a large-bore pipette to the embedment container, then the old GMA is pipetted off using a Pasteur pipette and fresh GMA is added. If capsules are being used, they are filled to the top and capped. For flat embedment, aluminium weigh-dishes or-boats are filled just to cover the specimens and another weigh-boat is floated on top of the first with the sample to create an oxygen-free sandwich. Pieces of paper containing sample identification in pencil can be included in the embedment if desired.

For rapid polymerization, the embedment containers are allowed to polymerize at room or low temperature either under vacuum or covered to eliminate oxygen.

For slow polymerization, the prepared embedding moulds are placed in an oven at approximately 45°C for two to five days. The blocks will be sufficiently polymerized after two days but may still be sticky to the touch. Excess GMA is blotted off and blocks are prepared for sectioning if desired at this point. An additional day or two in the oven will eliminate this. The oven may also be turned up to 60 °C after the first day to speed up polymerization. Polymerization may also be accomplished under a low-energy (370 nm) UV lamp; a container transparent to ultraviolet will he necessary.

If polymerization is too rapid the mixture will boil, creating bubbles which will remain in the polymerized tissue block. Tissues are recoverable after this happens, but with difficulty, GMA monomer mixture is added to the polymerized block and allowed to soak for several days, then it is re-polymerized (GMA polymer is slightly soluble in GMA monomer).

GMA-embedded samples should be stored in a container over desiccant overnight prior to sectioning. GMA is very hygroscopic and will pick up atmospheric moisture readily which will make the block softer and reduce its sectioning quality. Likewise, if a GMA block is too brittle, it should be stored in a small humidity chamber for a few hours prior to sectioning.

If the samples are polymerized in gelatine capsules, a flat surface is simply filed at the tissue end and the block is inserted into an appropriate microtome block holder (chuck). If Beem capsules are used, it will first be necessary to peel off the capsule. For flat-embedded samples, the aluminium weigh-boats are peeled off and discarded. The polymerized block containing the tissues is placed in a vice and the desired samples are cut out with a jeweller's saw. One side is filled to flatten it (if necessary to orient the sample). It is attached with rapid-curing epoxy or cyanoacrylic glue to an appropriate substrate made in advance by polymerizing epoxy or GMA (without tissue) in an empty capsule. The shelf-life of cyanoacrylic glue can be extended by storing in the freezer. After allowing 5–10 min for the glue to dry, the GMA block can then be trimmed with a fine file in a vice or the special specimen holder which accompanies some microtomes. Unlike epoxy-embedded tissue blocks, GMA is slightly too brittle for trimming with a razor blade.

The type of microtome available will determine how the samples will finally be mounted for sectioning. Most of us are familiar with ultramicrotomes and their associated chucks (sample holders). Empty epoxy capsules may be used as sample holders for ultramicrotomes. Beem- or gelatine-embedded capsules may be mounted directly into ultramicrotome chucks. However, because GMA is somewhat soft, deformation of the embedded capsule due to the pressure needed to hold the capsule in the chuck may occur. The deformation will cause sections to be uneven in thickness but this can be avoided by keeping the sample in a desiccator prior to sectioning.

Lipid preservation and enzyme histochemistry are areas which are greatly improved or made possible by using low-temperature embedding. Structural preservation is generally better than that in cryosections. There is less extraction of lipid, and enzyme activity can be retained in the polymerized block.

Tissues are dehydrated using concentrations of 5, 10, 20, 40, 60, and 80 per cent aqueous GMA monomer mixture at 0°C and 90 and 95 per cent at –25°C. Specimens should be infiltrated with 100 per cent monomer mixture at –25 or –35°C. The time requirements for infiltration depend on the specimen density but this generally takes longer because of the increased GMA viscosity at lower temperatures. The Sorvall embedding kit can be used for low-temperature embedding. The addition of the initiator (*N,N*-dimethylaniline) in the kit makes it unnecessary to irradiate the GMA monomer mixture with a low-energy UV lamp (370 nm).

GMA (and any plastic-embedded) tissues are most efficiently cut to appropriate section thickness (0.1–5 µm) using glass knives, although steel knives and razor blades have also been used successfully. There are two types of instruments available for making glass knives. One is produced by Sorvall and the knives can be used in the Sorvall JB-4 microtome. It will cut glass that is ½ inch (12.7 mm) thick which makes it possible to section material almost as wide as ½ inch. The other type, which makes knives from glass which is about ¼ inch (6.35 mm) thick, is used for conventional ultramicrotomes and is readily available from several manufacturers.

Glass knives can also be made by hand using knife pliers, a scoring rod and a straight edge. Making glass knives by hand takes some practice and usually results in only one usable knife per square. A commercial glass-knife maker will routinely produce two knives per square.

Now let us try to gather some details about sectioning.

Specimen blocks should be 'faced' prior to sectioning. This is done by coarsely advancing the knife and taking a few thick sections off. Sometimes, especially if the specimen is brittle, the sample may start falling apart during coarse sectioning. If so, several thin sections (*i.e.* 4 μm) can be removed, a process which will smooth off the specimen block face and prevent further breaking up of the sample.

Trimming devices can also be used to face the blocks. A TM-60 trimmer by Reichert-Jung (previously A.O. Spencer) was used to trim the large face block of a halved barley kernel embedded in GMA. In this particular case if you want to look at the total exposed area of half-seed, it is impossible to obtain a thin section of such a large surface or to trim it with a microtome without leaving knifemarks. The trimmer, on the other hand, mills the specimen evenly and when equipped with a rotating diamond miller cutter even a large surface does not get scored.

Several types of microtomes are available which work well for sectioning GMA-embedded tissue. In addition to various ultramicrotomes, which allow best control of section thickness, older rotary microtomes can be used with a stainless steel knife, razor blade or glass knife. Glass-knife holders are commercially available or one can be fabricated. Stainless steel knives produce more scratches than glass knives. Glass knives are extremely sharp, easy to prepare, relatively inexpensive, and disposable.

Each section should be picked up with fine forceps (the curved type being preferred), by the bottom as it comes off the knife whether using manual or automatic advance on the microtome. Care must be taken so that the section does not wrinkle. A little pressure is needed to pull the section while it is coming off the knife.

The section is placed in a dish (*e.g.* a 250 ml evaporating dish filled to the top) of distilled water on a dark background. Once several sections have been made and dropped into the dish, they can be collected on glass microscope slides.

Although GMA will not ribbon, a carefully trimmed block can be made to ribbon when treated with contact cement. First, the block is trimmed into a pyramid as for TEM sectioning. The top of the block should be shorter than the bottom and parallel; the sides should be angled. The top and bottom are painted with a light layer of contact cement using a wooden applicator stick, it is allowed to dry to tackiness then sectioned as usual.

In routine GMA embedding, lipids are usually extracted by solvents used during dehydration. Osmium tetroxide (O_SO_4) is routinely used in TEM as a secondary fixative to preserve lipids and to enhance contrast in samples. However, the use of O_SO_4 is not recommended for fluorescence microscopy as it masks primary fluorescence and eliminates the staining ability of the tissues for secondary fluorescence. Therefore, to observe and localize lipid droplets in tissues, it becomes necessary to adapt alternative procedures. Hand sections or cryosections may be used as alternatives to routine GMA embedding. Where higher resolution is required, a GMA embedding procedure for preserving hexane-soluble lipids developed by Pease and modified by Hargin *et al.* may be employed.

The modified GMA method involves fixing and rinsing tissues as usual followed by passing tissues through increasing concentrations of neutralized glutaraldehyde at 10 per cent increments until infilter with 50 per cent glutaraldehyde. At least 1 h (at room temperature) should be allowed in each successive step although dense tissues require a longer time, up to 24 h in each step. Tissues are then infiltrated with GMA–glutaraldehyde mixture by following the protocol of Pease. The final plastic block is often very brittle and difficult to section. Increasing the final moisture content to 35 per cent prior to embedding or placing the polymerized block in a humidity chamber for a few hours or overnight prior to sectioning may alleviate sectioning difficulties.

Many food constituents are naturally fluorescent. Natural fluorescence, which is also known as primary or autofluorescence, occurs in foods of both plant and animal origin. In plants, it is usually due to phenolic compounds of various types in the vascular tissue and epidermis in vegetative tissue, and in many specialized seed structures. The spectral characteristics of this fluorescence are diagnostic of the particular phenolics present, and the intensity is usually sufficient to be easily detected and photographed. Many plant pigments (especially chlorophyll) are also fluorescent and some proteins of plant and animal origin (*e.g.* connective tissue, bone and cartilage) frequently exhibit fluorescence in the microscope.

The majority of food constituents, however, are not autofluorescent and must be converted to fluorescent compounds by chemical treatment (secondary, or induced, fluorescence). Secondary fluorescence may be accomplished by (a) treating with specific fluorescent stains (fluorochromes), (b) producing specific fluorescent reaction products in the tissue sections.

The fluorochromes mostly used in food products include;

Fluorochrome	*Applications*
Aqueous acriflavine HCl	Phytic acid (*myo*-inositol hexaphosphoric acid)
Acid fuchsin	Storage proteins
ANS (1-anilino-8-naphthalene sulphonic acid)	Storage proteins
Fluorescamine	Storage proteins
Safranin	Starch
Acridine Orange	Starch
Periodic acid–Schiff's	Starch and periodale-positive substances
Aniline Blue	Cell walls
Calcofluor White M2R New	β-Glucans
Congo Red	β-Glucans
Aqueous Nile Blue A	Storage lipids
Cyanogen bromide	Nicotinic acid
2,4-Dimethylaminobenzadehyde or dimethylaminocinnamaldehyde	Aromatic amine
Diphenylborinic acid	Flavonoids

The Fluorochromes Used for Microorganisms

The following are the most common fluorochromes used for microorganisms.

Acridine Orange

Acridine Orange, one of the most common fluorochromes used for microbiology, has been described for staining of bacteria in soil:

the samples are shaken with five different concentrations of Acridine Orange (1:1000, 1:2000, 1:3000, 1:4000 and 1:5000) to achieve an optimal concentration to give sufficient fluorescence of the bacteria without having excess fluorescent stain in the sample.

In marine microbiology epifluorescence microscopic techniques involving membrane filtration of the seawater samples and staining with Acridine Orange have been widely adopted since the mid-1970s.

In 1980 Pettipher *et al.* described a membrane filtration technique applicable to microorganisms of milk samples. In this case treatment of the sample prior to filtration is needed. The technique was further developed to include other food products such as meat, fish, vegetables, etc.

Subsequently a fully automated equipment, Bactoscan (Foss Electric), was developed on the basis of Acridine Orange staining of bacteria in raw milk samples. After lysing the protein and the somatic cells, the bacteria are trapped between two gradients by centrifugation, treated with enzymes, and stained with Acridine Orange. A very thin film is dispensed on a rotating disc and the emission of fluorescence light is detected on a four-channel photodetector. The pulses from bacteria are counted and presented on a display and printout.

Acridine Red

Acridine Red is described by Seholefield *et al.*, who found a significant reduction in background fluorescence at pH 2 versus pH 3.1 when examining *Proteus vulgaris* added to milk samples, whereas the fluorescence of the bacteria was almost independent of the pH range.

Acridine Yellow

Different pure cultures of bacteria stained for 30 s in a 0.02 per cent aqueous solution of Acridine Yellow showed clear fluorescence. In contrast to Acridinc Orange stained slides, Afifi and Muller noticed that slides stained with Acridine Yellow could be stored for months without fading. Due to the good contrast between fluorescent bacteria and faintly stained food particles (meat, vegetables), Afifi and Muller suggested the use of Acridine Yellow for further investigations. In the previously described investigations by

Scholefield *et al.* the highest cell-to-background ratio was found after staining with Acridine Yellow, compared with the other fluorochromes tested.

Acriflavine

Acriflavine is also described by Scholefield *et al.*, to stain *Escherichia coli* and *Staphylococcus aureus* in inoculated meat washings. A comparison with colony count showed a reasonable correlation, although at low bacterial counts the precision of the microscopic results was reduced.

Mg-ANS

The magnesium salt of 1-anilino-8-naphthalenesulphonic acid fluoresces when bound to proteins but is non-fluorescent in aqueous solution. Mayfield described a staining technique to detect microorganisms in soil samples: after staining for 1 min with solutions of Mg-ANS (1.0, 2.0, 3.0, 3.5 and 4.0 mg/ml), excess stain is removed by blotting and the slide is examined under incident illumination. Although some fading occurs, microorganism detection is still possible after a 10 min exposure. A similar technique can be applied for the detection of microorganisms on dead algae. The microorganisms can easily be seen on the surface of the algae particles without destroying the obvious connection of the bacteria to the surface of the algae. This staining technique is suggested for examination of microorganisms in other intact natural habitats (soil, water, some food materials, etc.). However, food particles containing larger amounts of proteins will also fluoresce when stained with Mg-ANS and often make the detection of bacteria almost impossible.

Mg-ANS is also recommended as a yeast viability assessment procedure. A 0.03 per cent aqueous solution of Mg-ANS makes non-viable yeast cells fluoresce green, whereas viable cells only show very faint fluorescence.

Auramine

Auramine is described for detecting bacteria in different food materials of animal or vegetable origine. Staining for 15 m. with a 0.2 per cent solution of Auramine differentiates the yellow-green fluorescent bacteria from the food particles.

Calcofluor M_2R New

Calcofluor M_2R New is described for staining *Bacillus cereus* and *Pseudomonas* spp. in soil samples. Experiments revealed that the protoplasmic constituents of bacterial cells bind the fluorochrome whereas cell walls do not show fluorescence.

Calcofluor White CFW

Calcofluor White CFW is used for detecting fungal elements in tissue of animal origin as well as in moulded cheese. It stains non-specifically a wide variety of fungi and, to a much lesser extent, bacteria. Collagen, elastin and creatine in animal tissues also show bright fluorescence when stained with Calcofluor White CFW.

Two other optical brighteners, *Tinopal AN* (a general stain for most bacteria and fungi) and *CH3558* (a specific stain for yeast), are described by Paton and Jones. Both are used at 0.1 per cent concentration in water. If the food material itself absorbs the optical brighteners a more suitable contract may be obtained by first counterstaining the material with a 1:100 dilution of 5 per cent Erythrosin and 5 per cent phenol.

Euchrysme 2GNX

Euchrysme 2GNX is described for detecting yeast and bacteria in wine samples. After retaining the microorganisms on a polycarbonate filter, a 0.004 per cent Euchrysine 2GNX solution is used for staining. At pH 7.4 it is possible to distinguish between the green fluorescent viable cells and the bright orange fluorescent dead cells as also described by Hobbie *et al.* Pettipher *et al.* also tried Euchrysine 2GNX for staining bacteria in milk samples but found Acridine Orange/Tinopal AN a better stain due to decreased staining time and clarity of preparations.

Fluorescein diacetate (FDA)

Fluorescein diacetate (FDA) is used to detect selectively viable microorganisms. Free fluorescein is liberated due to esterase activity making viable cells fluoresce under 520 nm. Dead cells do not hydrolyse the ester bond and thus remain non-fluorescent. To obtain optimal esterase activity, the sample can be pretreated with 0.5 per cent w/v sodium acetate for 2 h at 20°C. After staining yeast with freshly prepared 0.01 per cent FDA in phosphate buffer, pH 7.2, followed by rinsing, Molzahn and Portno suggest counterstaining with 0.125 per cent Rhodamine B to mask autofluorescent yeast cells as well as other debris associated with beer samples. The FDA-staining technique for detecting small numbers of yeast cells in filtered drinks has been re-evaluated by Wackerbauer and Rinck. To increase the sensitivity of the technique the yeast cells collected on the membrane filter are pre-cultured for 16 h prior to staining. With this method as few as 12 yeast cells per filtered sample could be detected. By pre-culturing simultaneously in a general medium (PYG Broth) and a selective medium (Lysine-Broth) it is possible to differentiate between various types of yeast.

Spectrofluorometric detection of Clostridium, Lactobacillus and yeast in tomato juice as well as *Bacillus globigii* has been described, utilizing the liberation of fluorescent fluorescein from fluorescein diacetate.

Fluorscein Isothiocyanate (FITC)

Fluorscein isothiocyanate (FITC) in 0.01 per cent aqueous solution is used for assessing the viability of yeast cells, in contrast to Acridine Orange staining.

Primuline

Primuline is also used to determine yeast viability. Micromanipulative selection of fluorescent and non-fluorescent yeast cells shows good correlation between non-fluorescence and the ability to form microcolonies. Primuline staining has been further evaluated on different bacteria strains but found inferior to other fluorochromes used.

Rose Bengale

Rose Bengale was found superior in a comprehensive study of several different fluorochromes to differentiate between living and dead yeast cells, when examining the stained yeast at a wavelength of 540 nm.

Tinopal 4BMT

Tinopal 4BMT, together with other optical brighteners has been described for the staining of fungal mycelium and spores. The use of Tinopal 4BMT, also described by Jarvis *et al* permits easier detection of mould in food that achieved by using traditional stains.

To utilize the above-mentioned staining techniques in practical microbiological quality control of food it is, as already stated, of extreme important to differentiate between stained microorganisms and the background. As fluorescent-stained food particles will often mask the fluorescence of the microorganisms several attempts have been made either to counterstain these food particles or to remove them from the sample prior to staining.

The direct epifluorescent filter technique described below is an example of several efforts to overcome some of the many problems encountered. DEFT was developed for the examination of milk samples at the National Institute for Research in Dairying, Reading, UK, by Pettipher and colleagues. This technique is based on a pretreatment of the sample followed by filtration through a membrane filter. The microorganisms collected on the filter are stained with Acridine Orange and examined with an epifluorescence microscope visually or with the use of an image analyser. For routine quality control the method is still mainly used for raw milk, but its application in the analysis of other food products, like meat, fish and beverages, is increasing.

In the technique described by Pettipher *et al.*, whole milk samples are mixed with trypsin and a surfactant. After incubation for 10 min at 50°C the mixture can be filtered through a preheated polycarbonate filter. The filter is rinsed with 50°C Triton X-100 solution followed by a staining for 2 min with Acridine Orange and Tinopal AN. The surplus stain is removed by vacuum and the filter is rinsed with citrate/NaOH buffer followed by 95 per cent ethanol. The filter is air-dried and examined with incident UV light in a fluorescence microscope.

Pettipher concluded that the major barrier to the filtration of whole-milk samples is the presence of somatic cells. Several different enzymatic treatments were tried and a preparation of freeze-dried extract of crude trypsin in combination with the Triton X-100 surfactant proved to be most effective.

In a later publication a modification of the treatment prior to filtration is described for cream, concentrated whey and butter, involving a greater volume of a more dilute Triton X-100 solution and an increased incubation time. Using this technique it is possible to filter significant amounts of the sample. However, with ice cream only 0.1 ml could be filtered due to blocking of the filter by insoluble materials.

The DEFT technique has further been tested on other types of food samples, such as fresh and frozen meat and fish, frozen vegetables, etc. To remove food debris, Pettipher suggests prefiltering the homogenized food suspensions through nylon filters of 5 μm pore size, causing only a slight reduction in the recovery of microorganisms. Similar debris problems have been encountered when examining ground beef. These problems can be overcome by homogenizing the sample in a gauze pouch within a plastic bag during the treatment in the homogenizer (stomacher). Again, the recovery of microorganisms is only slightly reduced by the gauze pouch.

To evaluate the keeping quality of pasteurized milk, samples are preincubated at 30°C for 18 h after addition of benzalkonium chloride/Crystal Violet, which inhibits the growth of Gram-positive bacteria. The DEFT count correctly classifies 80–95 per cent of the pasteurized milk samples on the basis of keeping quality. Further increase in the sensitivity of the DEFT technique on milk samples can be achieved by adding citrate buffer, pH 3, to the sample during filtration. This allows 10 ml of milk to be filtered whereas only 4 ml could be filtered reliably without buffer addition.

Bacteria staining with Acridine Orange is normally very effective but the possibility of differentiating between living and dead microorganisms is debatable. The theory behind the differentiation is that stained RNA will fluoresce orange wheras DNA will fluoresce given. The RNA/DNA is higher in active growing microorganisms, in principle, living microorganisms should fluoresce orange. However, several other factors are involved in the staining of microorganisms and several observations strongly question the possibility of distinguishing between living and dead microorganisms.

In techniques directly based on the ability of microorganisms to form colonies, the problem of differentiation between living and dead cells is obviously solved.

The Fluorescent Microcolony Method

The microbial plate-counting method is a long process because of the time necessary for the microorganisms to form visible colonies.

To shorten this period, optical brightening agents (OBA) have been incorporated in the culture medium. During their growth, the microorganisms will pick up the OBA and can be detected by their fluorescence. Paton and Ayres described a method for evaluating the passage of *Salmonella* bacteria through eggshells. The bacteria were 'stained' by growing them in Calcofluor White MR2 New-containing media, and were later used in penetration experiments. In food microbiology fluorescent microcolony methods have been described mainly for detecting yeast in filtrable products such as wine and beer. The samples are filtered through membrane filters, which are then incubated on solid media containing the OBA. After a short incubation period (generally less than 24 h) the filters are examined with an epifluorescence microscope at rather low magnification. Several different OBAs of the Uvitex or Tinopal type are found to give good fluorescence with a variety of yeast strains normally found as contaminants in beer. Euchrysine 2GNX has been described as a better stain than the above-mentioned OBA for detecting *Saccharomyces bailii* in wine; however, Jacobsen and Lillie found only weak fluorescence even after incubating on a Uvitex- or Euchrysine 2GNS-containing medium. Practical experience with the fluorescence microcolony method has been mentioned for monitoring packaging of sterile beer. To isolate the important *Saccharomyces diastaticus*, a 37°C incubation on OBA media is recommended.

The fluorescence microcolony technique has also been described for the detection of bacteria in beer samples and on the surface of raw meat. The number of colonies found from meat rinsing water after 8 h incubation corresponded well with total counts on PCA.

The Characteristics of Fluorescent Compounds

The structure of fluorescent chormophores has been attributed to the crosslinking of oxidation-produced malonaldehyde with amino groups of proteins to form intra- or inter-molecular conjugated Schiff bases with the chromophoric system *N,N'*-disubstituted 1-amino-3-imino-propene. The proposed mechanism involves the reaction of one molecule of malonaldehyde with two molecules of primary amines initially to form the monomer amine-malonaldehyde (RN=CH–CH=CHOH) followed by the formation of dimer imine compound (RN=CH–CH=CH–NHR). Mass-spectral analysis upon reduction of Schiff bases with sodium borohydride confirmed the molar ratio of amino acid to aldehyde as 2:1. The structure required for fluorescence consists of an electron-donating group in conjugation with an imine. Hence, the monomeric amine-malonaldehyde products are not fluorescent, while the dimer compounds, even at a low level of one nanogram per gram, are easily detected by their fluorescence. Chio and Tappel characterized the conjugated Schiff base chromophores derived from the reaction of aliphatic primary amines with malonaldehyde on the basis of their characteristic absorption in the UV and visible regions; their excitation, emission, and absorption maxima occurring at 370, 450 nm, and 256 and 435 nm, respectively. Observed spectral shifts (isobestic points at 401–404 nm) result from the *cis-trans* isomerization about the C=C bond or C=N bond, which occurs as the solutions are left standing at room temperature.

Amino acid loss, specifically lysine, occurs from the modification of proteins with malonaldehyde and the consequent Schiff base formation. Examples are the loss of ε-aminolysine in frozen Baltic herring and the loss of ε-aminolysine and the *N*-terminal amino group of aspartic acid in thc of reactions of malonaldehyde with bovine plasma albumin. As Chino and Tappal have shown, the formation of yellow fluorescent compounds correlates well with the disappearance of ribonnuclease activity and with the loss of lysine and histidine in the enzyme–lipid reaction mixtures; the excitation and emission maxima for the fluorescing monomer and the oligomers of the inactivated enzyme occur at 395 and 470 nm, respectively. In the reaction of malonaldehyde with collagen, lysine participates in the crosslinkage reaction. In bovine serum albumin (BSA), basic amino acids are modified in the reaction with 12-keto-oleic acid, detected by polyacrylamide-gel electrophoresis.

There is a correlation between the formation of TBA-reactive substances and the development of fluorescence in oxidizing systems, as shown by Dillard and Tappel in the *in vitro* oxidation of microsomes, mitochondria, and sarcosomes from rats fed various levels of α-tocopherol. With the increase in the production of TBA-reactants, oxygen absorption find development of fluorescence (excitation and emission maxima 360 and 430 nm. respectively) had an inverse relationship with the amount of dietary α-tocopherol.

Reconstitute freeze-dried beef samples to initial moisture content

↓ **Vortex and store (15 min at room temperature)**

Add 25 ml $CHCl_3$:MeOH (2:1)

↓ **Mix (15 min) and transfer to centrifuge tube**

Rinse with 10 ml H_2O

↓

Centrifuge (10^4 G for 5 min at room temperature)

↓ **Remove aqueous phase (aspiration)**

Collect solvent layer

↓ **Filter (2×) SS #595**

Fluorometry assay

Figure 7.5: Step-by-step Preparation of Freeze-dried Beef for Fluorescence Study

There is a 100 per cent TBA recovery of mono- and di-substituted malonaldehyde addition products (RN=CH–CH=CHOH and RN=CH–CH=CH–NHR) while TBA recovery is much less in reactions of malonaldehyde with cyclic products. Fluorescing compounds formed during the oxidation of rat's microsomal membrane were also reported to be correlated with TBA-reactants in the work of Bidlack and Tappel.

Schiff base structures are pH-dependent. At alkaline pH, the fluorescence is quenched reversibly. Metal-chelating compounds also decrease the conjugated Schiff base fluorescence.

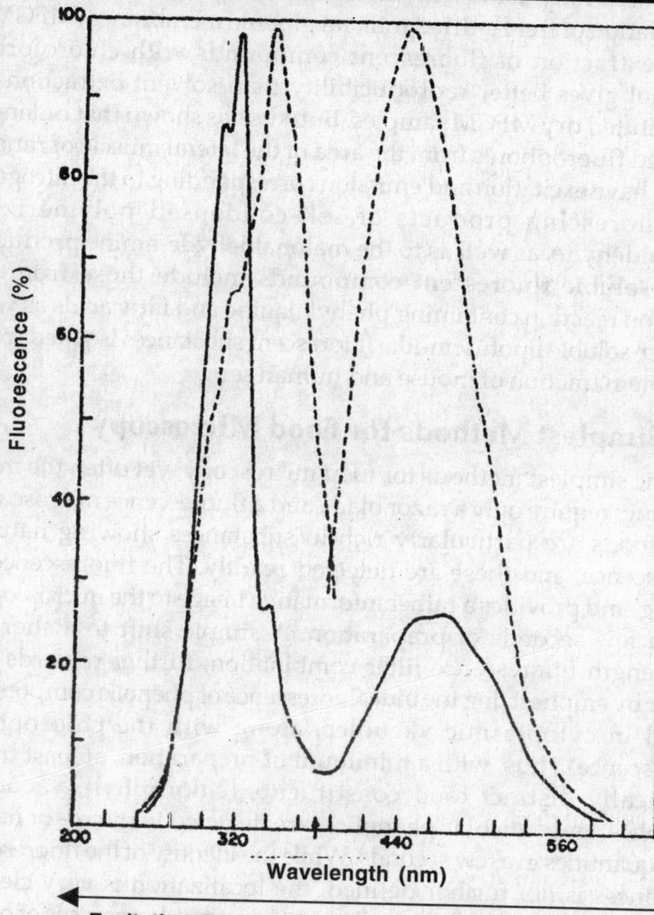

Figure 7.6: Typical Excitation and Emission Spectra of Unoxidized (——) vs oxidized (stored) (- - -) Freeze-dried Beef

Fluorescent products can be extracted with chloroform-methanol. Fluorescent chromophores are either lipid- or water-soluble, or insoluble, and a major portion of the fluorescent compounds in oxidizing biological tissues extract in the lipid-soluble phase of the chloroform-methanol mixture. Examples of lipid-soluble fluorophores are those, from the oxidation of unsaturated fatty acids with phosphatidyl ethanolamine, or from the oxidation of freeze-dried milk fat globule membranes (MFGM). Direct extraction of fluorescent compounds with chloroform-methanol gives better reproducibility than solvent extraction of reconstituted dry MFGM samples. Buttkus has shown that butanol-extracted fluorophores from the area of the lateral muscle of rancid herring have excitation and emission corresponding to the nitrogen-free fluorescing products of self-condensed polymerized malonaldehyde, as well as to the malonaldehyde-amine products. Water-soluble fluorescent compounds include those from an oxidation reaction containing phenylalanine and fatty acids as well as water-soluble lipofuscin-like fluorescent substances isolated from the protein fraction of mouse and human sera.

The Simplest Methods for Food Microscopy

The simplest methods for food microscopy, yet often the most revealing, require only a razor blade and a fluorescence microscope. Plant foods are particularly rich in substances showing natural fluorescence, and these are detected readily. The fluorescence is striking, and provides a rather informative image to the microscopist after a few seconds of preparation. A simple shift to a shorter-wavelength fluorescence filter combination, further rewards the viewer by emphasizing the blue fluorescence of phenolic compounds stored in cytoplasmic vacuoles, along with the chlorophyll fluorescence. Thus, with a minimum of preparation, at least three chemically distinct food constituents (chlorophyll, vacuolar phenolics, and cuticular phenolics) are detected in micro- or nano-gram quantities in a few seconds. While the identity of the fluorescing substances is not further defined, the localization is very clearly indicated, with reasonable resolution. Comparable analyses of other hand-cut or cryo-cut tissues, such as the cucumber and broccoli stem reveal the diversity of phenolic distribution in foods of plant origin, the latter being primarily associated with vascular (conducting) tissues. While all of these tissues may be prepared equally well with fixation, dehydration and embedding steps added to the protocol, such a process is clearly not necessary for many observations.

For higher-resolution images, it is preferable to use fixed, embedded specimens. In this example, the distribution of phenolic esters such as ferulic acid in the aleurone cell wall of wheat is very easily visualized, even in the relatively thin section. This example is similar to one which we have used subsequently for various quantitative exercises. It is important to note that some of the naturally fluorescing material normally present in such a specimen would have been extracted during processing with most other microscopic preparation techniques. This is often the case, especially with low-molecular-weight compounds, and even some larger complexes. Users of such approaches are cautioned that alternative methods such as hand-sectioning should be used in parallel studies to ensure that significant changes in the patterns of primary fluorescence have not occurred during sample processing.

So far, our examples include only those based on detection of primary (auto-) fluorescence. Many compounds are not detectable by these means, but a wide range of fluorescent staining methods are available for virtually any other food constituent. These may range from the totally empirical to the well-defined, from compounds with decades of historical application to newly synthesized compounds, and even those which have arisen by serendipity.

The advantages of fluorescence are in no way restricted to the microscopist: they have become equally important to chemists, cell biologists, and medical technologists. Consequently, there is a rapidly increasing catalogue of potential fluorescent probes, and many of these will no doubt find their way into microscopic applications in food research and elsewhere. One class of compounds which we expect to see increase in popularity involves the use of enzyme-specific probes which we have briefly mentioned earlier. In the presence of a suitable enzyme, a fluorescent component is released at the site of hydrolysis, and in some cases it is retained in the cell where it was hydrolysed. This is the case with fluorescein diacetate, as shown being enzymatically hydrolysed in the aleurone cells and scutellar epithelium of a germinating barley grain. While this procedure is generally useful only for esterases, numerous other substrates are available commercially for detection of a wide range of enzymes. In many cases, the fluorescent product is not retained at the site of hydrolysis, but in combination with quantitative microscopic techniques the enzymatic activity can be estimated. Similarly, a wide range of fluorescently labelled lectins are now available and these too have considerable potential for structural, and perhaps chemical specificity, providing suitable safeguards are included in the procedures. Several lectins been identified with useful specificity for cereal starch, rapeseed coat mucilage, and rapeseed cotyledonary cell walls. Others are available, and further exploration is necessary. Commercial lectins are not cheap, but they appear to have considerable promise in food microscopy.

We cannot conclude our brief discussion of applications without a few additional points. First, the accompanying micrographs should underscore the fact that those who pursue fluorescence microscopy in a reasonably systematic way are quickly and relatively easily rewarded with a most pleasant result: the micrographs are often among the most striking obtainable, and the chemical information is usually unobtainable by other means. With judicious use, the instrument is quite capable of telling the food technologist not only 'what', but 'how much', and 'where'. For those who enjoy an increase in complexity, it is even possible to combine several fluorochromes in one tissue section for simultaneous detection of several constituents such as starch β-glucan and protein. Nor is the microscopist restricted with these methods to cereal tissues. They are equally applicable to many other raw or processed foods.

The Methods Used for Quantification

Traditional methods for quantification using optical microscopes invariably employed some form of absorption measurement–that is, measurement of substances based on the relative absorption of specific illumination wavelengths, usually in systems employing transmitted (substage) illumination. Piller and Dhillon *et. al.* have provided excellent reviews of the principles and selected applications of absorption microspectrophotometry; for those analyses in which the target substance is non-fluorescent or in which there has not been a specific fluorescence probe developed, absorption techniques are obviously preferred. Indeed, while fluorescence techniques have many marked advantages, it should not be assumed from this discussion that other quantitative approaches are not equally useful. A wide range of alternative techniques are available to the optical microscopist, including scanning microinterferometry, integrating microdensitometry and image analysis of various microscopic images.

A major advantage of the fluorescence techniques is due to the fact that a fluorescent substance behaves as a self-luminous object–

it is viewed and measured against a dark field (excitation light is prevented from entering the objective by the barrier filter), thereby providing a high level of contrast which translates directly into increased sensitivity (perhaps up to 100, times that of absorption techniques). In addition, most fluorescent molecules emit light of the same intensity in all directions and a constant fraction of the emitted light, independent of object size, enters the objective. Theoretically then, there is no lower limit to the size of the fluorescent object which can be measured by microfluorometry, and measurement of fluorescence in objects smaller than the optical limit of resolution of the microscope is possible. In practical terms, limits are imposed by the sensitivity of the detector, the fluorescence efficiency (quantum yield) of the substance, the intensity of the excitation light, and the transmittance characteristics of the other optical components.

A further advantage of the fluorescence approach to quantification is the measurement of heterogeneous specimens (such as food materials). In absorption measurements, the object of interest must be differentiated from other, absorbing, components and the sensitivity of the method, therefore decreases as specimen thickness decreases. Furthermore, more complex methods must be applied to deal with the sampling requirements associated with avoiding distributional error. In fluorescence techniques, the high contrast reduces non-specific detection and the intensity of the signal is proportional to excitation intensity as well as in epi-illumination techniques being independent of specimen thickness. Therefore, thin specimens are conducive to maximum resolution and detection, and the total fluorescence emanating from a particular substance can be measured quite easily.

Until recently, quantification with optical microscopes has been the prerogative of the tenacious, the tinkerer, and the imaginative. Early microspectrophotometers were often difficult and expensive to build, they were limited to a narrow range of applications, and they were applicable to fluorescence detection only in those instances where the fluorescent signal was of unusually high intensity. Rarely were such instruments applied to food materials.

In the past few years, there has been an accelerating interest by some microscope manufacturers in developing attachments or modifications which will permit precise quantification of fluorescent images, and it is now a relatively simple (albeit expensive) matter to define the spectral characteristics of fluorescent structures in foods (as small as 0.5 μm) with spectral resolution approaching 0.5 nm. Furthermore, the distribution of any particular fluorescent substance can be mapped with equal structural precision, and other types of quantification (analysis of fluorescence decay rates) are available to the microscopist.

Many of the advances in quantitative fluorescence microscopy are due to the marriage of microcomputers and optical equipment. Data can be acquired rapidly, and elegant programs are available commercially which will simultaneously define monochromator, filter, scanning stage, and photomultiplier functions, and calibration procedures. With these additions, the flexibility of quantitative instruments has increased dramatically, and data are recorded, analysed and stored digitally and rapidly. It is now quite possible to scan spectrally 100 or more fields on a single specimen throughout the entire fluorescence spectrum, and perform a wide range of mathematical analyses on these spectra in a short period of time. Similarly, the precise distribution of a fluorescent component in a specimen can be mapped digitally and the data manipulated endlessly to provide distribution profiles and relative concentrations in any portion of the sample. The data also can be transferred from the controlling microcomputer to a larger mini- or mainframe computer for more detailed analyses.

Now let us learn more details about Zeiss UMSP 80 microspectroflurometer.

The instrument is of a relatively new and modular design and the examples included have been chosen to illustrate some of the typical functions of such an instrument based on primary applications within cereals. They are by no means exhaustive, but describe basic measuring routines which can be applied in a wide range of food applications. The experienced microscopist will not doubt to imagine many more uses than we describe, and in the next few years we hope that similar quantiative approaches will become an integral part of food research activities. Only with high-speed quantiative measurements will fluorescence microscopy realize its full potential as a research instrument.

The UMSP 80 (Carl Zeiss, Oberkochen, FRG) is an excellent example of a module microspectrophotometer designed specifically for fluorescence quantification.

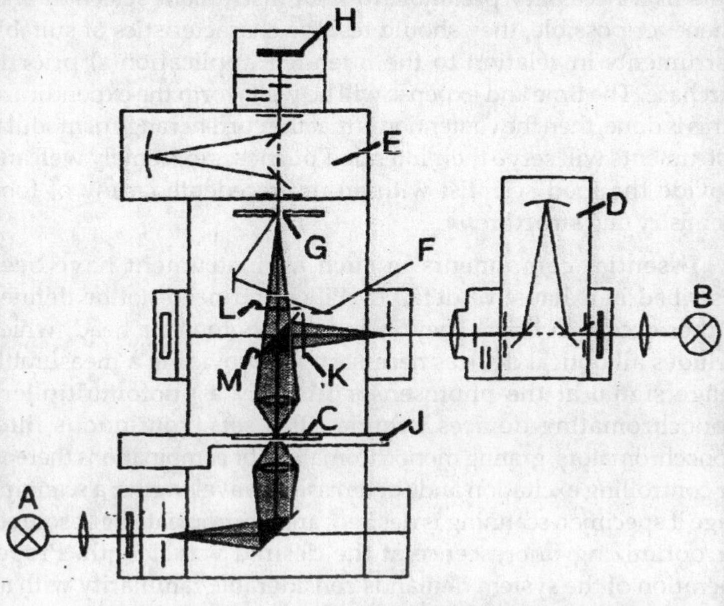

Figure 7.7: A Diagrammatic Representation of the UMSP 80 Microspectrometer

This instrument is capable of ultraviolet absorption (230-350 nm) and near-infrared (800-2100 nm) detection as well as fluorescence analysis in the normal, visible range (350-700 nm). Adjustment to any of these modes is a relatively simple procedure and the UMSP 80 responds quickly to the various measuring requirements imposed by a multidisciplinary establishment. The components shown here are by no means essential for all types of fluorescence quantification-only one monochromator may be adequate for scanning emission spectra (indeed, different types of monochromators may be used, *e.g.* grating or prism), a scanning stage is required only when distribution data are desired, quartz optics are used primarily for examining ultraviolet spectra, and a limited range of fluorescence filters might be quite adequate for many routine analyses. Consequently, the cost of such instruments varies widely, and many different manufacturers provide one or more types of machines which can be tailored to the needs of the customer.

Potential users should include discussions with experienced users as a necessary preamble to final instrument selection and, whenever possible, they should test the characteristics of suitable instruments in relation to the intended application(s) prior to purchase. The time and expense will be well worth the expenditure. If this is done, then the contention is that the current range of modular instruments will serve their intended purposes extremely well and provide the food scientist with an unprecedented view of food chemistry and structure.

Essential components in such an instrument have been described in exhaustive detail by Piller and need not be defined further except in brief. They include: a photometer head, which includes all optical devices necessary for providing a measurable image signal at the photosensor (usually a photomultiplier); monochromating devices (simple filter sets, continuous filter monochromators, grating monochromators, or combinations thereof) for controlling excitation and / or emission wavelengths; a scanning stage if specimen scanning is desired; and appropriate light sources for optimizing fluorescence at the desired wavelength. Proper operation of the system demands considerable familiarity with all relevant components if errors are to be minimized, and readers are encouraged to consult Piller's book (and references therein) for further discussion. Because microspectrophotometry involves examination of exceedingly small concentrations and amounts of material, and because the optics associated with their measurement are quite complex, the potential for error is enormous. Due attention to instrumentation and theory, however, will yield extraordinary results.

Scanning Electron Microscopy

Scanning electron microscopy (SEM) of biological specimens has several advantages over light microscopy (LM) and fluorescence microscopy (FM). These are a great depth of field, high resolution and the three-dimensional characteristics of its images. To date, however, it is impossible to obtain qualitative assessments from SEM micrographs beyond quantification and distribution of the chemical elements by X-ray microanalysis and back scattering.

Now let us study about some preliminary experiments regarding the interchangeable use of fluorescence and scanning electron microscopy looking at the same specimen with both techniques which have been performed in the laboratory. The technique is based on the fact that the primary or secondary fluorescence of a specimen can be observed even after the specimen has been gold coated for subsequent SEM. Both SEM and FM complement each other remarkably well, so that:

- ☆ Topographical changes observed with SEM in a given sample can be analytically identified by means of FM.
- ☆ Information provided by FM can be easily mapped and related to the sample's morphological structures.
- ☆ SEM used as an extension of FM can provide a better axial and spatial resolution to a fluorescent image.
- ☆ Localization and identification of a cell or small specimen in a mixed population, or even of apart of a specimen for subsequent SEM observation, can be greatly simplified by preliminary FM.

There are three possibilities for the combination of FM and SEM microscopic techniques:

(*i*) Examination of two different preparations with two separate microscopes.

(*ii*) Examination of the same preparation with two separate microscopes.

(*iii*) Examination of one preparation using one instrument which combines both techniques.

Of these, the examination of two different preparations with a fluorescence microscope and a scanning electron microscope, case (*i*) is the most common application found in the literature. However, there are very few examples reported on cereal grains or seeds. In addition, one instrument for the combined used of FM and SEM, case (*iii*), has been described but has not been used extensively. The main drawback of this last possibility is the cost of the instrument.

Chapter 8
Spectroscopy

Spectroscopy was originally the study of the interaction between radiation and matter as a function of wavelength (λ). In fact, historically, spectroscopy referred to the use of visible light dispersed according to its wavelength, *e.g.* by a prism. Later the concept was expanded greatly to comprise any measurement of a quantity as a function of either wavelength or frequency.

Spectroscopy is the study of light as it breaks into its constituent colors. This is because light is a wave, and different energies have different wavelengths. These different wavelengths correlate to different colors. By examining these different colors, one can determine any number of properties of the object being studied, as the colors of the light reflect the energy states. In other words, spectrophotometry is the study of the reflection or transmission properties of a substance as a function of wavelength. It is the quantitative study of electromagnetic spectra of a material. More technically, spectroscopy looks at the interaction between any matter and radiation. During the process, the transmittance or reflectance of the substance is measured through the careful geometrical and spectral consideration.

Spectrometry is the spectroscopic technique used to assess the concentration or amount of a given chemical (atomic, molecular, or ionic) species. In this case, the instrument that performs such measurements is a spectrometer, spectrophotometer, or spectrograph.

The data that is obtained from spectroscopy is called a spectrum. A spectrum is a plot of the intensity of energy detected versus the wavelength (or mass or momentum or frequency, etc.) of the energy. A spectrum can be used to obtain information about atomic and molecular energy levels, molecular geometries, chemical bonds, interactions of molecules, and related processes. Often, spectra are used to identify the components of a sample (qualitative analysis). Spectra may also be used to measure the amount of material in a sample (quantitative analysis).

Spectroscopy/spectrometry is often used in physical and analytical chemistry for the identification of substances through the spectrum emitted from or absorbed by them. It is also heavily used in astronomy and remote sensing.

Classification of Methods of Spectroscopy

It generally depends upon:

1. Nature of excitation measured
2. Measurement process

Nature of Excitation Measured

The type of spectroscopy depends on the physical quantity measured. Normally, the quantity that is measured is an intensity, either of energy absorbed or produced.

- ☆ Electromagnetic spectroscopy involves interactions of matter with electromagnetic radiation, such as light.
- ☆ Electron spectroscopy involves interactions with electron beams. Auger spectroscopy involves inducing the Auger effect with an electron beam. In this case the measurement typically involves the kinetic energy of the electron as variable.
- ☆ Acoustic spectroscopy involves the frequency of sound.
- ☆ Dielectric spectroscopy involves the frequency of an external electrical field.
- ☆ Mechanical spectroscopy involves the frequency of an external mechanical stress, *e.g.* a torsion applied to a piece of material.

Measurement Process

Most spectroscopic methods are differentiated as either atomic or molecular based on whether or not they apply to atoms or molecules. Along with that distinction, they can be classified on the nature of their interaction:

- ☆ Absorption spectroscopy uses the range of the electromagnetic spectra in which a substance absorbs. This includes atomic absorption spectroscopy and various molecular techniques, such as infrared, ultraviolet-visible and microwave spectroscopy.
- ☆ Emission spectroscopy uses the range of electromagnetic spectra in which a substance radiates (emits). The substance first must absorb energy. This energy can be from a variety of sources, which determines the name of the subsequent emission, like luminescence. Molecular luminescence techniques include spectrofluorimetry.
- ☆ Scattering spectroscopy measures the amount of light that a substance scatters at certain wavelengths, incident angles, and polarization angles. One of the most useful applications of light scattering spectroscopy is Raman spectroscopy.

General Types of Spectra

There are two main spectra of light that are looked at in spectroscopy:

1. Continuous
2. Discrete

With discrete spectra, one sees only bright or dark lines at very distinct and sharply-defined colors (energies). As we'll discover shortly, discrete spectra with bright lines are called emission spectra, those with dark lines are termed absorption spectra.

Continuous Spectra

A spectrum in which all wavelengths are present between certain limits; it is produced by electrons undergoing free-bound transitions in a hot gas. White light for example can be dispersed by a prism to give a continous spectrum in the optical region of the spectrum from red to violet. Dark absorption lines crossing a continuous spectrum are caused by the absorption of radiation at specific wavelengths.

For a continuous spectrum, the light is composed of a wide, continuous range of colors (energies). Continuous spectra arise from dense gases or solid objects which radiate their heat away through the production of light. Such objects emit light over a broad range of wavelengths, thus the apparent spectrum seems smooth and continuous. Stars emit light in a predominantly continuous spectrum. Other examples of such objects are incandescent light bulbs, electric cooking stove burners, flames, cooling fire embers etc.

Discrete Spectra

A spectrum in which the component wavelengths (and wavenumbers and frequencies) constitute a discrete sequence of values (finite or infinite in number) rather than a continuum of values. Discrete spectra are the observable result of the physics of atoms.

There are two types of discrete spectra, emission (bright line spectra) and absorption (dark line spectra).

(*i*) Emission Line Spectra

Emission is a process by which a substance releases energy in the form of electromagnetic radiation. Emission can occur at any frequency at which absorption can occur, and this allows the absorption lines to be determined from an emission spectrum. The emission spectrum of a chemical element or chemical compound is the relative intensity of each frequency of electromagnetic radiation emitted by the element's atoms or the compound's molecules when they are returned to a ground state.

Unlike a continuous spectrum source, which can have any energy it wants, the electron clouds surrounding the nuclei of atoms can have only very specific energies dictated by quantum mechanics. Each element on the periodic table has its own set of possible energy levels, and with few exceptions the levels are distinct and identifiable. Atoms will also tend to settle to the lowest energy level (ground state). This means that an excited atom in a higher energy level must 'dump' some energy. The way an atom 'dumps' that energy is by emitting a wave of light with that exact energy.

In the Figure 8.1, a hydrogen atom drops from the 2nd energy level to the 1st, giving off a wave of light with an energy equal to the difference of energy between levels 2 and 1. This energy corresponds to a specific color, or wavelength of light and thus we see a bright line at that exact wavelength, an emission spectrum is born.

Tiny changes of energy in an atom generate photons with small energies and long wavelengths, such as radio waves. Similarly, large changes of energy in an atom will mean that high-energy, short-wavelength photons (UV, x-ray, gamma-rays) are emitted. Each element's emission spectrum is unique. The emission spectrum of a body or substance is the characteristic range of radiations it emits when it is heated, bombarded by electron or ions, or absorbs photons.

Therefore, spectroscopy can be used to identify the elements in matter of unknown composition. Similarly, the emission spectra of molecules can be used in chemical analysis of substances.

(*ii*) Absorption Line Spectra

A material's absorption spectrum is the fraction of incident radiation absorbed by the material over a range of frequencies. The absorption spectrum is primarily determined by the atomic and molecular composition of the material. Radiation is more likely to be absorbed at frequencies that match the energy difference between two quantum mechanical states of the molecules. The absorption that occurs due to a transition between two states is referred to as an absorption line and a spectrum is typically composed of many lines.

A spectrum showing dark lines at some narrow color regions (wave-lengths) is called absorption line spectrum. The lines are formed by atoms absorbing light, which lifts their electrons to higher orbits. If a star with a 'continuous' spectrum is shining upon an atom, the wavelengths corresponding to possible energy transitions within that atom will be absorbed and therefore an observer will not see them. In this way, a dark-line absorption spectrum is born.

The frequencies where absorption lines occur, as well as their relative intensities, primarily depend on the electronic and molecular structure of the molecule. The frequencies will also, though, depend on the interactions between molecules in the sample, the crystal structure (in solids) and on several environmental factors (*e.g.*,

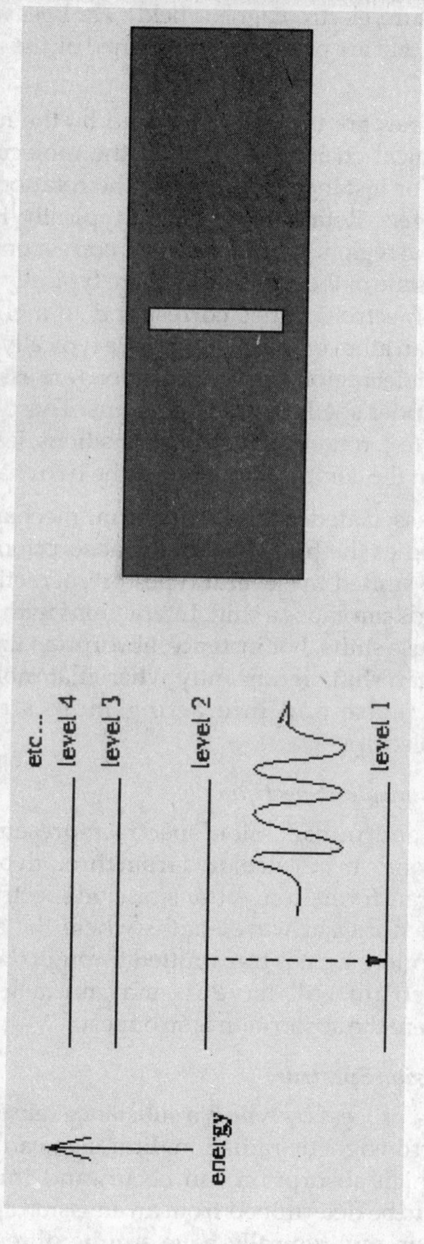

Figure 8.1: An Excited Hydrogen Atom Relaxes from Level 2 to Level 1, Yielding a Photon. This results in a bright emission line.

temperature, pressure, electromagnetic field). The lines will also have a width and shape that are primarily determined by the environment of the sample.

Absorption lines are typically classified by the nature of the quantum mechanical change induced in the molecule or atom. Rotational lines, for instance, occur when the rotational state of a molecule is changed. Rotational lines are typically found in the microwave spectral region. Vibrational lines correspond to changes in the vibrational state of the molecule and are typically found in the infrared region. Electronic lines correspond to a change in the electronic state of an atom or molecule and are typically found in the visible and ultraviolet region. X-ray absorptions are associated with the excitation of inner shell electrons in atoms. These changes can also be combined (*e.g.* rotation-vibration transitions, leading to new absorption lines at the combined energy of the two changes.

The energy associated with the quantum mechanical change primarily determines the frequency of the absorption line but the frequency can be shifted by several types of interactions. Electric and magnetic fields can cause a shift. Interactions with neighboring molecules can cause shifts. For instance, absorption lines of the gas phase molecule can shift significantly when that molecule is in a liquid or solid phase and interacting more strongly with neighbouring molecules.

Relation to Transmission Spectrum

Absorption and transmission spectra represent equivalent information and one can be calculated from through other through a mathematical transformation. A transmission spectrum will have its maximum intensities at wavelengths where the absorption is weakest because more light is transmitted through the sample. An absorption spectrum will have its maximum intensities at wavelengths where the absorption is strongest.

Relation to Emission Spectrum

Emission is a process by which a substance releases energy in the form of electromagnetic radiation. Emission can occur at any frequency at which absorption can occur, and this allows the absorption lines to be determined from an emission spectrum. The emission spectrum will typically have a quite different intensity pattern from the absorption spectrum, though, so the two are not equivalent. The absorption spectrum can be calculated from the emission spectrum using appropriate theoretical models and additional information about the quantum mechanical states of the substance.

Relation to Scattering and Reflection Spectra

The scattering and reflection spectra of a material are influenced by both its index of refraction and its absorption spectrum. In an optical context, the absorption spectrum is typically quantified by the extinction coefficient, and the extinction and index coefficients are quantitatively related through the Kramers-Kronig relation. Therefore, the absorption spectrum can be derived from a scattering or reflection spectrum. This typically requires simplifying assumptions or models, and so the derived absorption spectrum is an approximation.

Principle of Spectrophotometry and its Measurement

Light is quantized into tiny packets called photons, the energy of which can be transferred to an electron upon collision. However, transfer occurs only when the energy level of the photon equals the energy required for the electron to get promoted onto the next energy state, for example from the ground state to the first excitation state (Boyer, 1993). This said process is the basis for absorption spectroscopy. Generally, light of a certain wavelength and energy is illuminated on the sample, which absorbs a certain amount of energy from the incident light. The energy of the light transmitted from the sample afterwards is measured using a photodetector, which registers the absorbance of the sample.

To carry out spectrophotometry, a spectrophotometer is required which is used to measure intensity of light as a function of the wavelength of light. A spectrophotometer, is the combination of two devices, a spectrometer and a photometer. Spectrometer is used for producing light of any selected wavelength or color while a photometer is used for measuring the intensity of light. The two devices are placed at either side of a cuvette filled with a liquid. Spectrometer produces the light of desired wavelength and it passes through the tube and reaches photometer that measures its intensity. Then the photometer produces a voltage signal to a display device, usually a galvanometer. As the amount of light absorbed by the liquid changes the signal also changes. The concentration of a substance in solution can be measured by calculating the amount of absorption of light at the appropriate wavelength or a particular color.

If development of color is linked to the concentration of a substance in solution then that concentration can be measured by determining the extent of absorption of light at the appropriate wavelength. For example hemoglobin appears red because the hemoglobin absorbs blue and green light rays much more effectively than red. The degree of absorbance of blue or green light is proportional to the concentration of hemoglobin.

When monochromatic light (light of a specific wavelength) passes through a solution there is usually a quantitative relationship (Beer's law) between the solute concentration and the intensity of the transmitted light, that is

$$I=I_0 10^{-kcl}$$

where,

I sub 0 is the intensity of transmitted light using the pure solvent, I is the intensity of the transmitted light when the colored compound is added, c is concentration of the colored compound, l is the distance the light passes through the solution, and k is a constant. If the light path l is a constant, as is the case with a spectrophotometer, Beer's law may be written

$$I/I_0 = 10^{-kc} = T$$

where,

k is a new constant and T is the transmittance of the solution. There is a logarithmic relationship between transmittance and the concentration of the colored compound. Thus,

$$-\log T = \log 1/T = kc = \text{optical density}$$

The O.D. is directly proportional to the concentration of the colored compound. Most spectrophotometers have a scale that reads both in O.D. (absorbance) units, which is a logarithmic scale, and in % transmittance, which is an arithmetic scale. As suggested by the above relationships, the absorbance scale is the most useful for colorimetric assays.

Parts of a Spectrophotometer and their Working

Spectrophotometry deals with visible light, near-ultraviolet, and near-infrared and involves the use of a spectrophotometer. The spectrophotometer is a complex instrument used in measuring the absorbance of biomolecules within the ultraviolet and visible light spectrum, similar to the one found in the laboratory. It is a conglomerate of light sources, wavelength selectors, optical systems, sample chambers, photodetectors, and meters functioning together to perform a specific task *i.e.* to measure the absorbance of a sample. They are commonly used in scientific fields such as physics, chemistry, biochemistry, human nutrition and molecular biology.

The most common spectrophotometers are used in the UV and visible regions of the spectrum, and some of these instruments also operate into the near-infrared region as well.

Visible region 400–700 nm spectrophotometry is used extensively in colorimetry science. Traditional visual region spectrophotometers cannot detect if a colorant or the base material has fluorescence. This can make it difficult to manage color issues if for example one or more of the printing inks is fluorescent. Where a colorant contains fluorescence, a bi-spectral fluorescent spectrophotometer is used. There are two major setups for visual spectrum spectrophotometers, d/8 (spherical) and 0/45. The names are due to the geometry of the light source, observer and interior of the measurement chamber. Scientists use this machine to measure the amount of compounds in a sample. If the compound is more concentrated more light will be absorbed by the sample; within small ranges, the Beer-Lambert law holds and the absorbance between samples vary with concentration linearly.

Ultraviolet-visible spectroscopy or spectrophotometry involves the spectroscopy of photons in the UV-visible region and the instrument used is called a UV/vis spectrophotometer. This means it uses light in the visible and adjacent (near ultraviolet (UV) and near infrared (NIR)) ranges. The absorption in the visible ranges directly affects the color of the chemicals involved. In this region of the electromagnetic spectrum, molecules undergo electronic transitions. This technique is complementary to fluorescence spectroscopy, in that fluorescence deals with transitions from the excited state to the ground state, while absorption measures transitions from the ground state to the excited state.

There are two existing light sources within a UV-VIS spectrophotometer – one for each (UV and visible light) spectrum. The usual light source used to generate visible light is the tungsten-halogen lamp emitting 200-340 nm wavelengths (Boyer, 1993). The UV source can be either a high-pressure hydrogen lamp or deuterium lamp, the latter of which is the one found in the lab. When measuring absorbance at the UV spectrum, the other lamp has to be turned off. The same goes when measuring visible light absorbance. This is to prevent interference of unnecessary wavelengths in the incident light on the sample. Following the light source is a monochromator, the purpose of which is to filter light and select a specific wavelength by using either a prism or a diffraction grating. After the monochromator is a series of lenses, slits, mirrors, and filters that act as an optical system to concentrate, increase spectral purity of, and direct monochromatic light towards the sample chamber with cuvettes containing solutions to be tested. In the laboratory, the sample chamber is equipped with multiple slots to allow for continuous measurements of several sample replicates at a particular wavelength. However, since the instrument has only a single beam, every time the wavelength has to be changed a blank reading must precede any sample reading. With regards to cuvettes, which contain the sample solutions, there are three kinds available for use today. The first is made of glass and is often utilized for reading absorbance at wavelengths greater than 340 nm due to its undesirable absorption of UV light. The second is made of fused silica or quartz and is the one used in the experiment. It can be utilized in absorbance measurement throughout the UV-VIS spectrum (200 nm to 800 nm) because of its high grade of transparency. The last class is of disposable cuvettes, the material of which can vary. One example is made of polymethacrylate and is used only for measurement at 280 nm to 800 nm (Potter, 1995).

The light-sensitive detector follows the sample chamber and measures the intensity of light transmitted from the cuvettes and passes the information to a meter that records and displays the value to the operator on an LCD screen. Two kinds are of use in UV/VIS spectrophotometry today – the phototube and the photomultiplier tube. The phototube or photocell functions by generating an electric current. When a photon hits the cathode of the cell, an electron is ejected from the cathode and directed to the anode. This flow of electron produces a current, the magnitude of which is proportional to the energy of the photon. The photomultiplier tube, which is more sensitive, relies on Planck's Photoelectric Effect. Photons hitting the tube's photosensitive surface eject primary electrons, which then collide with another surface and release secondary electrons. These secondary electrons hit several other surfaces and eject more secondary electrons, which eventually get caught by an anode and produce an electric current. The current generated, however, is several-fold amplified so that even a single photon with very low energy can be detected and registered (Christian, 2004).

Spectrophotometers designed for the main infrared region are quite different because of the technical requirements of measurement. One major factor is the type of photosensors that are available for different spectral regions, but infrared measurement is also challenging because virtually everything emits IR light as thermal radiation, especially at wavelengths beyond about 5 μm. Another complication is that quite a few materials such as glass and plastic absorb infrared light, making it incompatible as an optical medium. Ideal optical materials are salts, which do not absorb strongly. Samples for IR spectrophotometry may be smeared between two discs of potassium bromide or ground with potassium bromide and pressed into a pellet. Where aqueous solutions are to be measured, insoluble silver chloride is used to construct the cell.

Spectrophotometer Calibration

Spectrophotometer calibration is a process in which spectrophotometer is calibrated to confirm that it is working properly. This is important, as it ensures that the measurements obtained with the instrument are accurate. The procedure varies slightly for different instruments, with most manufacturers providing a detailed calibration guide in the owner's manual so that people know how to calibrate the equipment properly. When this process is performed, the person doing it must make a note in the log attached to the equipment and in their experimental notes, so that people know when the device was last calibrated and handled, and by whom.

In spectrophotometer calibration, a reference solution is used to zero out the equipment. This solution provides a base or zero reading. The device is calibrated by placing the reference solution inside the spectrophotometer, zeroing out the settings, and running the instrument. Then, samples of an actual test material can be subjected to spectrophotometry in confidence that the machine has been calibrated and is working properly.

In a single beam spectrophotometer, a single beam of light is generated, and the device must be recalibrated for each use. In a double beam spectrophotometer, beams can be sent through a test sample and a reference sample at the same time to generate two sets of results which can be used for reference and calibration. In either case, spectrophotometer calibration can be done in the lab by someone working with the machine. If the machine develops serious problems, it may be sent to the manufacturer for maintenance, repair, and potential replacement.

In order for a spectrophotometer to work properly, it must be allowed to warm up before use. Many devices take around 10 minutes to warm up. It is important to avoid performing spectrophotometer calibration during the warmup phase as this will throw the settings off. It is also important to be aware that for certain types of wavelengths, special filters and attachments may be needed for the device to function.

Different Types of Spectrophotometers

Different types of spectrophotometers are found in the market. These instruments are available in many shapes, configurations and sizes. They are classified on various bases. The most important distinctions used to classify them are:

- The different measurement techniques.
- The wavelengths they work with.
- How they acquire a spectrum.
- The sources of intensity variation.

Two basic designs available in the market are the single and double beam spectrophotometer. As the name suggests this single beam spectrophotometer comprises of a single beam of radiation emanating from the source and travelling through the various components and sample until ultimately reaching the detector.

Sample absorbance is determined by measuring light intensity without the sample in the beam and comparing it with the intensity after passing through the sample (Figure 8.2). The way this is achieved in practice is to fill a sample cell with solution that contains

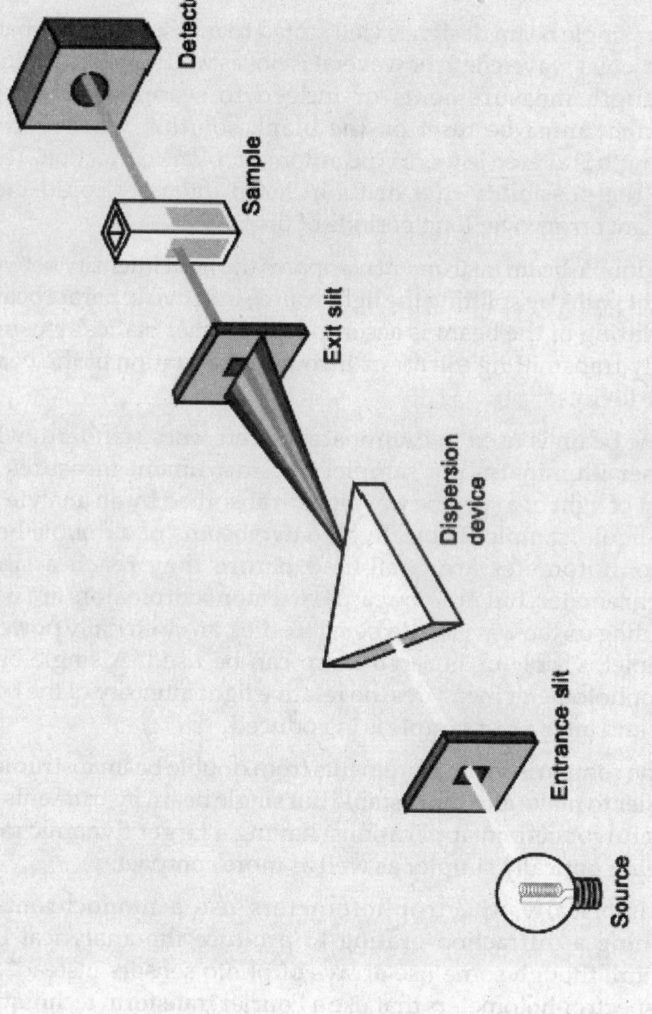

Figure 8. 2: Single Beam Spectrophotometer

all solvents / reagents minus the analytical species (the 'blank'). The cell is then placed in the sample compartment of the instrument and the readout is adjusted to zero absorbance (or 100% transmission) at the desired wavelength setting.

Solution containing the analytical species is replaced in the cell and its absorbance determined. The reading that is observed is attributed to the presence of the analyte alone.

The single beam design is well suited to measuring absorbance at a particular wavelength however it is not as well suited to multiple wavelength measurements or indeed to scanning. The zero absorbance must be reset on the blank solution whenever the wavelength is altered ie there is no automatic blank correction. There is also the possibility that drifts in lamp intensity could mean significant errors over long periods of time.

A double beam instrument compares the light intensity between two light paths by splitting the light source into two separate beams. The splitting of the beam is accomplished either statically using a partially transmitting mirror or through attenuation of the beams optical devices.

One beam is used to illuminate the reference standard, while the other illuminates the sample. The instrument measures the amount of light of a specific wavelength absorbed by an analyte in a gas or liquid sample. Typically, the two beams of a double beam spectrophotometer are combined before they reach a single monochromator, but in some cases two monochromators are used. Depending on the wavelength being studies, an electrically powered ultraviolet, visible or infrared lamp can be used. A single beam spectrophotometer measures the relative light intensity of the beam before and after a test sample is introduced.

The comparison measurements from double beam instruments are easier to make and more stable but single beam instruments still are useful for certain applications, having a larger dynamic range and being optically simpler as well as more compact.

Historically, spectrophotometers use a monochromator containing a diffraction grating to produce the analytical light spectrum, though some use arrays of photo sensors instead. Still other spectrophotometers that use a Fourier transform technique to acquire spectral information more quickly, a technique called Fourier Transform InfraRed.

A double beam spectrophotometer or single beam spectrophotometer quantitatively compares the fraction of light that passes through a reference solution and a test solution. Light from the source lamp is passed through a monochromator, diffracting the light into a "rainbow" of wavelengths. The outputs are narrow bandwidths of this diffracted spectrum. Discrete frequencies are transmitted through the test sample. Then the intensity of the transmitted light is measured with a photodiode or other brightness sensor. The transmittance value for this wavelength is then compared with the transmission through a reference sample.

Spectrophotometry routines consist of shining a light source into a monochromator. A particular output wavelength is then selected and beamed at the sample. The photodetector behind the sample responds to the light stimulus and outputs an analog electronic current which is converted to a usable format. The numbers are either plotted or (as is now most commonly the case) fed into a computer for further analysis.

The main advantages of a double beam instrument over the single beam spectrophotometer are an improvement in the stability of the light source, detectors and associated electronic devices. The disadvantages include the precision required in recombining the beams prior to reaching the monochrometer, the quality of the mirrors and other optics (if used) and their coatings and the problems which can created by dust buildup on these devices.

These disadvantages can make the double beam instruments somewhat more difficult to maintain than single beam devices, though the results they can provide make them ideal for certain spectrophotometry applications.

Types of Spectroscopy

There are many different types of materials analysis techniques under the broad heading of 'spectroscopy', utilizing a wide variety of different approaches to probing material properties, such as absorbance, reflection, emission, scattering, thermal conductivity, and refractive index.

One can divide spectroscopy into many sub-disciplines, depending on what is being measured, and how it is being measured. Some major divisions include mass spectrometry, electron spectroscopy, absorption spectroscopy, emission spectroscopy, x-ray spectroscopy, and electromagnetic spectroscopy. There are many other types of spectroscopy as well. Some of the commonly types and used more often are described as under:

Astronomical Spectroscopy

Energy from celestial objects is used to analyze their chemical composition, density, pressure, temperature, magnetic fields, velocity, and other characteristics. There are many energy types (spectroscopies) that may be used in astronomical spectroscopy.

Attenuated Total Reflectance Spectroscopy

This is the study of substances in thin films or on surfaces. The sample is penetrated by an energy beam one or more times and the reflected energy is analyzed. Attenuated total reflectance spectroscopy and the related technique called frustrated multiple internal reflection spectroscopy are used to analyze coatings and opaque liquids.

Electron Paramagnetic Spectroscopy

This is a microwave technique based on splitting electronic energy fields in a magnetic field. It is used to determine structures of samples containing unpaired electrons.

Electron Spectroscopy

There are several types of electron spectroscopy; all associated with measuring changes in electronic energy levels.

Gamma-ray Spectroscopy

Gamma radiation is the energy source in this type of spectroscopy, which includes activation analysis and Mossbauer spectroscopy.

Laser Spectroscopy

Absorption spectroscopy, fluorescence spectroscopy, Raman spectroscopy, and surface-enhanced Raman spectroscopy commonly use laser light as an energy source. Laser spectroscopies provide information about the interaction of coherent light with matter. Laser spectrocopy generally has high resolution and sensitivity.

Raman spectroscopy uses the inelastic scattering of light to analyse vibrational and rotational modes of molecules. The resulting 'fingerprints' are an aid to analysis.

Mass Spectrometry

Mass spectrometry (MS) is an analytical technique for the determination of the elemental composition of a sample or molecule. It is also used for elucidating the chemical structures of molecules, such as peptides and other chemical compounds. The MS principle consists of ionizing chemical compounds to generate charged molecules or molecule fragments and measurement of their mass-to-charge ratios.

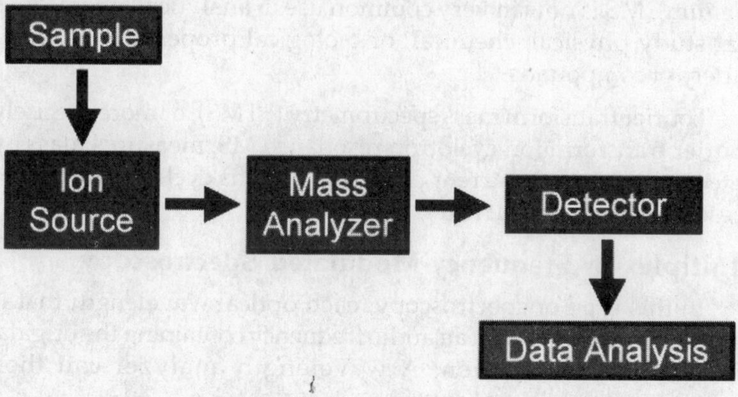

Main steps of measuring with a mass spectrometer include:

1. A sample is loaded onto the MS instrument, and undergoes vaporization.
2. The components of the sample are ionized by one of a variety of methods (*e.g.*, by impacting them with an electron beam), which results in the formation of positively charged particles (ions)
3. The positive ions are then accelerated by an electric field
4. Computation of the mass-to-charge ratio (m/z) of the particles based on the details of motion of the ions as they transit through electromagnetic fields, and

5. Detection of the ions, which in step 4 were sorted according to m/z.

MS instruments consist of three modules *i.e.* an ion source, which can convert gas phase sample molecules into ions (or, in the case of electrospray ionization, move ions that exist in solution into the gas phase), a mass analyzer, which sorts the ions by their masses by applying electromagnetic fields and a detector, which measures the value of an indicator quantity and thus provides data for calculating the abundances of each ion present. The technique has both qualitative and quantitative uses. These include identifying unknown compounds, determining the isotopic composition of elements in a molecule, and determining the structure of a compound by observing its fragmentation. Other uses include quantifying the amount of a compound in a sample or studying the fundamentals of gas phase ion chemistry (the chemistry of ions and neutrals in a vacuum). MS is now in very common use in analytical laboratories that study physical, chemical, or biological properties of a great variety of compounds.

Fourier transform mass spectrometry (FTMS), or more precisely Fourier transform ion cyclotron resonance MS, measures mass by detecting the image current produced by ions cyclotroning in the presence of a magnetic field.

Multiplex or Frequency-Modulated Spectroscopy

In this type of spectroscopy, each optical wavelength that is recorded is encoded with an audio frequency containing the original wavelength information. A wavelength analyzer can then reconstruct the original spectrum.

Fluorescence Spectroscopy

Fluorescence spectroscopy uses higher energy photons to excite a sample, which will then emit lower energy photons. This technique has become popular for its biochemical and medical applications, and can be used for confocal microscopy, fluorescence resonance energy transfer, and fluorescence lifetime imaging.

X-ray

This technique involves excitation of inner electrons of atoms, which may be seen as x-ray absorption. An x-ray fluorescence emission spectrum may be produced when an electron falls from a higher energy state into the vacancy created by the absorbed energy.

When X-rays of sufficient frequency (energy) interact with a substance, inner shell electrons in the atom are excited to outer empty orbitals, or they may be removed completely, ionizing the atom. The inner shell "hole" will then be filled by electrons from outer orbitals. The energy available in this de-excitation process is emitted as radiation (fluorescence) or will remove other less-bound electrons from the atom (Auger effect). The absorption or emission frequencies (energies) are characteristic of the specific atom. In addition, for a specific atom small frequency (energy) variations occur which are characteristic of the chemical bonding. With a suitable apparatus, these characteristic X-ray frequencies or Auger electron energies can be measured. X-ray absorption and emission spectroscopy is used in chemistry and material sciences to determine elemental composition and chemical bonding.

Flame

Liquid solution samples are aspirated into a burner or nebulizer/burner combination, desolvated, atomized, and sometimes excited to a higher energy electronic state. The use of a flame during analysis requires fuel and oxidant, typically in the form of gases. Common fuel gases used are acetylene (ethyne) or hydrogen. Common oxidant gases used are oxygen, air, or nitrous oxide. These methods are often capable of analyzing metallic element analytes in the part per million, billion, or possibly lower concentration ranges. Light detectors are needed to detect light with the analysis information coming from the flame.

(*i*) Atomic Emission Spectroscopy

This method uses flame excitation; atoms are excited from the heat of the flame to emit light. This method commonly uses a total consumption burner with a round burning outlet. A higher temperature flame than atomic absorption spectroscopy (AA) is typically used to produce excitation of analyte atoms. Since analyte atoms are excited by the heat of the flame, no special elemental lamps to shine into the flame are needed. A high resolution polychromator can be used to produce an emission intensity vs. wavelength spectrum over a range of wavelengths showing multiple element excitation lines, meaning multiple elements can be detected in one run. Alternatively, a monochromator can be set at one wavelength to concentrate on analysis of a single element at a certain emission line. Plasma emission spectroscopy is a more modern version of this method.

(*ii*) Atomic Absorption Spectroscopy (often called AA)

Energy absorbed by the sample is used to assess its characteristics. Sometimes absorbed energy causes light to be released from the sample, which may be measured by a technique such as fluorescence spectroscopy.

This method commonly uses a pre-burner nebulizer (or nebulizing chamber) to create a sample mist and a slot-shaped burner which gives a longer pathlength flame. The temperature of the flame is low enough that the flame itself does not excite sample atoms from their ground state. The nebulizer and flame are used to desolvate and atomize the sample, but the excitation of the analyte atoms is done by the use of lamps shining through the flame at various wavelengths for each type of analyte. In AA, the amount of light absorbed after going through the flame determines the amount of analyte in the sample. A graphite furnace for heating the sample to desolvate and atomize is commonly used for greater sensitivity. The graphite furnace method can also analyze some solid or slurry samples. Because of its good sensitivity and selectivity, it is still a commonly used method of analysis for certain trace elements in aqueous (and other liquid) samples.

(*iii*) Atomic Fluorescence Spectroscopy

This method commonly uses a burner with a round burning outlet. The flame is used to solvate and atomize the sample, but a lamp shines light at a specific wavelength into the flame to excite the analyte atoms in the flame. The atoms of certain elements can then fluoresce emitting light in a different direction. The intensity of this fluorescing light is used for quantifying the amount of analyte element in the sample. A graphite furnace can also be used for atomic fluorescence spectroscopy. This method is not as commonly used as atomic absorption or plasma emission spectroscopy.

Plasma Emission Spectroscopy

In some ways similar to flame atomic emission spectroscopy, it has largely replaced it.

- Direct-current plasma (DCP): A direct-current plasma (DCP) is created by an electrical discharge between two electrodes. A plasma support gas is necessary, and Ar is common. Samples can be deposited on one of the electrodes, or if conducting can make up one electrode.
- Glow discharge-optical emission spectrometry (GD-OES)
- Inductively coupled plasma-atomic emission spectrometry (ICP-AES)
- Laser Induced Breakdown Spectroscopy (LIBS), LIBS also called Laser-induced plasma spectrometry (LIPS)
- Microwave-induced plasma (MIP)

Spark or Arc (Emission) Spectroscopy

Emission spectroscopy is a spectroscopic technique which examines the wavelengths of photons emitted by atoms or molecules during their transition from an excited state to a lower energy state. Each element emits a characteristic set of discrete wavelengths according to its electronic structure, by observing these wavelengths the elemental composition of the sample can be determined. Emission spectroscopy developed in the late 19th century and efforts in theoretical explanation of atomic emission spectra eventually led to quantum mechanics.

There are many ways in which atoms can be brought to an excited state. Interaction with electromagnetic radiation is used in fluorescence spectroscopy, protons or other heavier particles in Particle-Induced X-ray Emission and electrons or X-ray photons in Energy-dispersive X-ray spectroscopy or X-ray fluorescence. The simplest method is to heat the sample to a high temperature, after which the excitations are produced by collisions between the sample atoms. This method is used in flame emission spectroscopy, and it was also the method used by Anders Jonas Ångström when he discovered the phenomenon of discrete emission lines in 1850s.

It is used for the analysis of metallic elements in solid samples. For non-conductive materials, a sample is ground with graphite powder to make it conductive. In traditional arc spectroscopy methods, a sample of the solid was commonly ground up and destroyed during analysis. An electric arc or spark is passed through the sample, heating the sample to a high temperature to excite the atoms in it. The excited analyte atoms glow emitting light at various wavelengths which could be detected by common spectroscopic methods. Since the conditions producing the arc emission typically are not controlled quantitatively, the analysis for the elements is qualitative. Nowadays, the spark sources with controlled discharges under an argon atmosphere allow that this method can be considered eminently quantitative, and its use is widely expanded worldwide through production control laboratories of foundries and steel mills.

Absorption Spectroscopy

Absorption spectroscopy is a technique in which the power of a beam of light measured before and after interaction with a sample is compared. Specific absorption techniques tend to be referred to by the wavelength of radiation measured such as ultraviolet, infrared or microwave absorption spectroscopy. Absorption occurs when the energy of the photons matches the energy difference between two states of the material.

The sample absorbs energy, *i.e.*, photons, from the radiating field. The intensity of the absorption varies as a function of frequency, and this variation is the absorption spectrum. Absorption spectroscopy is performed across the electromagnetic spectrum.

There are a wide range of experimental approaches to measuring absorption spectra. The most common arrangement is to direct a generated beam of radiation at a sample and detect the intensity of the radiation that passes through it. The transmitted energy can be used to calculate the absorption. The source, sample arrangement and detection technique vary significantly depending on the frequency range and the purpose of the experiment.

The most straight-forward approach to absorption spectroscopy is to generate radiation with a source, measure a reference spectrum of that radiation with a detector and then re-measure the sample spectrum after placing the material of interest in between the source and detector. The two measured spectra can then be combined to determine the material's absorption spectrum. The sample spectrum alone is not sufficient to determine the absorption spectrum because it will be affected by the experimental conditions—the spectrum of the source, the absorption spectra of other materials in between the source and detector and the wavelength dependent characteristics of the detector. The reference spectrum will be affected in the same way, though, by these experimental conditions and therefore the combination yields the absorption spectrum of the material alone.

A wide variety of radiation sources are employed in order to cover the electromagnetic spectrum. For spectroscopy, it is generally desirable for a source to cover a broad swath of wavelengths in order to measure a broad region of the absorption spectrum. Some sources inherently emit a broad spectrum. Examples of these include globars or other black body sources in the infrared, mercury lamps in the visible and ultraviolet and x-ray tubes. One recently developed, novel source of broad spectrum radiation is synchotron radiation which covers all of these spectral regions. Other radiation sources generate a narrow spectrum but the emission wavelength can be tuned to cover a spectral range. Examples of these include klystrons in the microwave region and lasers across the infrared, visible and ultraviolet region (though not all lasers have tunable wavelengths).

The detector employed to measure the radiation power will also depend on the wavelength range of interest. Most detectors are sensitive to a fairly broad spectral range and the sensor selected will often depend more on the sensitivity and noise requirements of a given measurement. Examples of detectors common in spectroscopy include heterodyne receivers in the microwave, bolometers in the millimeter-wave and infrared, mercury cadmium telluride and other cooled semiconductor detectors in the infrared, and photodiodes and photomultiplier tubes in the visible and ultraviolet.

If both the source and the detector cover a broad spectral region, then it is also necessary to introduce a means of resolving the wavelength of the radiation in order to determine the spectrum. Often a spectrograph is used to spatially separate the wavelengths of radiation so that the power at each wavelength can be measured independently. It is also common to employ interferometry to determine the wavelength. Fourier transform infrared spectroscopy is a widely used implementation of this technique.

Two other issues that must be considered in setting up an absorption spectroscopy experiment include the optics used to direct the radiation and the means of holding or containing the sample material. In both cases, it is important to select materials that have relatively little absorption of their own in the wavelength range of interest. The absorption of other materials could interfere with or mask the absorption from the sample. For instance, in several wavelength ranges it is necessary to measure the sample under vacuum or in a rare gas environment because gases in the atmosphere have interfering absorption features.

Absorption spectroscopy is employed as an analytical chemistry tool to determine the presence of a particular substance in a sample and, in many cases, to quantify the amount of the substance present. Infrared and ultraviolet-visible spectroscopy are particularly common in analytical applications. Absorption spectroscopy is also employed in studies of molecular and atomic physics, astronomical spectroscopy and remote sensing.

Visible

Many atoms emit or absorb visible light. In order to obtain a fine line spectrum, the atoms must be in a gas phase. This means that the substance has to be vaporised. The spectrum is studied in absorption or emission. Visible absorption spectroscopy is often combined with UV absorption spectroscopy in UV/Vis spectroscopy. Although this form may be uncommon as the human eye is a similar indicator, it still proves useful when distinguishing colours.

Ultraviolet

All atoms absorb in the Ultraviolet (UV) region because these photons are energetic enough to excite outer electrons. If the frequency is high enough, photoionization takes place. UV spectroscopy is also used in quantifying protein and DNA concentration as well as the ratio of protein to DNA concentration in a solution. Several amino acids usually found in protein, such as tryptophan, absorb light in the 280 nm range and DNA absorbs light in the 260 nm range. For this reason, the ratio of 260/280 nm absorbance is a good general indicator of the relative purity of a solution in terms of these two macromolecules. Reasonable estimates of protein or DNA concentration can also be made this way using Beer's law.

Infrared Spectroscopy (IR Spectroscopy)

Infrared spectroscopy offers the possibility to measure different types of inter atomic bond vibrations at different frequencies. It is the subset of spectroscopy that deals with the infrared region of the electromagnetic spectrum. It covers a range of techniques, the most common being a form of absorption spectroscopy. As with all

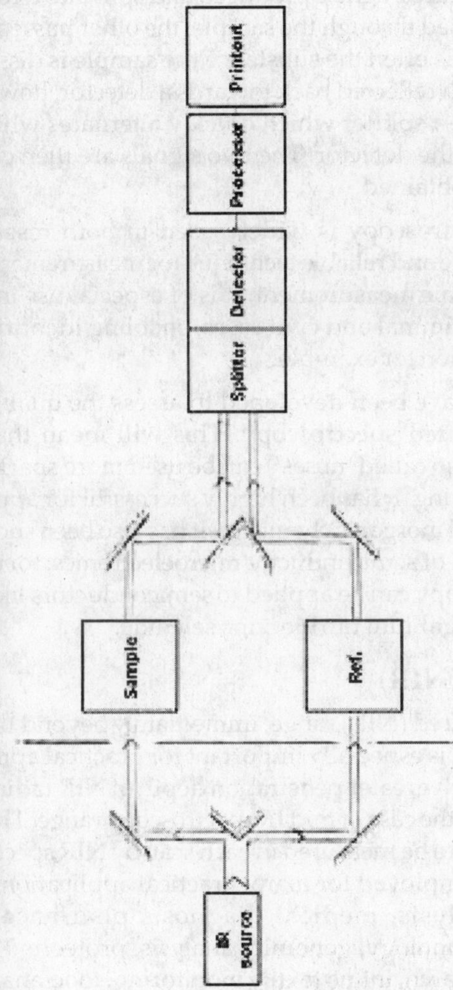

Figure 8.3: Typical Apparatus

spectroscopic techniques, it can be used to identify compounds and investigate sample composition. A common laboratory instrument that uses this technique is an infrared spectrophotometer.

A beam of infrared light is produced and split into two separate beams. One is passed through the sample, the other passed through a reference which is often the substance the sample is dissolved in. The beams are both reflected back towards a detector, however first they pass through a splitter which quickly alternates which of the two beams enters the detector. The two signals are then compared and a printout is obtained.

Infrared spectroscopy is widely used in both research and industry as a simple and reliable technique for measurement, quality control and dynamic measurement. It is of especial use in forensic analysis in both criminal and civil cases, enabling identification of polymer degradation for example.

Techniques have been developed to assess the quality of tea-leaves using infrared spectroscopy. This will mean that highly trained experts (also called 'noses') can be used more sparingly, at a significant cost saving. It has been highly successful for applications in both organic and inorganic chemistry. It has also been successfully utilized in the field of semiconductor microelectronics: for example, infrared spectroscopy can be applied to semiconductors like silicon, gallium arsenide, gallium nitride, zinc selenide.

Near Infrared (NIR)

The near infrared (NIR) range, immediately beyond the visible wavelength range, is especially important for practical applications because of the much greater penetration depth of NIR radiation into the sample than in the case of mid IR spectroscopy range. This allows also large samples to be measured in each scan by NIR spectroscopy, and is currently employed for many practical applications such as rapid grain analysis, medical diagnosis pharmaceuticals/ medicines, biotechnology, genomics analysis, proteomic analysis, interactomics research, inline textile monitoring, food analysis and chemical imaging/hyperspectral imaging of intact organisms, plastics, textiles, insect detection, forensic lab application, crime detection, various military applications, and so on.

Coherent Anti-Stokes Raman Spectroscopy (CARS)

CARS is a recent technique that has high sensitivity and powerful applications for *in vivo* spectroscopy and imaging.

Nuclear Magnetic Resonance Spectroscopy

Nuclear magnetic resonance spectroscopy, most commonly known as NMR spectroscopy, is the name given to a technique which exploits the magnetic properties of certain nuclei to determine different electronic local environments of hydrogen, carbon, or other atoms in an organic compound or other compound. This is used to help determine the structure of the compound.

It is a powerful and versatile spectroscopic technique for investigating molecular structure and dynamics of a sample subjected to a static magnetic field, from the analysis of the interaction between the magnetic moments of sample nuclei and an applied electromagnetic wave. It involves reorientations of nuclear spins with respect to an applied static magnetic field.

Of all the spectroscopic methods, it is the only one for which a complete analysis and interpretation of the entire spectrum is normally expected. Although larger amounts of sample are needed than for mass spectroscopy, NMR is non-destructive, and with modern instruments good data may be obtained from samples weighing less than a milligram.

Many types of information can be obtained from an NMR spectrum. Much like using infrared spectroscopy (IR) to identify functional groups, analysis of a NMR spectrum provides information on the number and type of chemical entities in a molecule. However, NMR provides much more information than IR. The impact of NMR spectroscopy on the natural sciences has been substantial. It can, among other things, be used to study mixtures of analytes, to understand dynamic effects such as change in temperature and reaction mechanisms, and is an invaluable tool in understanding protein and nucleic acid structure and function. It can be applied to a wide variety of samples, both in the solution and the solid state.

Much of the recent innovation within NMR spectroscopy has been within the field of protein NMR, which has become a very important technique in structural biology. One common goal of these investigations is to obtain high resolution 3-dimensional structures of the protein, similar to what can be achieved by X-ray crystallography. In contrast to X-ray crystallography, NMR is primarily limited to relatively small proteins, usually smaller than 35 kDa, though technical advances allow ever larger structures to be solved. NMR spectroscopy is often the only way to obtain high resolution information on partially or wholly intrinsically unstructured proteins.

Fourier Transform Spectroscopy

Fourier transform spectroscopy is a measurement technique whereby spectra are collected based on measurements of the coherence of a radiative source, using time-domain or space-domain measurements of the electromagnetic radiation or other type of radiation. It can be applied to a variety of types of spectroscopy including optical spectroscopy, infrared spectroscopy (FT IR, FT-NIRS), Fourier transform (FT) nuclear magnetic resonance, mass spectrometry and electron spin resonance spectroscopy. There are several methods for measuring the temporal coherence of the light, including the continuous wave Michelson or Fourier transform spectrometer and the pulsed Fourier transform spectrograph (which is more sensitive and has a much shorter sampling time than conventional spectroscopic techniques, but is only applicable in a laboratory).

Applications

(*i*) Analytical Chemistry

Absorption spectroscopy is useful in chemical analysis because of its specificity and its quantitative nature. The specificity of absorption spectra allows compounds to be distinguished from one another in a mixture. For example, absorption spectroscopy is used to identify the presence of pollutants in the air, distinguishing the pollutant from the nitrogen, oxygen, water and the other expected constituents. The specificity also allows unknown samples to be identified by comparing a measured spectrum with a library of reference spectra. In many cases, it is possible to determine qualitative information about a sample even if it is not in a library. Infrared spectra, for instance, have characteristics absorption bands that indicate if carbon-hydrogen or carbon-oxygen bonds are present.

An absorption spectrum can be quantitatively related to the amount of material present using the Beer-Lambert law. Determining the absolute concentration of a compound requires knowledge of the compound's absorption coefficient. The absorption coefficient for some compounds is available from reference sources, and it can also be determined by measuring the spectrum of a calibration standard with a known concentration of the target.

(*ii*) Remote Sensing

One of the unique advantages of spectroscopy as an analytical technique is that measurements can be made without bringing the instrument and sample into contact. Radiation that travels between a sample and an instrument will contain the spectral information, so the measurement can be made remotely. Remote spectral sensing is valuable in many situations. For example, measurements can be made in toxic or hazardous environments without placing an operator or instrument at risk. Also, sample material does not have to be brought into contact with the instrument thereby preventing possible cross contamination.

(*iii*) Astronomy

Astronomical spectroscopy is a particularly significant type of remote spectral sensing. In this case, the objects and samples of interest are so distant from earth that electromagnetic radiation is the only means available to measure them. Astronomical spectra contain both absorption and emission spectral information. Absorption spectroscopy has been particularly important for understanding interstellar clouds and determining that some of them contain molecules. Absorption spectroscopy is also employed in the study of extrasolar planets.

(*iv*) Atomic and Molecular Physics

Theoretical models, principally quantum mechanical models, allow for the absorption spectra of atoms and molecules to be related to other physical properties such as electronic structure, atomic or molecular mass, and molecular geometry. Therefore, measurements of the absorption spectrum are used to determine these other properties. Microwave spectroscopy, for example, allows for the determination of bond lengths and angles with high precision.

In addition, spectral measurements can be used to determine the accuracy of theoretical predictions. For example, the Lamb shift measured in the hydrogen atomic absorption spectrum was not expected to exist at the time it was measured. Its discovery spurred and guided the development of quantum electrodynamics, and measurements of the Lamb shift are now used to determine the fine-structure constant.

Chapter 9

Fluorescence Spectroscopy

Introduction

Fluorescence is one of the oldest analytical methods used, and it has just recently become quite popular as a tool in biological sciences related to food technology.

There are many advantages in the use of analytical fluorescence spectroscopy, as we will see later on in this chapter. However, many researchers shy away from this technique because of lack of knowledge of the fundamental principles of fluorescence.

Fluorescence refers to the light (luminescence) emitted by molecules during the period in which they are excited by photons. This emitted light is from the singlet state and ceases rather abruptly when the exciting energy source is removed. The afterglow then is less than 10^{-6}s, and it is independent of temperature. This is the contrary of phosphorescence which is light from the triplet state defined as the afterglow longer than 10^{-6}s and is temperature-dependent.

The fluorescence normally observed in solutions is called Stokes fluorescence. This is the re-emission of less energetic photons, which have a longer wavelength (lower frequency) than the absorbed photons.

If thermal energy is added to an excited state or a compound has many highly populated vibrational energy levels, emission at shorter wavelengths than those of absorption occurs. This is anti-Stokes fluorescence, often observed in dilute gases at high temperatures. A common example is the green emission from copper-activated cadmium sulphide excited by red light.

Resonance fluorescence is the re-emission of photons possessing the same energy as the absorbed photons. This type of fluorescence is never observed in solution because of solvent interactions, but it does occur in gases and crystals. If an electron is excited by an absorbed photon of energy to a higher vibrational level with no electronic transition, energy is entirely conserved and a photon of the same energy is re-emitted within 10^{-15} s as the electron returns to its original state. The emitted light has the same wavelength as the exciting light since the absorbed and emitted photons are of the same energy. The emitted light is referred to as Rayleigh scattering and occurs at all wavelengths. Its intensity, however, varies as the fourth power of the wavelength, so its effect can be minimized by working at longer wavelengths. It is a problem when the intensity of fluorescence is low in comparison with the exciting radiation and when the absorption and fluorescence spectra of a substance are close together.

Another form of scattering emission related to Rayleigh scattering is the Raman effect. Raman scatter appears in fluorescence spectra at higher and lower wavelengths (the former being more common) than the Rayleigh-scatter peak, and these Raman bands are satellites of the Rayleigh-scatter peak with a constant frequency difference from the exciting radiation. These bands are due to vibrational energy being added to, or subtracted from, this excitation photon. The Raman bands are much weaker than the Rayleigh-scatter peak but become significant when high-intensity sources are used.

Every molecule possesses a characteristic property that is described by a number called the quantum yield, or quantum

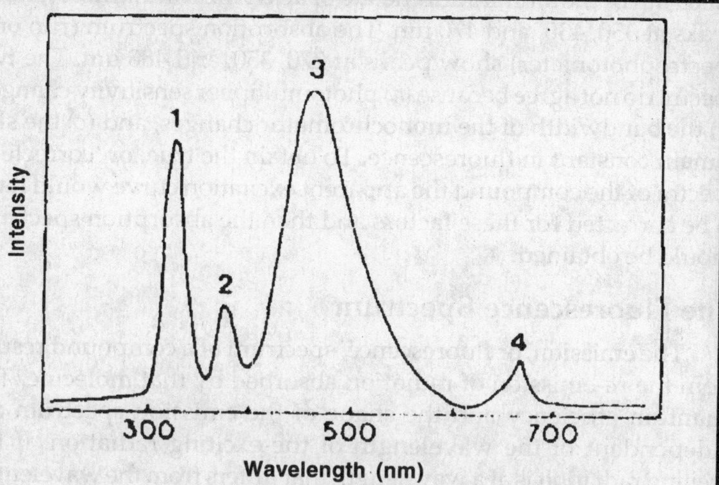

Figure 9.1: Fluorescence Spectra of Quinine Sulphate in 0.05 M-sulphuric Acid (λ_{ex} = 320 nm)

efficiency, ϕ. This is the ratio of the total energy emitted per quantum of energy absorbed.

$$\phi = \frac{\text{number of quanta emitted}}{\text{number of quanta absorbed}} = \text{quantum yield}$$

The higher the value of ϕ, the greater the fluorescence of a compound. A non-fluorescent molecule is one whose quantum efficiency is zero or so close to zero that the fluorescence is not measurable. All energy absorbed by such a molecule is rapidly lost by collisional deactivation.

Any fluorescent molecule has two characteristic spectra: the excitation spectrum (the relative efficiency of different wavelengths of exciting radiation to cause fluorescence) and the emission spectrum (the relative intensity of radiation emitted at various wavelengths).

The shape of the excitation spectrum should be identical with that of the absorption spectrum of the molecule and independent of the wavelength at which fluorescence is measured. However, this is seldom the case. The differences occur because of instrumental artifacts as we will see in the following example. The excitation spectrum of the aluminium chelate of acid Alizarin Garnet R shows peaks at 350, 430, and 470 nm. The absorption spectrum (run on a spectrophotometer) show peaks at 270, 350, and 480 nm. The two spectra do not agree because (*a*) photomultiplier sensitivity changes, (*b*) the bandwidth of the monochromator changes, and (*c*) the slits remain constant in fluorescence. To obtain the true, or 'corrected', spectra of the compound the apparent excitation curve would have to be corrected for these factors and then the absorption spectrum should be obtained.

The Fluorescence Spectrum

The emission, or fluorescence, spectrum of a compound results from the re-emission of radiation absorbed by that molecule. The quantum efficiency and the shape of the emission spectrum are independent of the wavelength of the exciting radiation. If the exciting radiation is at a wavelength that differs from the wavelength of the absorption peak, less radiant energy will be absorbed and hence less will be emitted. The emission spectrum of the aluminium-acid Alizarin Garnet R complex indicates a fluorescence peak at 580 nm.

Each absorption band at the first electronic state will have a corresponding emission, or fluorescence band. These two bands, or spectra, will be approximately mirror images of each other. In fact this mirror-image principle is useful in distinguishing whether an absorption band is another vibrational band in the first excited state or a higher electronic level. Fluorescence peaks other than the mirror image of the absorption spectrum indicate scatter or the presence of impurities. Rayleigh and Tyndall scatter can be observed in the emission spectrum at the same wavelength as the excitation wavelength and also at twice this value (second-order grating effect) in a grating spectrofluorometer. In very dilute solutions one may also observe Raman scatter. The wider the fluorescence band, the more complex and less symmetrical the compound.

Following shows the absorption and emission spectra of anthracene and quinine. Four major absorption peaks are observed in the anthracene spectrum; all correspond to transitions from S_0 to S_1^* (* = excited state) but denote transitions to different vibrational levels. Four major emission peaks, each a mirror image of the peaks in the absorption spectrum, are likewise observed. For quinine two

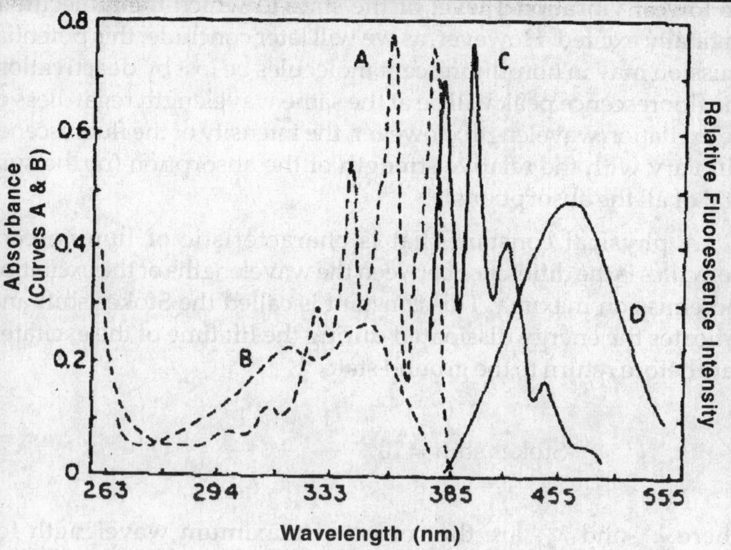

Figure 9.2: Absorption and Fluorescence Spectra of Anthracene (in ethanol) and Quinine (in 0.5 M-sulhuric acid)

excitation peaks are observed, one at 250 nm corresponding to an $S_0 \rightarrow S_2$ transition and a second at 350 nm corresponding to an $S_0 \rightarrow S_1$ transition. Only one emission peak, corresponding to the $S_1 \rightarrow S_0$ transition, is observed.

The fact that some compounds possess several excitation and/or emission peaks is of analytical usefulness. If two compounds have overlapping excitation bands, as in the case of anthracene and quinine, both could be excited together and then differentiated by their emission spectra. Quinine could be measured at a λ_{em} of 450 nm, whereas anthracene could be monitored at a λ_{em} of 400 nm. Similarly, if two compounds emit radiation at the same wavelength, they can still be measured together in the same solution if they have different, non-overlapping, excitation peaks. This, in fact, is one of the major advantages that fluorescence spectroscopy has over absorption spectroscopy.

Any portion of the spectrum where absorption occurs can produce fluorescence since emission almost always takes place from the lowest vibrational level or the state to which the molecule is originally excited. However, as we will later conclude, this potential emission may in non-fluorescent molecules be lost by deactivation. The fluorescence peak will be at the same wavelength regardless of the excitation wavelength; however, the intensity of the fluorescence will vary with the relative strength of the absorption (or the sum total of all the absorptions).

A physical constant that is characteristic of luminescent molecules is the difference between the wavelengths of the excitation and emission maxima. This constant is called the Stokes shift and indicates the energy dissipated during the lifetime of the excitated state before return to the ground state:

$$\text{Stokes shift} = 10^7 \quad \frac{1}{\lambda_{ex}} - \frac{1}{\lambda_{em}}$$

where λ_{ex} and λ_{em} are the corrected maximum wavelength for excitation and emission, and are expressed in nanometres. The Stokes shift is of interest to analytical chemists since the emission wavelength can be greatly shifted by varying the state of the molecule being excited. The fluorescence maximum shift of 5-hydroxyindole from 330 nm at pH 7 to 550 nm in strong acid occurs with no change in the excitation peak (295 nm) and is due to excited-state protonation.

The basic equation defining the relationship of fluorescence to concentration is

$$F = \phi I_0 (1 - e)^{-ebc}$$

where ϕ is the quantum efficiency, I_0 is the incident radiant power, ε is the molar absorptivity, *b* is the path length of the cell, and *c* is the molar concentration.

The basic fluorescence intensity–concentration equation indicates that there are three major factors other than concentration that affect the fluorescence intensity:

- ☆ The quantum efficiency ϕ. The greater the value of ϕ, the greater will be the fluorescence, as already discussed.
- ☆ The intensity of incident radiation, I_0. Theoretically, the more intense source will yield the greater fluorescence. In actual practice a very intense source can cause

photodecomposition of the sample. Hence one compromises on a source of moderate intensity (*i.e.*, a mercury or xenon lamp is used).

☆ The molar absorptivity of the compound, e. In order to emit radiation a molecule must first absorb radiation. Hence, the higher the molar absorptivity, the better will be the fluorescence intensity of the compound. It is for this reason that saturated non-aromatic compounds are non-fluorescent.

A plot of fluorescence versus concentration should be linear at low concentrations and reach a maximum at higher concentrations. At high concentrations the observed fluorescence signal decreases in relation to the concentration of the fluorophore; this is called quenching. The decrease is in part caused by an attenuation of the excitation beam in the areas of the solution in front of the detection system and by the absorption of thc emitted fluorescence within the solution. This is defined as the inner-cell (inner- filter) effect. The linearity of fluorescence as a function of concentration holds over a very wide range of concentration. Measurements down to 10^{-5} µg/ml are feasible, and linearity extends up to 100 µg/ml or higher.

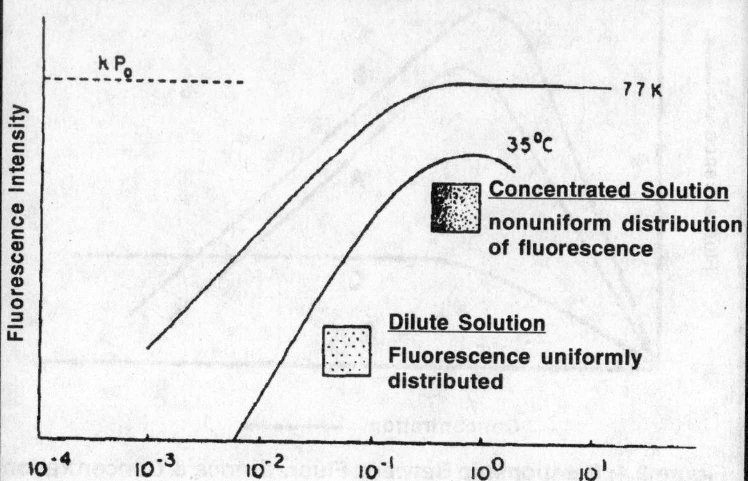

Figure 9.3: Dependence of Fluorescence on the Concentration of a Fluorophore (naphthalene) and Temperature

Generally a linear response will be obtained until the concentration of the fluorescent species is large enough to absorb significant amounts of exciting light. For a linear response to be obtained the solutions must absorb less than 5 per cent of the exciting radiation. At higher concentrations light scattering as well as the inner-cell effect become important. In the concentration regions where fluorescence is proportional to concentration, fluorescence is measured in the absence of significant radiation. In this region the energy available for excitation is uniformly distributed through the solution. Thus, at low concentrations, when the absorbance is less than about 0.05, there is a linear relationship between fluorescence and concentration. At intermediate concentrations the light is not evenly distributed along the light path. The portion of the solution nearest the light source absorbs so much radiation that less and less is available for the rest of the solution.

The Reflection Spectrofluorometry

In order for fluorescence to be observed, absorption must occur. As we have already seen, the fluorescence intensity is proportional

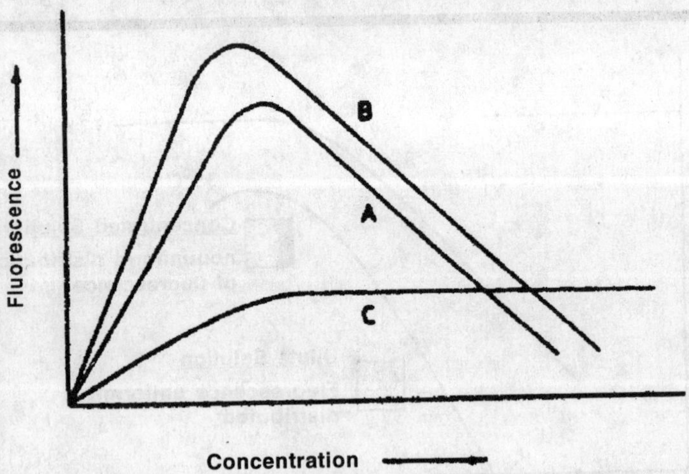

Figure 9.4: Relationship Between Fluorescence & Concentration

A: End-on detector; Curve B: Right-angle detector (transmission spectrofluorometry); Curve C: Surface detector (reflectance spectrofluorometry).

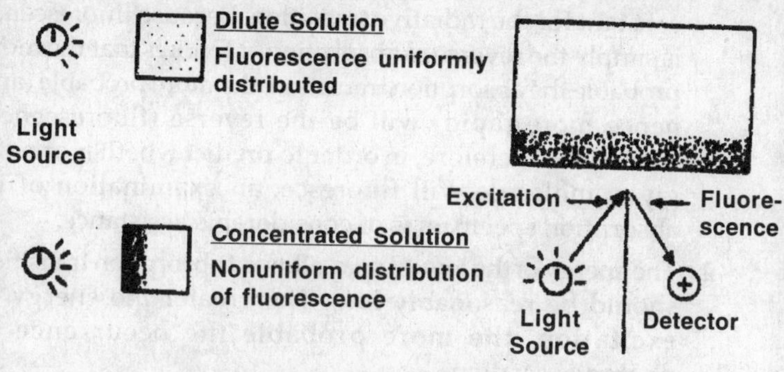

Figure 9.5: Effect of Concentration on Fluorescence

to the molar absorptivity: the more highly absorbing the substance, the greater its fluorescence. However, as previously described, quenching and inner-cell effects tend to occur at high concentrations. As a result, considerable excitation occurs at the front of the solution, but less and less occurs throughout the rest of the cell.

Fluorescence phenomena are not sensitive to the finer details of molecular structure; fluorescence is not generally useful as a 'fingerprinting' technique. Of the huge number of known organic and inorganic compounds, only a small fraction exhibits intense fluorescence. In order to understand how molecular structure affects fluorescence, one must realize that fluorescence always competes with a variety of other processes. When a molecule is promoted to an electronically excited state, it may divest itself of its excess energy in a number of different ways, the principal decay processes being (*a*) fluorescence, (*b*) non-radiative decay (internal conversion of intersystem crossing), and (*c*) photochemical reaction. Which of these three processes dominates depends entirely on their relative rates. Thus, for fluorescence to dominate, one desires that the rate constant for radiative transitions be large relative to those for non-radiative decay or photodecomposition.

In general, therefore, strongly fluorescent molecules possess the following characteristics:

1. The spin-allowed electronic absorption transition of lowest energy is very intense, *i.e.*, has a large ε_{max}. The

intensity of absorption is directly proportional to the rate constant for the radiative transition. Because fluorescence is simply the reverse of absorption, it follows that the more probable the absorption transition, the more probable (and hence more rapid) will be the reverse (fluorescence) transition. Therefore, in order to predict whether or not a given molecule will fluoresce, an examination of its absorption spectrum is of considerable assistance.

2. The energy of the lowest spin-allowed absorption transition should be reasonably low. The greater the energy of excitation, the more probable the occurrence of photodissociation.
3. The electron that is promoted to a higher level in the absorption transition should be located in an orbital not strongly involved in bonding. Otherwise, bond dissociation may accompany excitation, and fluorescence is unlikely to be observed.
4. The molecule should not contain structural features or functional groups that enhance the rates of radiationless transitions. Although the theory of non-radiative processes is still in the process of development, we observe that certain structural features greatly increase the rates of radiationless processes and therefore, adversely affect fluorescence intensities.

The Aromatic Hydrocarbons

On the basis of these few simple considerations one can easily understand why aromatic hydrocarbons are usually very intensely fluorescent. In these systems π-electrons, which are less strongly held than σ-electrons, can be promoted to π* anti bonding orbitals by absorption of electromagnetic radiation of fairly low energy without extensive disruption of bonding. Furthermore, $\pi \rightarrow \pi^*$ transitions in most aromatic hydrocarbons are strongly allowed (ε_{max} 10^4). The combination of these two factors signifies that aromatic compounds possessing low-lying (π, π*) singlet states usually fluoresce strongly.

In saturated hydrocarbons there are no π-bonding or non-bonding electrons; thus all electronic transitions involve σ-bonding electrons. Transitions involving σ-electrons can be expected to occur at very high energies and, in addition, significantly to disrupt bonding in the molecule. In fact saturated hydrocarbons do fluoresce, though the fluorescence is very weak (fluorescence quantum efficiencies, are in the order of 10^{-3}) and occurs in the 140–170 nm region (vacuum ultraviolet). In aliphatic carbonyl compounds $n \rightarrow \pi^*$ transitions can occur, and these compounds consequently can exhibit fluorescence in the 'normal' ultraviolet or even the visible region, though the quantum efficiencies are likewise very small. Some non-aromatic, but highly conjugated, compounds, such as β-carotene, vitamin A, and vitamin A aldehyde are fluorescent, due to the occurrence of $\pi \rightarrow \pi^*$ transitions.

In general, however, the vast majority of intensely fluorescing organic compounds are aromatic, and it is with such systems that we shall be mainly concerned.

Most unsubstituted aromatic compounds exhibit an intense fluorescence in the ultraviolet or visible region. As the degree of conjugation increases, the intensity of fluorescence often increases and a bathochromic shift is observed.

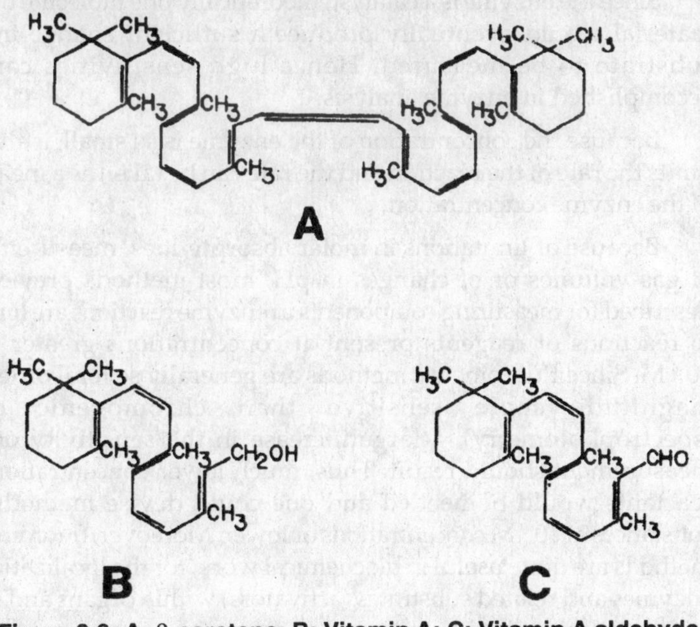

Figure 9.6: A: β-carotene; B: Vitamin A; C: Vitamin A aldehyde

Table 9.1: Luminescence of Condensed Linear Aromatics in EPA[a] Glass at 77 K

Compound	ϕF	λ_{ex}*(nm)*	λ_{em}*(nm)*
Benzene[b]	0.11	205	278
Naphthalene[b]	0.29	286	321
Anthracene[c]	0.46	365	400
Tetracene[d]	0.60	390	480
Pentacene[e]	0.52	580	640

[a] A mixture of diethyl ether, isopentane, and ethanol, 5:5:2 (by vol.).

[b] Fluoresces in the ultraviolet.

[c] Fluoresces in the blue.

[d] Fluoresces in the green.

[e] Fluoresces in the red.

The Fluorometric Assay Methods for Enzymes

Since the enzyme is a catalyst, theoretically one molecule of this material would eventually produce a sufficient change in the substrate to be measured. Hence high sensitivities can be accomplished in enzyme analysis.

Because the concentration of the enzyme is so small, it always limits thc rate of the reaction and the rate can be taken as a measure of the enzyme concentration.

Because of limitations in molar absorptivities, measurements of gas volumes or of changes in pH, most methods previously described for measuring components in enzyme reactions are limited to reactions of reagents present at concentrations greater than 10^{-6} M. Since fluorometric methods are generally several orders of magnitude more sensitive than chromogenic ones (spectrophotometry), a large increase in the sensitivity of the measurement should result. Thus, much lower concentrations of reactants would be needed and one could devise methods for substances at 10^{-9} M concentrations or lower. Moreover, fluorometric methods are quite useful in biochemical work, for the localization of enzymes and related substrates (activators) within organs and even within individual cells.

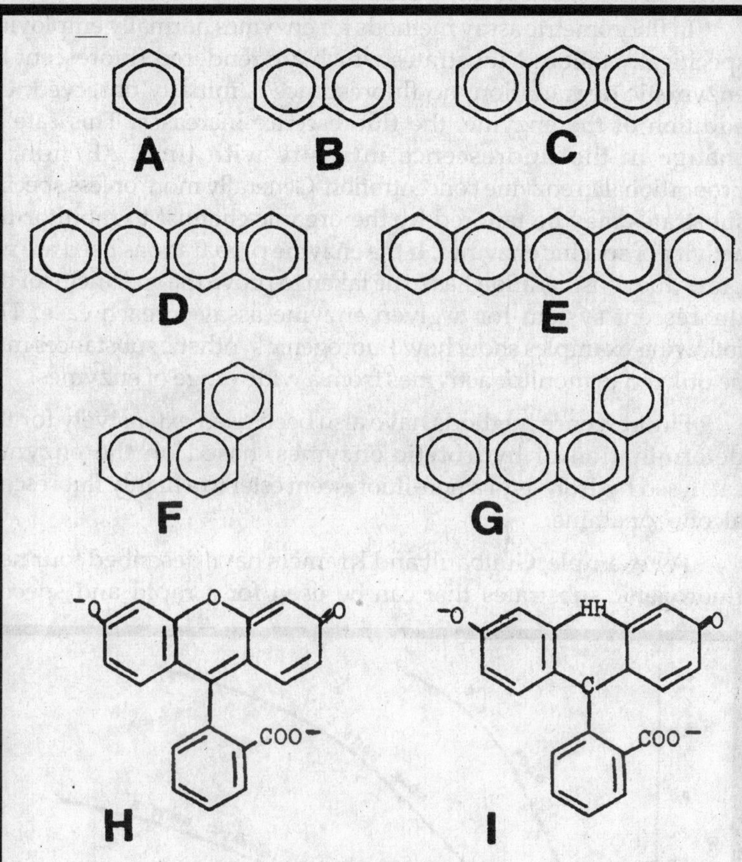

Figure 9.7: A: Benzene; B: Naphthalene; C: Anthracene; D: Tetracene; E: Pentacene; F: Phenanthrene; G: Benzanthracene; H: Phenolphthalein; I: Fluorescein

Fluorescence methods have found increasing use in enzymology because of their sensitivity and specificity. For example, NADH and NADPH, the reduced forms of nicotinamide adenine dinucleotide (NAD) and nicotinamide adenine dinucleotide phosphate (NADP), are highly fluorescent. Thus, all NAD- and NADP-dependent reactions involved in enzymatic analysis can be measured fluorometrically, with an increase of two to three orders of magnitude in sensitivity over colorimetric techniques.

In fluorometric assay methods for enzymes normally employing specifically tailored substrates which are rendered fluorescent by enzymatic degradation, no fluorescence is initially observed. On addition of the enzyme, the fluorescence increases. This rate of change in the fluorescence intensity with time, ΔF/min, is proportional to enzyme concentration. Generally more or less specific substrates may be tailored by the organic chemist to monitor the activity of specific enzymes. If the enzyme preparations used are not pure, due consideration has to be taken to prove the specificity of the fluorescent system for a given enzyme assay in each case. The following examples show how fluorogenic synthetic substances may be utilized to monitor activities from a wide range of enzymes.

Fluorescence methods have also been used extensively for the determination of hydrolytic enzymes, based on the enzyme-catalysed hydrolysis of a non-fluorescent ester to a highly fluorescent alcohol or amine.

For example, Guilbault and Kramers have described four new fluorogenic substrates that can be used for a rapid and specific

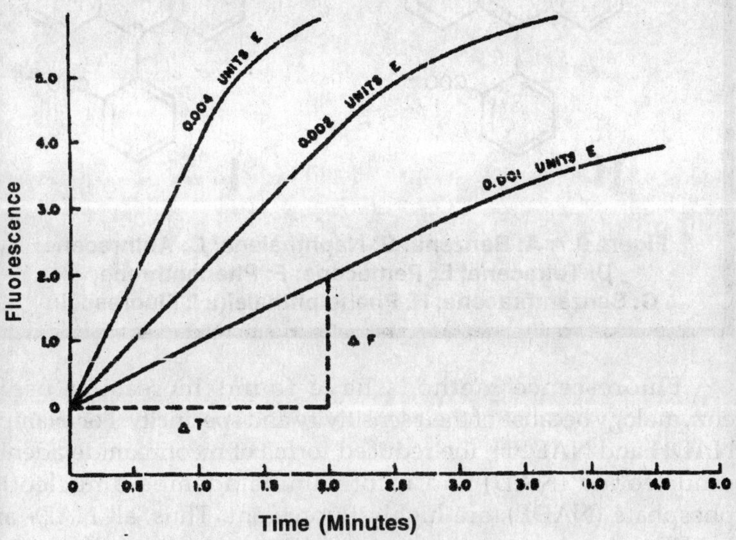

Figure 9.8: Rate of Increase in Fluorescence with Time on Addition of an Enzyme to a Fluorochrome

determination of cholinesterases: resorufin butyrate, indoxyl acetate, and 1- and 2-naphthyl acetate. All of these are non-fluorescent, but they are hydrolysed by cholinesterase to highly fluorescent compounds.

The substrates resorufin acetate and butyrate are hydrolysed by cholinesterase, acid phosphatase, and chymotrypsin to the highly fluorescent resorufin (λ_{ex} 540 nm, λ_{em} 580 nm). The rate of resorufin production with time is proportional to the concentration of cholinesterase from 0.0001 to 0.123 unit/ml, with a deviation of only 1 per cent. By the choice of substrates, some specificity is possible. For example, resorufin acetate is not hydrolysed by lipase nor by acetylcholinesterase (from bovine erythrocytes), but resorufin butyrate is hydrolysed by lipase. Similar concentrations of cholinesterase can be determined with a slightly lower deviation (0.9 per cent) by using indoxyl acetate as substrate.

Guilbault and Kramer found that indoxyl acetate could be used as a fluorogenic substrate for cholinesterase, by a proper control of experimental conditions. Indoxyl acetate is hydrolysed first to indoxyl, which is fluorescent. Air then rapidly affects the oxidation of indoxyl to Indigo White, which is twice as fluorescent as indoxyl, and then to the non-fluorescent Indigo Blue.

A fluorometric assay for nucleases has been suggested by Stevens, who synthesized sulphonyl chlorides of fluorescent compounds and showed that they reacted with the amino groups of deoxyribonuclease to yield non-dialysable fluorescent derivatives. Stevens pointed out that should such a fluorescent derivative be acted on by deoxyribonuclease, it will yield dialysable fluorescent products as a measure of the nuclease activity.

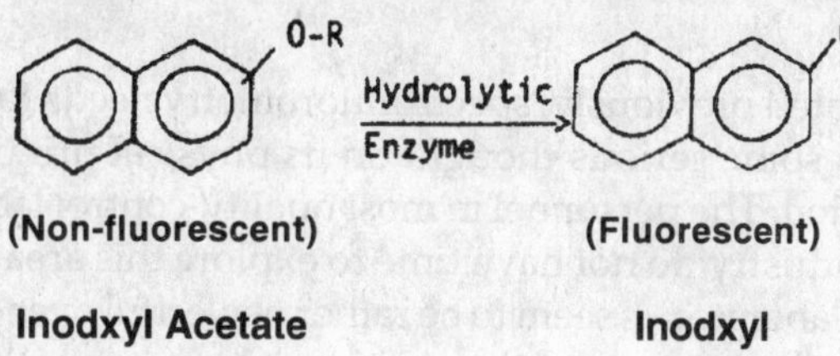

Figure 9.9: Indoxyl Acetate Hydrolysed to Indoxyl

Analytical fluorescence is a particularly useful technique because of its high sensitivity and specificity. However, it is of paramount importance to be aware of the limitations of the system, as slight environmental changes, such as pH, temperature etc. can and will cause fluorescence perturbation.

Analytical fluorescence has already provided much new information about biological systems, especially about food products. The use of kinetic methods of analysis in combination with fluorescence opens up a new field which can be tailored to provide an invaluable tool for the food industry.

Similarly, quite complicated fluorescent characteristics of food components, pure or in mixtures, might be used for the evaluation of the composition of foods, provided that the environmental factors can be controlled and that the data obtained can be analysed by sufficient and powerful data evaluation programs.

The Fluorometric Analysis

For most routine applications where reliable data on the excitation and emission wavelengths for a certain assay are given in the literature, the filter fluorometer is the optimal tool because of its simplicity and reasonable price. Modern filter technology is very advanced and it is, therefore, possible to obtain filters which are quite accurately translucent for distinct wavelengths while they effectively stop other light. In fact, filter fluorometers are in several applications superior to spectrofluorometers because the accuracy in wavelength definition can be compromised by the amount of energy which is allowed through the filter, giving advantages when a high level of energy is needed. In development of new analyses the spectrofluorometer is used to set specifications for the filters. If the ideal filter is not available in the market, it is possible to have special filters made.

As indicated previously, spectrofluorometry needs for the sake of usefulness some serious thought on its physical principles and instrumentation. The personnel in most quality-control laboratories in the food industry do not have time to explore this area and even several R&D laboratories seem to be rather neglectful over coming to grips with the fluorescence options. This might be one of the reasons why fluorescence techniques have taken so long to penetrate the food technology field.

The initial problems of joining the field of fluorescence analysis should not be difficult to overcome at most laboratories if today's available literature is consulted and if one works systematically.

Key factors to be considered for successful spectrofluorometry are the characteristics, lifetime and cost of xenon lamp. This is primarily so when whole spectra, and not just separate readings at fixed wavelengths, are recorded and calibrated to a known standard.

The intensity of fluorescence is proportional to the intensity of the excitation energy, and the intensity of the light source varies from day to day. In ratio spectrofluorometers a beam splitter is provided in the excitation light path, and a small proportion of the light is directed onto a reference cell containing a stable fluorophore. In the Perkin-Elmer instrument, this fluorophore is Rhodamine 101 dye, which absorbs energy at wavelengths in the range 230–630 nm and fluoresces at about 650 nm with constant quantum efficiency.

The measured intensity of the reference channel is proportional to the intensity of the exciting light, and the reference signal is used to correct for changes in lamp output. However, the light intensity of the exciting light is a function of wavelength, and even in ratio instruments the response of the reference may be dependent upon wavelength. Thus, to ensure reproducible spectra over a period of time, the use of fluorescence standards are essential. For standardization of the instrument, the use of solid fluorescence standards is recommended. A set of six different fluorescent compounds in a polymer matrix is available from Perkin-Elmer. Any wavelength region can be standardized by using one of the six standards.

One disadvantage of fluorescence as an analytical tool is its serious dependence on the factors such as temperature, pH, ionic strength, etc. The extreme sensitivity of fluorescence spectrofluorometry demands a very high standard of experimental work, if good results are to be achieved. Extreme precautions must be observed with regard to cleanliness of cells and glassware (although they must not be cleaned in chromic acid baths which fluoresce). Fluorescence spectrofluorometers should be used in dust-free laboratories with small temperature variations. Thermostatically controlled cell holders are available for most spectrofluorometers; a constant-temperature room is not always sufficient. Also, if samples are stored in freezers or refrigerators, care must be taken to bring the sample back to room temperature before measurement. The effects of changing the temperature of the whole measuring system from 15 to 25°C and the effect of changing the sample temperatures from 10 to 30°C (while the spectrophotometer but not the sample holder was kept at 20°C).

Fluorescence methods can be applied successfully only when environmental factors are controlled and proper standards are used. However, recent developments, especially of the electronic part of the instruments, have made it easier to use fluorescence for quantitative determinations. The Perkin-Elmer spectrofluorometer has an automatic gain control system, and the expansion factor used to obtain a response of a certain magnitude is automatically recorded, which is necessary especially when the reproducibility of whole spectra is required.

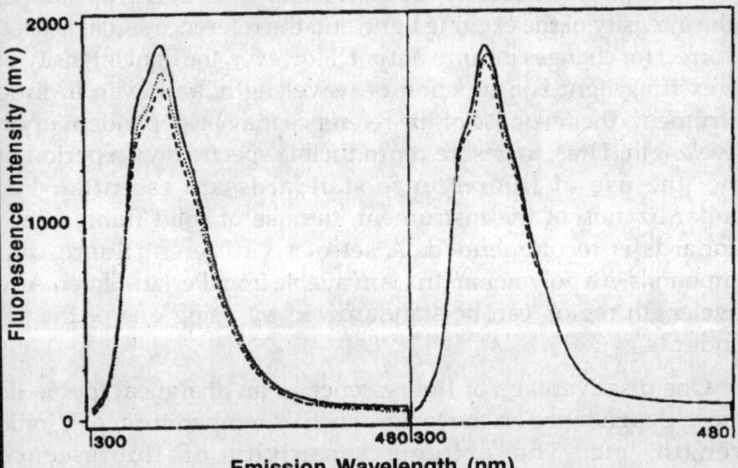

Figure 9.10: Variation in fluorescence emission spectra (excitation 275 nm, emission 300-400 nm) of a solid fluorescence standard (*p*-terphenyl) as a function of lamp burning time for Aminco SPF-500 ratio spectrofluorometer (left side) and Perkin-Elmer LS-5B fluorescence spectrometer (right side). Lamp burning time: 100 h (- - -), 200 h (· · ·), and 300 h (—)

The Autofluorescence

Autofluorescence is a very useful method which is used to detect heat endurance in plants. When chloroplasts are heat-damaged they display specific fluorescence in the red area at 686 nm optimally excited at 420 nm. Gibbons and Smillie utilized this mechanism to study the heat-sensitivity of the temperate pea (Pe) compared to the tropical papaya (Pa). The leaves were treated in the dark at different temperatures (35, 45, 48, and 54°C), illuminated with a mercury lamp and photographed using normal daylight colour film and a band-pass BP 600–700 mm emission filter. It is clearly seen that the fluorescence of the heat-resistant papaya develops at higher

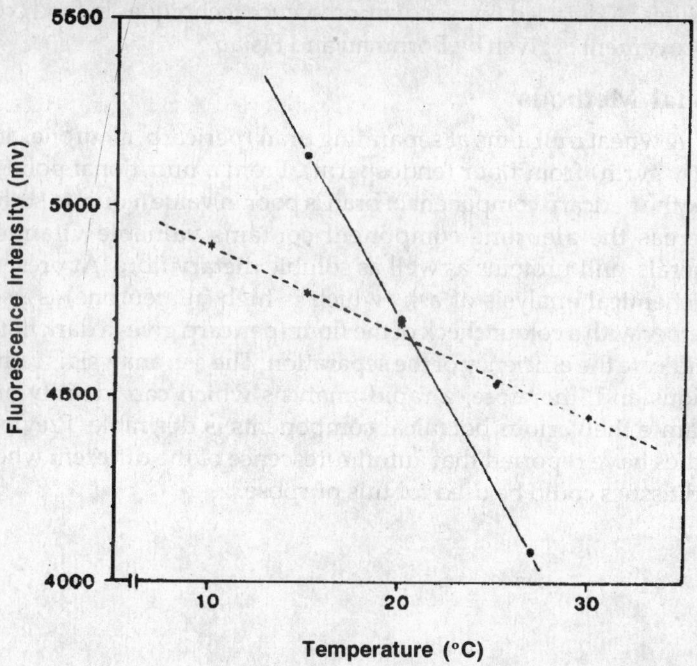

Figure 9.11: Variation in fluorescence emission intensity (excitation 275 nm, emission 340 nm) of a wheat flour sample as a function of room temperature of equipment and sample (-   -) and sample temperature (- * -) with a constant equipment temperature (20°C). Measured by Perkin-Elmer LS-5B fluorescence spectrometer

temperatures (54°C) than the heat-sensitive pea, where some autofluorescence can be seen already at 35°C.

Quantification by Fluorometry

The above morphological observations were quantified in a Jasco FP 550 spectrofluorometer at 686 nm emission showed which the relative heat sensitivity of pea over papaya. These changes in chlorophyll fluorescence are also valid for cold-temperature sensitivity, and a simple hand-held apparatus was devised to record this phenomenon out in the field. This example points out a few of the great possibilities in the use of fluorescence to record the conditions of economically important plants by remote sensing which can be carried out in the field or with aeroplanes or even satellites. A detailed review of fluorescence techniques in food crop improvement is given by Bornman and Hsiao.

Visual Methods

A wheat mill aims at separating bran (pericarp, aleurone, and partly germ) from flour (endosperm). From a nutritional point of view the pericarp component of bran is poor in value (equal to straw) whereas the aleurone component contains valuable vitamins, minerals, and proteins as well as soluble dietary fibre. At present, the chemical analysis of ash (which is high in aleurone) is used together with a colour check of the flour (pericarp gives a dark flour) to indicate the efficiency of the separation. The ash analysis is rather tedious and, therefore, a rapid analysis which can identify and separate the various botanical components is desirable. Previous studies have reported that autofluorescence of the different wheat seed tissues could be used for this purpose.

Chapter 10

Gas Liquid Chromatography: Application in Aroma Investigation

Introduction

Today Gas Chromatography has emerged as the cornerstone analytical technique in the field of general volatile analysis. Given this importance, it is not surprising that gas chromatography is of particular importance to the specialized field of aroma investigation. By definition aroma questions involve the range of chemical compounds that are of a sufficient volatility to reside in the vapor space surrounding a particular matrix. In even its most elemental form, gas chromatography is capable of revealing several pieces of key information regarding the volatile composition of a fragrant sample. This basic process, involving the single column separation of a volatile mixture followed by detection at a single universal detector, can be referred to as single dimension gas chromatography (SDGC) for the sake of reference. Among the key pieces of information that can be extracted from basic SDGC separations are the following:

- ✰ Absolute retention times for a set of compounds on a particular column operating under a specific set of operating parameters.
- ✰ General indications of the relative concentrations of the various components in the mixture.
- ✰ General indications of the relative volatilities of the various components in the mixture.

Conspicuously absent from this list is the capability of assigning definitive identification, structural, or functional group information to the peaks in a chromatogram. Therein lies one of the major limitations of SDGC-its limited usefulness in providing definitive qualitative information regarding the analyzed sample. This factor is especially important in the specialized field of aroma or odor analysis, since within this field the single most important characteristic of interest is qualitative in nature, namely, the relationship between a chromatographic peak and the olfactory response. As a result of this limitation, various techniques have been employed in an attempt to extract increased qualitative information from the SDGC process. These include the use of retention indices or sample spiking and absolute retention time matching. At best, however, these techniques can only serve to narrow the field of possible matches to what, on a completely unknown sample, is still a very large group of possible "hits."

Another major limitation of SDGC relates to its limited usefulness as even an absolute volatile separation technique. This limitation is understandable considering the tremendous number of volatile components potentially present in the headspace surrounding natural products. It has been proposed (1,2), for example, that for an analysis at a target concentration level of 10 parts per trillion (ppt) there is the theoretical possibility of a total component population ranging between 10^6 and 10^9. This possibility must then be considered in relation to the fact that there are at best several hundred theoretical resolution "windows" available for the complete separation of such a complex mixture under SDGC limitations. The actual number of these windows available from any chromatographic system depends on a number of factors, including column efficiency, system performance, column temperature limits, and system operating parameters. H͜wever, these limits can be assumed to typically number considerably less than 1000. In addition, since this number assumes perfect spacing of theoretical peaks, it is obvious that this level of optimal resolution will never exist for a real-world sample representing random peak distribution. The added separation challenge presented by the random peak distribution factor was recently proposed and shown to be formidable. It was proposed, by way of example, that although only approximately 40,000 plates are required for the separation of 100 ordered (*i.e.*, perfectly spaced) components, a 100-fold plate count increase (*i.e.*, approximately 4 million plates) is required for the separation of only 82 of 100 peaks representing random distribution. Unfortunately, as this relates to aroma volatiles analysis, all of these factors are brought to bear in the extreme-component concentration levels of significance to low ppt coupled with highly disordered peak distribution. An excellent of this limitation was shown in one study, which revealed in excess of 1500 resolved or partially resolved peaks from tobacco essential oil extracts. In this case, multidimensional gas chromatographic techniques were utilized to enhance these complex separations, making possible the mass special identification of 80 compounds not previously reported for these extracts.

A number of different techniques have been developed and utilized to offset the limitations of SDGC and increase both the quality and quantity of information that can be extracted from gas chromatographic separations. These techniques represent a number of hardware configurations and are loosely bound under the broad definitions that have become known as multidimensional gas chromatography (MDGC). W.Bertsch in his 1978 review of multidimensional techniques stated that, in the strictest sense, for a technique to qualify for inclusion into the MDGC field it must meet one of two principles:

1. Two columns of different selectivity in combination with a system [integration, mass spectroscopy (MS) identification etc.] which will permit assignment of retention indexes.

or

2. Two columns of different selectivity and a device (prep scale collection tube, valve etc.) to selectively transfer a

portion of a chromatographic run from one into another column.

In practice such restrictive definitions leave out a number of techniques and concepts that are very useful in overcoming the previously stated limitations of SDGC. As a result, prefers to include many techniques under the general heading of MDGC that do not meet the strictest limits of the Bertsch definitions. In these cases, the overriding consideration is whether a concept, when added onto the basic SDGC technique, serves to overcome the limitations of SDGC. In other words, to qualify under the somewhat broader definition of MDGC, the concept or technique under consideration should accomplish one of the following:

1. Provide increased qualitative information regarding peak identification, functionality, or other characteristics (*e.g.*, sensory) than could otherwise be provided by SDGC alone.

or

2. Increase peak resolution beyond that which would be achievable through simple column efficiency increases on a single column type.

The Detector Strategies for Chemical Analysis

There are several important analytical techniques that meet the above broadened definitions of multidimensional gas chromatography. Among these are included several hyphenated GC techniques which link a single GC column effluent with primary chemical structure characterization devices. Among the most important of these configurations are GC-MS, GC-Fourier transform infrared spectroscopy (GC-FTIR), GC-atomic emission detector (GC-AED), and GC-inductively coupled plasma (GC-ICP). Coupling these detectors with even single-dimension chromatographic separations permit detailed chemical structure data to be assigned to eluting peaks. This information ranges from actual peak identification or confirmation in the case of GC-MS and GC-FTIR to functional group identification or elemental analysis in the case of GC-FTIR, GC-AED, and GC-ICP.

Another detector strategy that can be used to expand the qualitative information provided by a single GC column separation is the use of multiple selective detectors operated in parallel. In this process the effluent from a single chromatographic column is split between two or more detectors representing different selectivities. The simplest hardware devices used to effect this effluent splitting are very simple fixed splitters which are based on fixed restrictor transfer lines and low dead volume connectors. Alternatively, somewhat greater flexibility is provided by variable splitter control devices, which are based on a combination of fixed restrictor transfer lines and needle valve control. Regardless of the mechanism used to effect the effluent splitting, this process makes it possible to utilize detector response ratios from the two detectors to confirm peak identification or possibly assign chemical functionality or sensory characteristics. Detector combinations that have found particularly wide spread usage in the environmental field are photoionization detector/flame ionization detector (PID/FID), PID/electron capture detector (ECD), and PID/Hall electrolytic conductivity detector (ELCD). Configurations that are particularly important to the field of aroma profiling are PID/flame photometric detector (FPD), PID/nitrogen phosphorus detector (NPD) and PID/olfactory detector. Utilizing the latter, for example, it is possible to determine the aroma characteristics of a peak eluting at the olfactory detector and match that to an electronic signal that is simultaneously generated at the PID operating in parallel.

One of the most useful detector strategies for the specialized field of aroma and odor profiling is the series coupling of detectors representing different selectivities. These techniques are a logical outgrowth of the previous category and are made possible if one of the two detectors is nondestructive in principle. Thermal conductivity (TCD) and photoionization detectors both meet this criteria and have often been used as the first detector in a variety of series coupled detector configurations. However, according of few researchers TCD has limited usefulness in the field of aroma and odor investigations due to both its limited sensitivity and its limited selectivity. In contrast, these same factors make the photoionization detector the single most generally useful to this field. In practice it is found that the PID exhibits excellent sensitivity towards most compounds and classes of compounds that are also important to the human olfactory response. Correspondingly, the PID exhibits relatively poor response to lower molecular weight saturated hydrocarbons, thereby eliminating a relatively large pool of potential interference peaks which might otherwise obscure the critical early regions of aroma profile chromatograms. The end result of these factors is that the PID represents the best overall match to the human olfactory response in both detection thresholds and detector selectivity.

Several configurations that incorporate the PID as part of a series coupled detector system have applications to the field of aroma profiling. These include PID-flame photometric PID-nitrogen-phosphorus, and PID-chemluminscence; in each of these, PID serves as a high-sensitivity general detector, which responds to most of the classes of compounds that are important to olfactory response. The PID can be coupled to a high-sensitivity and highly selective detector, which responds to a much narrower range of compounds that have been shown to be strong respondents to the human olfactory senses: the FPD and chemulminescence detectors selectively responding to sulfur species and the NPD selectively responding to nitrogen containing species. In this experience of some scientists, however, is that the single most useful detector system in the aroma-profiling application is the series coupling of the PID and the olfactory detector (*i.e.*, sniffport). In this case the effluent from the PID is swept immediately through a heated interface link to a heated and air-swept external vent port. This port is configured such that an investigator can conveniently sniff the effluent and assign aroma or odor descriptors to the peaks as they elute from the PID. If the PID-olfactory coupling is properly designed, the end result is the virtually simultaneous generation of an electronic signal at the PID and a corresponding sensory response at the sniff port for the effluent of the chromatographic column. This process permits the assignment of aroma characteristics to at least a retention region of a chromatographic profile and in some cases the isolated peak that is responsible for the aroma characteristics.

The creative detector strategies can be used to overcome the limitations of SDGC as a qualitative analytical technique. Without question these detector strategies can be extremely useful when applied to the special challenges of aroma profiling. However, in and of themselves, creative detector strategies can do very little towards offsetting the limitations of SDGC as an absolute separations technique. The focus of this work is to explore the application of those forms of MDGC that do address the limitations of SDGC as a separations tool. In doing so, an attempt is made to illustrate how MDGC-based detector strategies can be coupled to MDGC-based separations strategies to develop integrated aroma profiling systems.

There are few, if any, specialized fields of chemical analysis that have a greater requirement for complex volatile separations than does the field of aroma and odor investigation. This results from a combination of the extremes in both sensitivity and selectivity that are characteristic of the human olfactory response. It is not surprising that the importance of these factors is magnified several-fold if the area of interest is extended to other members of the animal kingdom. There are many examples in the literature in which key aroma or off-odor components from both natural and synthetic samples are detectable down to low ppt levels by the human olfactory response. An excellent example is 2-acetyl-l-pyrroline (2-AP), which, at the ppb level, is responsible for the characteristic "popcorn" aroma of the aromatic Basmati rice varieties. When these particular varieties of rice are cooked, trace amounts of 2-AP are either released from some bound precursor form or possibly chemically generated and released to the vapor space surrounding the rice. The result is a very pungent and characteristic aroma, which is also very desirable from culinary and marketing standpoints. The chromatographic separation challenge presented for the isolation of 2-AP from rice and other food products results from the fact that the detection threshold for 2-AP has been estimated to be approximately 100 ppt for the human olfactory response. The analytical challenge results not so much from these extremely low concentration levels of significance, but rather from the fact that, as we are forced to examine such low levels, the "forest grows." When concentrating the volatile organic compounds from the headspace surrounding any natural product, large amounts of potential interference compounds are inevitably collected and introduced into the GC system. As a result, we find that it is the rule rather than the exception that under SDGC conditions the most significant aroma peaks will be covered up by the surrounding mass of peaks, which may have little or no significance from an aroma standpoint. To address this limitation of SDGC it is necessary to explore the family of techniques which relate to the second of the previously staled MDGC definitions–to increase peak resolution beyond that which would be achievable through simple column efficiency increases on a single column type.

The major elements of this basic two-dimensional GC system are the injection device, a first column for preliminary separation, a flow switch device at the juncture of the first column and second column, a first detector for profiling the first column separation, and a second detector for profiling the second column separation. The first column and detector are commonly referred to as the precolumn and monitor detector, while the second column and detector are commonly referred to as the analytical column and analytical detector. Of the six basic elements shown, five elements can be viewed as being common to both MDGC and SDGC systems. If, for example, the switching device is replaced by a splitter tee, the effluent from the precolumn is simply split in its entirety between the monitor detector and the analytical column. The end result is then two SDGC chromatograms generated on two different detectors but with no additional qualitative information developed regarding the volatiles composition.

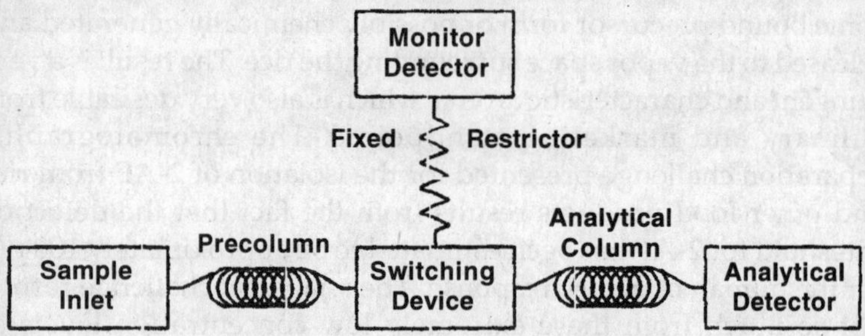

Figure 10.1: Basic MDGC Components.

Schematic diagram illustrating the key elements of a general MDFC separation system. This illustration is general in that it is equally representative of both rotary valve and Deans switch-based systems.

The critical difference between such a configuration and a true MDGC configuration is the presence of the flow switching device, which is located at the juncture of the precolumn, analytical column, and monitor detector transfer line. It is the presence of this device that enables the tremendous increase in separation power that is made possible through the MDGC techniques. Utilizing this critical device, the MDGC technique can be viewed as involving the following basic steps;

1. Injection of sample onto a precolumn for preliminary separation

2. Transferring those portions of the precolumn effluent that are adequately separated or are of no particular interest directly to the monitor detector
3. Shunting those portions of the precolumn effluent that are incompletely resolved or are of particular interest onto the analytical column for additional separation.

The last of these steps is generally referred to as heartcutting and is called on to address a number of chromatographic separation problems. These problems may arise as the result of matrix complexity due to the large number of peaks present or in some cases may be the result of gross difference in concentration between the components of interest and other matrix components. In either case these configurations permit the precolumn to serve, in essence, as an extension of the sample preparation or sample clean-up steps thereby affording the option of injecting much larger sample volumes than would be permitted under a conventional SDGC configuration. This is only possible since, under MDGC operation, the appearance of the precolumn separation at the monitor detector can be largely ignored. Mechanically transferring a small selected fraction of the resulting grossly overloaded perks or peak groups usually results in the desired separation at the analytical column/analytical detector. Obviously, the most dramatic separation enhancements result when the heartcut transfers are carried out between columns of considerable polarity or selectivity difference (*e.g.*, a non-polar-bonded polydimethylsiloxane precolumn to a polar-bonded Carbowax 20 M analytical column). In many cases these types of MDGC operations enable a particular separation to be pushed to lower detection limits, and in most cases these improvements can be achieved while at the same time increasing the speed of analysis. Among modern separation techniques in the field of analytical chemistry, few have enjoyed more success in enabling "needle-in-the-haystack" separations.

Given the importance of these techniques, it is not surprising that several different mechanical approaches have been developed for performing the critical stream selection flow switch. This operation is carried out, either through the use of one of the new-generation low dead volume rotary switching valves or, alternately, by one of the variations on the pressure balancing concept first proposed by D.R. Deans. Each of these approaches carries with it certain advantages and disadvantages; the rotary valve is a simpler mechanical approach, which is somewhat limited in flexibility, while the various pneumatic balance-based systems are considerably more flexible but are based on somewhat less intuitive concepts. Additional differences of note between these two approaches are the typical lower thermal mass and greater inertness possible for the pressure balance flow path connections compared to those of the rotary valve equivalents. The inertness is particularly important to aroma studies considering the extremely low levels of interest and the adsorption sensitivity of the functional groups typically present. The thermal mass is important in that it off sets the requirement for placing the Deans switch hardware components in a separate valve oven maintained at elevated temperatures. The separate valve oven is definitely a requirement for larger thermal mass rotary valves, which perform poorly when installed directly into a column oven operated under temperature-programmed conditions. These two mechanical approaches were evaluated in detail in a comparison study and shown to be equally effective in performing straightforward MDGC heartcutting applications. However, considering the various comparison factors relating to these two approaches and the unique requirements of aroma profiling, some of the researchers prefer to apply the Deans pressure balance-based approach to this specialized application area. That is why Deans switch is the focus for the information presented in this Chapter. It is understood, however, that there are valid alternatives to this approach, which in some instances may offer simpler and less costly solutions.

The Basic MDFC System for Aroma Separations

The flow switch mechanism for the Deans switch principle is less intuitive than that of the rotary switching valve. Switching a flow path with a rotary valve simply involves the mechanical shifting of a flow channel between one of two positions. In contrast, under the Deans switch principle, there are no moving parts present at the point of flow switch but rather a simple four-way tee. Flow switching in this case is fluid rather than mechanical in principle and is enabled by the addition of a second, independently regulated carrier gas supply to the juncture between the two columns. Under this configuration it is possible to tune the two carrier gas pressure inputs to the system to a state referred to as pressure balanced. This condition is essence which involves supplying a balancing carrier gas pressure to the juncture between the two columns; a pressure slightly higher than that which would exist at that point if the precolumn and analytical column were simply joined together with a low dead volume union. Once this pressure-balanced condition is reached, three very useful flow switch options are made available:

1. If the system is balanced and the precolumn vent line is open, the precolumn effluent takes the path of least resistance and flows directly to the monitor detector. This flow path option is normally referred to as bypass mode.
2. If the system is balanced and the precolumn vent line is closed, the precolumn effluent is shunted across the midpoint restrictor to the second column. This flow path option is normally referred to as heartcut mode.
3. The third flow switch option is referred to as backflush and is enabled when the carrier gas pressure supply to the injector is shut off and the inlet split vent is opened. Under these conditions the balancing carrier gas supply to the midpoint restrictor takes over and reverses the direction of carrier gas flow through the precolumn. Any chromatographing component that has not reached the flow switch juncture is simply carried back to the injector and passed out the split vent line. During this time the carrier gas supply to the analytical column continues uninterrupted, with the result that any component that has been transferred past the flow switch juncture onto the analytical column continues to chromatograph in the normal manner. This function permits those heavy components of no interest to the analysis at hand to be removed from the system prior to the analytical column.

Two basic elements must be present for the Deans switch system to make possible the toggling between heartcut and bypass modes of operation. The first of these is the presence of the balancing carrier gas feed to the midpoint restrictor, while the second is a device to open and close the precolumn vent line. The second of these two requirements can be met using a pneumatically actuated high temperature on/off valve in the transfer line linking the midpoint restrictor and the monitor detector. Activation of this valve permits the instantaneous toggling of the precolumn flow between the

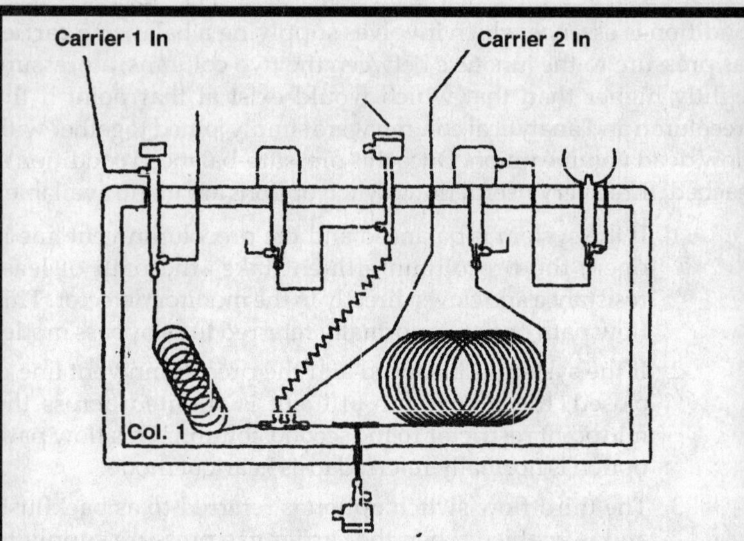

Figure 10.2: Basic MDGC System for Aroma Separations

heartcut and bypass flow paths. This device, referred to as the heartcut valve, is equipped with a make-up gas provision to ensure a rapid and complete transfer of the precolumn effluent to the monitor detector. The precolumn vent transfer line is another key element of the Deans switch system that requires special consideration. This line is, in reality, a fixed restrictor tube whose length and internal diameter are selected such that it matches the restriction of the analytical column. Relatively small ID fused silica capillary tubing is utilized to ensure that a desired level of restriction can be achieved in a short, inert, low-volume transfer line. If the restrictor is precisely matched and balancing carrier gas is fed into the midpoint restrictor at a constant pressure, equal flow rates are established through the fixed restrictor tube and the analytical column. In practice. the fixed restrictor tube is matched to the analytical column such that there is an approximate 10 per cent bias of gas flow to the fixed restrictor/ monitor detector pathway.

The last key hardware component required for the basic Deans switch system is the cryogenic trap. In a variety of forms and designs, these devices represent a very important element of state-of-the-art Deans switch-based MDGC systems. The cryotrap capability is useful in a number of situations, not the least of which is the refocusing of groups of unresolved heartcut components at the head of the analytical column prior to their release from the cryotrap for a separate run on a column of different polarity. A second application for the cryotrap in these configurations is the sharpening of chromatographic peaks, which may have broadened in the precolumn pathway for one of a number of reasons. These factors can range from injector-induced effects (*e.g.*, adsorption, dead volumes, or large volume injections) to column-induced effects (*e.g.*, adsorption, dead volumes, column flooding, or reverse solvent effects). In any case, if the cryotrap is properly designed and if the chromatographing components fall within the trapping range of the coolant selected, the end result is the injection of the heart cut components from the sharpest possible injection band.

Moving down from the system level to the component level, we find that design considerations are common to both MDGC and SDGC systems. If these systems are to deliver chromatographic separations which are quantitative, reproducible, and of highest possible efficiency, a number of fundamental performance requirements must be met. To meet these requirements, hardware components must be designed such that they maximize inertness while minimizing both thermal mass and flow path dead volumes. It should not be surprising that, given the low concentration levels of interest and the adsorption sensitivity of many key aroma components, these design requirements are extremely critical when the application area is aroma profiling.

The Application of MDGC Techniques

When examining the range of options made possible by the basic Deans switch principle, it is easy to understand the separation power of these systems. Instead of the single opportunity for resolving any particular group of components, as is the case with SDGC configurations, the basic MDGC configuration described above offers three:

1. There is a possibility of separating the components of interest on the precolumn by itself.
2. Through the use of the heartcut option and without cryotrapping, there is the possibility of separating the components of interest based on the combined selectivity of the precolumn and analytical column.

3. Through the use of the heartcut and cryotrap options, there is the possibility of separating the components of interest on the analytical column by itself.

After the desired chromatographic separation has been achieved through the use of one of these options, the backflush function can then be called on to quickly remove uninteresting higher boilers from the precolumn. Doing so often results in the reduction in turnaround time between chromatographic runs and eliminates the requirement for a high-temperature bake-out of the columns between runs. The following series of chromatograms illustrates how these processes can be used to advantage for difficult chromatographic separations. This example is taken from an actual method development project and presents an excellent demonstration of the evolution of a Deans switch-based MDGC procedure, which in this case was developed for an aroma critical component.

Example Application: 2-Acetyl-l-Pyrroline from Rice Extracts

The thrust of this project was the development of a method for the separation and quantification of 2-acetyl-l-pyrroline (2-AP) from crude rice extract. In this project the previously described MDGC techniques were used to develop an analytical procedure for this analysis, which met some very stringent requirements. The challenge, in this case, was to develop a chromatographic procedure which could be used for the rapid quality control screening of rice cultivars from a cross-breeding program. The goals for the project were not unlike those usually encountered in the development of GC methodologics. Simply stated, these goals were "rapid but complete resolution of a sub ppb level component from a complex matrix which was obtained directly from a natural product and doing so without the necessity for pre GC sample clean up or column oven temperature programming." Although these goals can be stated simply enough, actually achieving them in the laboratory is quite another matter. Several of these goals clearly run counter to each other and when limited to an SDGC approach, meeting such a challenge would not be possible. However, through the application of the MDGC techniques of heartcutting, cryotrapping, and backflushing, these goals are shifted within range. In this particular case only a few grains of rice are available from each cultivar for analysis, resulting in a sample size limitation of 0.3 g. The small, ground rice sample is cooked directly in a small amount of methylene chloride solvent to promote the release and extraction of the 2-AP. This is followed by the direct injection of up to 8 μl of the methylene chloride extract without additional clean-up, followed by the MDGC-based chromatographic separation at 110°C isothermal.

Chapter 11

High Performance (Pressure) Liquid Chromatography (HPLC): Application

Introduction

High performance liquid chromatography is basically a highly improved form of column chromatography. Instead of a solvent being allowed to drip through a column under gravity, it is forced through under high pressures of up to 400 atmospheres. That makes it much faster. It also allows you to use a very much smaller particle size for the column packing material which gives a much greater surface area for interactions between the stationary phase and the molecules flowing past it. This allows a much better separation of the components of the mixture. The other major improvement over column chromatography concerns the detection methods which can be used. These methods are highly automated and extremely sensitive.

Principle

Chromatography is the term used to describe a separation technique. Separation is based on the analyte's relative solubility between two liquid phases in which a mobile phase carrying a mixture is caused to move in contact with a selectively absorbent stationary phase. Different components of the sample are carried forward at different rates by the moving liquid phase, due to their differing interactions with the stationary and mobile phases. There are a number of different kinds of chromatography, which differ in the mobile and the stationary phase used. In HPLC the mobile phase is a solvent. This solvent is pumped under high pressure through a column. The stationary phase is a finely divided solid held inside the column.

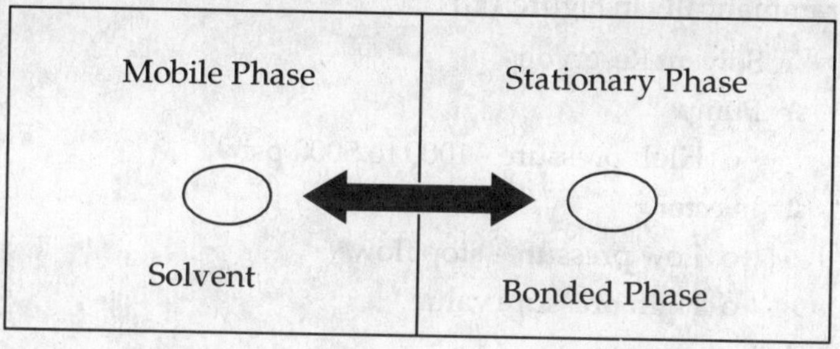

Theory

As in other forms of liquid chromatography, separation in High Performance Liquid Chromatography or High Pressure Liquid Chromatography (HPLC) is also obtained on the basis of partitioning, adsorption, ion exchange or molecular sieving phenomena. The conventional column chromatography suffers from two major drawbacks; namely it is generally a time consuming process and quality of resolution is poor. This is mainly because of the fact that in conventional column chromatography the mobile phase percolates through the column under the force of gravity or by small pressure applied by peristaltic pump. This accounts for the slow flow rate which in addition to extending the time required for elution of the sample creates the problem of peak broadening through diffusion phenomenon resulting in poor resolution. In general, resolution of individual components can be improved by decreasing the particle size of stationary phase. However, in conventional column chromatography, this is not feasible because the use of finer gel material will further lower the permeability of the column contributing to decreasing flow rate thereby providing greater time for band broadening. The resistance to flow of mobile phase can be overcome by use of high pressure. In recent years, stationary phases of smaller particle size which can withstand high pressures, have been developed, which has facilitated the development of a new chromatographic technique called HPLC, which gives faster and superior resolution with sharp and compact peaks.

HPLC Instrumentation

The basic HPLC equipment consists of the following components. The essential features of HPLC equipment are shown diagrammatically in Figure 11.1.

- ☆ Solvent Reservoir
- ☆ Pump
  - o High pressure - 1000 to 5000 psi
- ☆ Injector
  - o Low pressure - stop flow
  - o High pressure value
- ☆ Column
  - o Normal Phase - organic (water-free) mobile phase
    - — Silica gel - non-aqueous
    - — Adsorption
  - o Reverse phase (C8, C18) - aqueous mobile phase
    - — Partitioning
  - o Ion-exchange - aqueous mobile phase
  - o Molecular sieve - aqueous mobile phase
    - — Size
- ☆ Detector
  - o Specific
    - — Absorbance
    - — Fluorescence
    - — Electrochemical

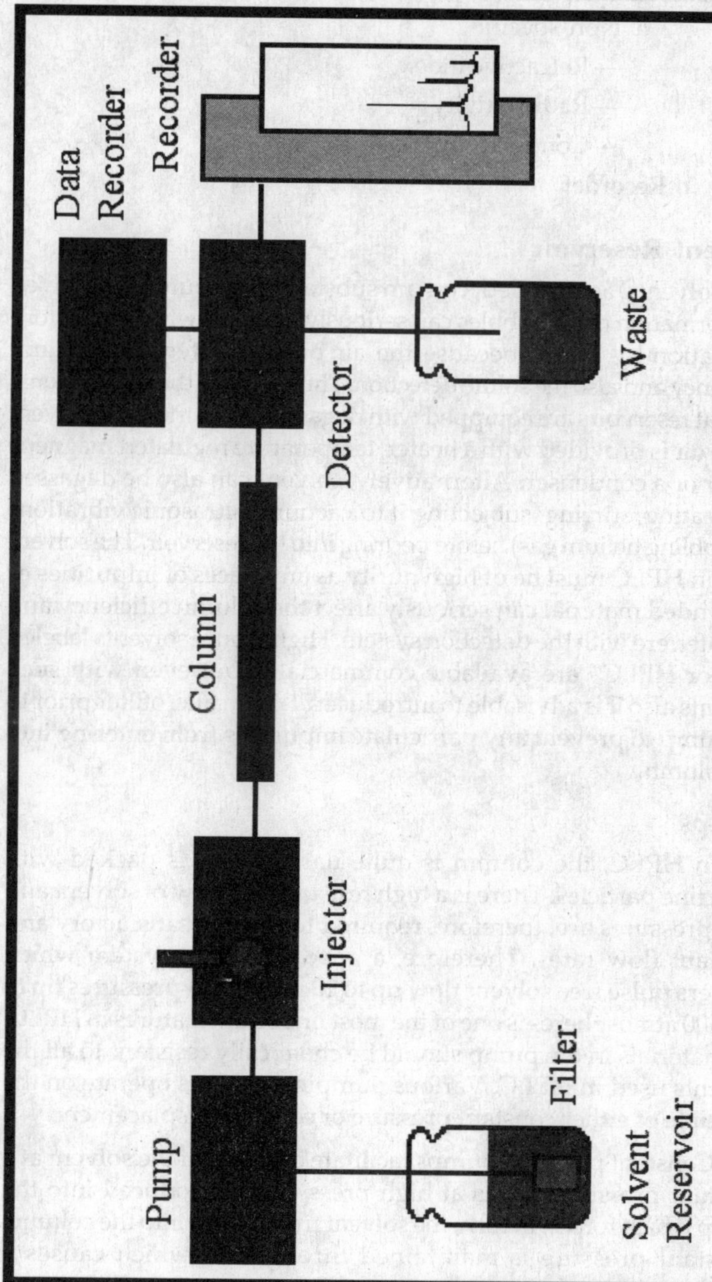

Figure 11.1: Diagram of Essential Components of HPLC

- o Non-specific
  - — Refractive index
  - — Radioactivity
  - — Conductivity
- ☆ Recorder

Solvent Reservoir

Solvents, as supplied, contain substantial amount of dissolved air. Formation of air bubbles can seriously interfere with satisfactory separation by HPLC because the air bubbles affect the column efficiency and also the solute detection. Thus some of the conventional solvent reservoirs are equipped with degassifiers. In these the solvent reservoir is provided with a heater, temperature regulated magnetic stirrer or a condenser. Alternatively, solvent can also be degassed (by heating, stirring, subjecting it to vacuum, ultrasonic vibrations or bubbling helium gas) before pouring into the reservoir. The solvent used in HPLC must be of high purity as any traces of impurities or suspended material can seriously affect the column efficiency and can interfere with the detection system. Highly pure solvents labeled as "For HPLC" are available commercially, but even with such solvents also it is advisable to introduce a 1-5 μm microfilter prior to the pump to prevent any particulate impurities from entering into the column.

Pumps

In HPLC, the column is quite narrow and is packed with superfine particles. There is a high resistance to flow of solvent and high pressures are, therefore, required to achieve satisfactory and constant flow rates. Therefore, a good pumping system which delivers pulse free solvent flow up to 20 ml/min at pressures up to 300-400 atmospheres is one of the most important features in HPLC. All materials in the pump should be chemically resistant to all the solvents used in HPLC. Various pumping systems operate on the principle of either constant pressure or constant displacement.

Constant pressure pumps facilitate delivery of the solvent at a constant pressure. A gas at high pressure is introduced into the pump which forces, in turn, the solvent from pump into the column. Constant pressure is maintained throughout, which causes a decrease in permeability of the column with time w' ich in turn results in decreased flow rates. Such pumps do not compensate for this decrease in flow rate and so provide uniform and pulse less solvent flow.

The second type of pumps is the constant displacement pump. Such pumps displace a constant amount of the solvent from the pump into the column and so maintain a constant flow rate irrespective of the changing conditions within the column. These pumps produce small pulses of flow between two displacements and so pulse dampeners are usually introduced between the pump and the column to smoothen the flow and to minimize the pulsing effect. Two commonly used constant displacement pumps are: (*i*) motor driven syringe type pump and (*ii*) reciprocating pump which deliver a fixed and constant volume of the solvent onto the column at each stroke.

Sampling Device

Sample can be introduced into the column either by a syringe injection through a septum of an injection port into eluent stream or by a sample loop from which it is swept into the column by the eluent. The sample is loaded directly on top of the column to avoid appreciable mixing of the sample with the eluent. In the syringe injection mode, the sample is injected with the help of a microsyringe (which can withstand high pressures) directly onto the column bed. While loading the sample, the pump is turned off and when the pressure is dropped near atmospheric pressure, the sample is introduced. After the sample has been injected, the pump is switched on again. This procedure is known as stop flow injection.

The second type of system is loop injection. Here the sample is introduced with the help of a metal loop of fixed small volume. The loop is filled with the sample and by the appropriately adjusting the sample valve, the solvent from the pump is channeled through the loop. The sample is thus flushed by the solvent from the loop whose outlet opens directly at top of the column bed.

Columns

Since glass tubing cannot withstand pressures in excess of 70 atm, stainless steel precision bored columns with an internal mirror finish for efficient packing, are normally used. These straight columns of 15-50 cm length and 1-4 mm diameter can withstand very high pressures of up to 5.5×10^7 Pa and are relatively corrosion resistant. At the end of the column, homogenously porous plugs of stainless steel or teflon are used to retain the packing material and to ensure the uniform flow of the solvent through the column. At times, repeated application of impure samples such as urine, blood or crude cell extracts results in clogging and the loss of resolving power of the column. To prevent this, a short column of length 1-2 cm and internal diameter equal to that of analytical column is generally introduced between the injector and the analytical column. This short column is called guard column and is packed with material with which analytical column is packed. The guard column retains the solid particles in the sample before sample enters the main column. The guard columns can be replaced at regular intervals.

Matrices and Stationary Phases

One of the basic requirements for HPLC is that the packing material which serves as stationary phase or support for stationary phase should be pressure stable, *i.e.* it must be designed to withstand the operating pressure applied during separation. Three forms of column packing materials are available based on nature of the rigid solid structure:

(*i*) Totally Porous Materials or Microporous Supports

In these supports the micropores ramify through particles which are generally 5-10 μm in diameter.

(*ii*) Porous Layer Beads or Pellicular Supports

These are superficially porous supports where a thin, porous, active layer is coated onto a solid core such as impervious glass beads. The thickness of the porous layer is generally 1-3 μm. The size of glass beads used is between 25-50 μm.

(*iii*) Bonded Phases

The stationary phase is chemically bonded to an inert support such as silica. The type of particular stationary phase will depend on the separation principle. Some of these stationary phases, with their commercial names, which can be used for different types of chromatographic separations are listed in Table 11.1.

Table 11.1: Examples of HPLC Stationary Phases

Chromatographic Separation Principle	*Commercial Name*	*Nature of Stationary Phase*	*Type of Support*
Partition	ULTRA Pak TSK	Octadecylsilane	Porous
	ODS ULTRA Pak	Alkylamine	Porous
	TSK NH_2	Octadecylsilane	Pellicular
	Bondapak-C_{18}/ Corasil	Alkylamine	Porous
	μ Bondapak-NH_2		
Adsorption	Corasil	Silica	Pellicular
	Partisil C_8	Octylsilane	Porous
	Pellumina	Alumina	Pellicular
	Micropak	Alumina	Microporous
Exclusion	Superose	Agarose	Soft gel
	Fractogel TSK	Polyvinylchloride	Semi-rigid gel
	Bio-Gas	Glass	Rigid solid
	Styragel	Polystyrene divinyl benzene	Semi-rigid gel
Ion exchange	Perisorb-KAT	Strong acid	Pellicular
	Partisil-SAX	Strong base	Porous
	Micropak-NH_2	Weak base	Porous
	Partisil-SCX	Strong acid	Porous

Detectors

Detectors are the devices which continuously monitor changes in the composition of the eluent coming out of the column. Most commonly used detectors are refractive index detectors, UV detector, electrochemical and fluorometric detectors.

Refractive Index Detector (RID)

Refractive index (RI) of dilute solutions changes proportionally with solute concentration. This relationship is exploited for quantitative detection of solutes in the column eluate. The relationship between change of RI and solute concentration is only moderately dependent on the type of solute, making this a quite universal, yet not very sensitive detection principle. RIC can, therefore, be applied to general purpose. This detector suffers from many defects including low sensitivity, tendency to be affected by temperature or flow speeds and incompatibility for being used in gradient elution unless chosen solvents are of identical RI. It measures the bulk RI of sample eluent system. Hence any substance whose RI differs sufficiently from that of eluent can be detected. To attain adequate sensitivity, the temperature of the eluent and measuring cell is held constant to ±0.001°C. Variations in flow rates also interfere with response of differential refractometer. Hence very good damping is essential for the pumps producing pulsating flow.

UV-VIS-absorption Detectors

The basis of quantitative absorbance photometry is Lambert-Beer's law, *i.e.* the absorbance of a solution is proportional to the concentration of the absorbing solute, the light path length and the extinction coefficient. Fixed wavelength detectors utilize lamps which emit light of a few discrete wavelengths. The most common of these lamps is the low pressure mercury lamp emitting over 90 per cent of its light at 254 nm. Lower wavelength lamps are available such as zinc lamps (214 nm) and cadmium lamps (229 nm). The combination of the lamp and a filter determines the fixed operating wavelength of the detector. Variable wavelength (VW) detectors use a light source with a continuous emission spectrum and a continuously adjustable (narrow) band filter, called monochromator. The most common light source for these detectors is the deuterium lamp whose usable emission spectrum ranges from about 190 nm to about 350 nm, with an intensity maximum between 220 and 240 nm. Above 300 nm, the output intensity is low, therefore, some VW detectors have an additional or optional tungsten lamp, which can be used at wavelength above 350 nm. In recent years, specially designed VW detectors for HPLC have been introduced which allow automatic rapid change of wavelength setting within 1 to 2 seconds or less across their entire wavelength span, which typically ranges from about 190- nm to about 600 nm.

Electrochemical Detectors

Methods used in HPLC based on electroanalysis can be classified as bulk property and solute property electrochemical detectors. Bulk property electrochemical detectors respond to a change in an electrochemical property of the bulk liquid flowing through the measuring cell, whereas the solute property electrochemical detectors respond to a change in voltage (potentiometry) or current (voltammetry or coulometry) when an analyte passes through the cell. The potentiometric detectors have not been commercialized. Voltammetric and coulometric detectors on the contrary are offered by various manufacturers.

Fluorescence Detectors

The quantity of fluorescent light emitted from excited molecules in dilute solutions is proportional to intensity of excitation source, illuminated volume of the sample solution, quantum efficiency of fluorescence of sample and the concentration of the solute to be detected. Ideally, fluorescence radiation, as a result of suitable excitation of the sample molecules, is measured against a dark background. Therefore, the main source of detector noise is dark current noise of the photodetector, which is mainly determined by temperature. As a rule for every 10 °C increase in temperature the dark current noise of the photodiode gets doubled.

Operation

High performance liquid chromatography (HPLC) is a separation technique utilizing differences in distribution of compounds to two phases, called stationary phase and mobile phase. The stationary phase designates a thin layer created on the surface of fine particles and the mobile phase designates the liquid flowing over the particles. Under a certain dynamic condition, each component in a sample has different distribution equilibrium depending on solubility in the phases and/or molecular size. As a result, the components move at different speeds over the stationary phase and are thereby separated from each other. This is the principle behind HPLC. The column is a stainless steel (or resin) tube which is packed with spherical solid particles. Mobile phase is constantly fed into the column inlet at a constant rate by a liquid pump. A sample is injected from a sample injector, located near the column inlet. The injected sample enters the column with the mobile phase and the components in the sample migrate through it, passing between the stationary and mobile phases. Compounds move in the column only when is in the mobile phase. Compounds that tend to be distributed in the mobile phase therefore migrate faster through the column while compounds that tend to be distributed in the stationary phase migrate slower. In this way, each component is separated on the column and sequentially elutes from the outlet. Each compound eluting from the column is detected by a detector connected to the outlet of the column.

When the separation process is monitored by the recorder starting at the time the sample is injected, a graph is obtained. This graph is called a chromatogram. The time required for a compound to elute (called retention time) and the relationship between compound concentration (amount) and peak area depend on the characteristics of the compound. Retention time is therefore used as an index for qualitative determination and peak surface area (or height) as an index for quantitative determination. The retention time of the target compounds and the concentration for each unit of peak area are based on data obtained in advance by analyzing a sample with known quantities of the reference standards. Normally, the reference standards are highly purified target compounds.

Sample Preparation

The sample is normally reconstituted in the solvent to maximize binding to the column. The sample should not be dissolved in an organic solvent or it may not stick to the stationary phase. The sample should not be dissolved in detergent containing solutions. Some detergents may bind to reverse phase columns and modify them irreversibly. In addition detergents preferentially ionize in electrospray mass spectrometry and can obscure the detection or suppress the ionization of the analyte.

Injection of the Sample

Details given in sampling device.

Retention Time

The time taken for a particular compound to travel through the column to the detector is known as its retention time. This time is measured from the time at which the sample is injected to the point at which the display shows a maximum peak height for that compound.

Different compounds have different retention times. For a particular compound, the retention time will vary depending on:

- The pressure used (because that affects the flow rate of the solvent) the nature of the stationary phase (not only what material it is made of, but also particle size)
- The exact composition of the solvent
- The temperature of the column

That means that conditions have to be carefully controlled if you are using retention times as a way of identifying compounds.

The Detector

There are several ways of detecting when a substance has passed through the column which has been discussed earlier. A common method which is easy to explain uses ultra-violet absorption. Many organic compounds absorb UV light of various wavelengths. If you have a beam of UV light shining through the stream of liquid coming out of the column, and a UV detector on the opposite side of the stream, you can get a direct reading of how much of the light is absorbed. The amount of light absorbed will depend on the amount of a particular compound that is passing through the beam at the time.

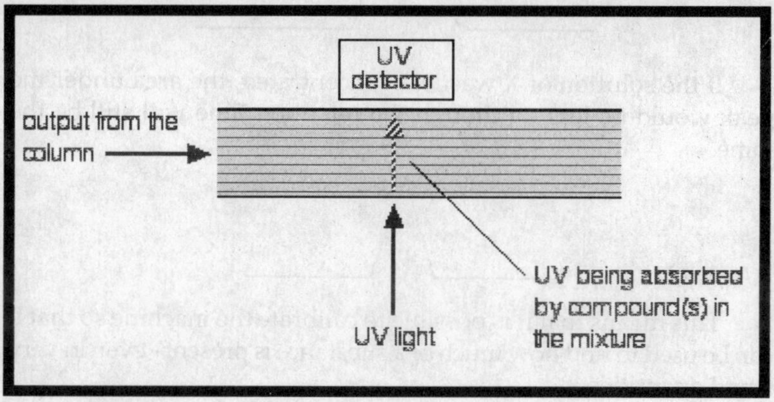

Interpreting the Output from the Detector

The output will be recorded as a series of peaks - each one representing a compound in the mixture passing through the detector and absorbing UV light. As long as you were careful to control the conditions on the column, you could use the retention times to help to identify the compounds present - provided, of course, that you (or somebody else) had already measured them for pure samples of the various compounds under those identical conditions.

For example, you can also use the peaks as a way of measuring the quantities of the compounds present. Let's suppose that you are interested in a particular compound, X. If you injected a solution containing a known amount of pure X into the machine, not only could you record its retention time, but you could also relate the amount of X to the peak that was formed.

The area under the peak is proportional to the amount of X which has passed the detector, and this area can be calculated automatically by the computer linked to the display. The area it would measure is shown below in the (very simplified) diagram.

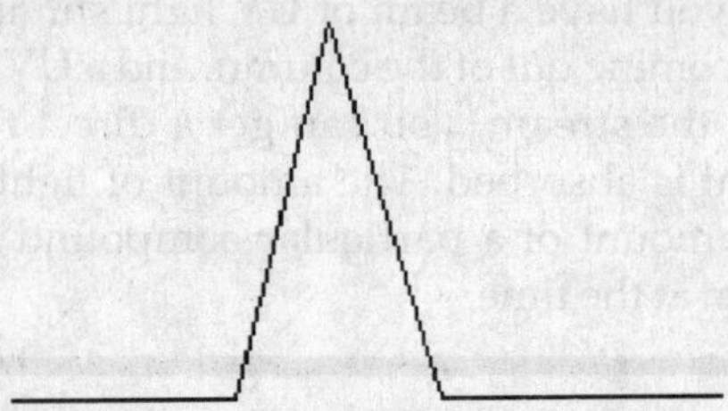

If the solution of X was less concentrated, the area under the peak would be less - although the retention time will still be the same.

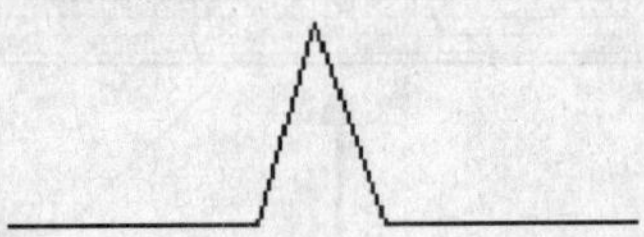

This means that it is possible to calibrate the machine so that it can be used to find how much of a substance is present - even in very small quantities.

Be careful, though! If you had two different substances in the mixture (X and Y) could you say anything about their relative amounts? Not if you were using UV absorption as your detection method.

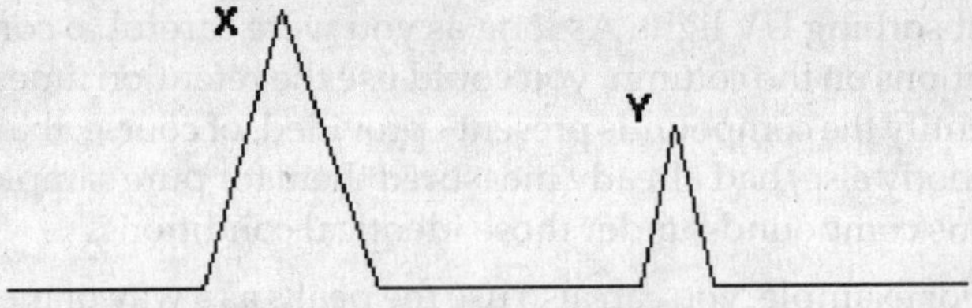

In the above diagram, the area under the peak for Y is less than that for X. That may be because there is less Y than X, but it could equally well be because Y absorbs UV light at the wavelength one is using less than X does. There might be large quantities of Y present, but if it only absorbed weakly, it would only give a small peak.

HPLC–Modes

- ☆ Normal phase: Polar stationary phase and non-polar solvent.
- ☆ Reverse phase: Non-polar stationary phase and a polar solvent.

1. Normal Phase HPLC

Normal phase HPLC (NP-HPLC), or adsorption chromatography, this method separates analytes based on adsorption to a stationary surface chemistry and by polarity.

The column is filled with tiny silica particles, and the solvent is non-polar - hexane, for example. A typical column has an internal diameter of 4.6 mm (and may be less than that), and a length of 150 to 250 mm. Polar compounds in the mixture being passed through the column stick longer to the polar silica than non-polar compounds. The non-polar ones therefore pass more quickly through the column.

It was one of the first kinds of HPLC that chemists developed. NP-HPLC uses a polar stationary phase and a non-polar, non-aqueous mobile phase, and works effectively for separating analytes readily soluble in non-polar solvents. The analyte associates with and is retained by the polar stationary phase. Adsorption strengths increase with increased analyte polarity, and the interaction between the polar analyte and the polar stationary phase (relative to the mobile phase) increases the elution time. The interaction strength depends not only on the functional groups in the analyte molecule, but also on steric factors. The effect of sterics on interaction strength allows this method to resolve (separate) structural isomers.

The use of more polar solvents in the mobile phase will decrease the retention time of the analytes, whereas more hydrophobic solvents tend to increase retention times. Very polar solvents in a mixture tend to deactivate the stationary phase by creating a stationary bound water layer on the stationary phase surface. This behavior is somewhat peculiar to normal phase because it is most purely an adsorptive mechanism (the interactions are with a hard surface rather than a soft layer on a surface).

NP-HPLC fell out of favor in the 1970s with the development of reversed-phase HPLC because of a lack of reproducibility of retention times as water or protic organic solvents changed the hydration state of the silica or alumina chromatographic media. Recently it has become useful again with the development of Hydrophibic Interaction Chromatography (HILIC) bonded phases which improve reproducibility. However, HILIC has the advantage of separating acidic, basic and neutral solutes in a single chromatogram.

2. Reversed Phase HPLC

Reversed phase HPLC (RP-HPLC) has a non-polar stationary phase and an aqueous, moderately polar mobile phase. One common stationary phase is a silica which has been treated with RMe_2SiCl, where R is a straight chain alkyl group such as $C_{18}H_{37}$ or C_8H_{17}. With these stationary phases, retention time is longer for molecules which are more non-polar, while polar molecules elute more readily. An investigator can increase retention time by adding more water to the mobile phase; thereby making the affinity of the hydrophobic analyte for the hydrophobic stationary phase stronger relative to the now more hydrophilic mobile phase. Similarly, an investigator can decrease retention time by adding more organic solvent to the eluent.

In this case, the column size is the same, but the silica is modified to make it non-polar by attaching long hydrocarbon chains to its surface - typically with either 8 or 18 carbon atoms in them. A polar solvent is used - for example, a mixture of water and an alcohol such as methanol.

There will be a strong attraction between the polar solvent and polar molecules in the mixture being passed through the column. There won't be as much attraction between the hydrocarbon chains attached to the silica (the stationary phase) and the polar molecules in the solution. Polar molecules in the mixture will therefore spend most of their time moving with the solvent.

Non-polar compounds in the mixture will tend to form attractions with the hydrocarbon groups because of van der Waals dispersion forces. They will also be less soluble in the solvent because of the need to break hydrogen bonds as they squeeze in between the water or methanol molecules, for example. They therefore spend less time in solution in the solvent and this will slow them down on their way through the column.

That means that now it is the polar molecules that will travel through the column more quickly. Reversed phase HPLC is the most commonly used form of HPLC.

Application of HPLC to Food Analysis

High performance liquid chromatography (HPLC) is used increasingly in the analysis of food samples. Modern HPLC has many applications including separation, identification, purification, and quantification of various compounds. It is now one of the most powerful tools in analytical chemistry, with the ability to separate, identify and quantitate the compounds that are present in any sample that can be dissolved in a liquid. Today, trace concentrations of compounds, as low as "parts per trillion" (ppt), are easily obtained. This method breaks downs complex mixtures into individual compounds, which in turn, are identified and quantified by suitable detectors. Normal-phase HPLC is best applied to the separation of compounds that are highly soluble in organic solvents such as fat soluble vitamins and highly hydrophilic species such as carbohydrates may also be resolved by normal-phase chromatography. Amino bonded-phase HPLC columns are utilized for the separation of carbohydrates. Whereas reversed-phase HPLC is widely used for analysis of cereal proteins, both water and fat soluble vitamins. The availability of fluorescence detectors has enabled researchers to quantitate very small amounts of the more than six possible forms of vitamin B_6 (vitamers) in foods and biological samples. It can be used to resolve carbohydrates on C_{18} bonded-phase columns. The constituents of soft drinks (caffeine, aspartame etc.) can be rapidly separated. Reversed-phase HPLC with a variety of detection methods including R1, UV, light scattering and LC-MS has been applied to analysis of lipids. Antioxidants such as butylated hydroxyanisole (BHA) and butylated hydroxytoluene (BHT) can be extracted from dry foods and analyzed by reversed-phase HPLC with simultaneous UV and fluorescence detection. Phenolic flavor compounds (such as vanillin) and pigments such as chlorophylls, carotenoids and anthocynins) are also amenable to reversed-phase HPLC. Reversed-phase ion-pair chromatography also is used for the separation of synthetic food colours, preservatives, artificial sweeteners etc.

Carbohydrates

Food carbohydrates like glucose, galactose, raffinose, fructose, mannitol, sorbitol, lactose, maltose, cellobiose, and sucrose are characterized by a wide range of chemical reactivity and molecular size. Because carbohydrates do not possess chromophores or fluorophores, they cannot be detected with UV-visible or fluorescence techniques. Nowadays, however, refractive index detection can be used to detect concentrations in the low parts per million (ppm) range and above, whereas electrochemical detection is used in the analysis of sugars in the low parts per billion (ppb) range.

Sample Preparation and Chromatographic Conditions

Degassed drinks can be injected directly after filtration. More complex samples require more extensive treatment, such as fat extraction and deproteination. Sample cleanup to remove less polar impurities can be done through solid-phase extraction on C18 columns. HPLC method is the method of choice for analysis of mono- and oligosaccharides and can be used for analysis of polysaccharides after hydrolysis. HPLC gives both qualitative analysis (identification of carbohydrate) and with peak integration, quantitative analysis. The HPLC method presented here is used to analyze mono, di-, tri and oligosaccharides as well as sugar alcohols.

Sample preparation	Samples were directly injected
Column	300 x 7.8 mm Bio-Rad HPXP, 9 μm
Mobile phase	water
Column compartment 80°C	
Flow rate	0.7 ml/min
Detector	refractive index
HPLC method performance	
Limit of detection	<10 ng with S/N = 2
Repeatability of RT over 10 runs areas over 10 runs 2%	<0.05%

Lipids

Lipids are mixtures of fatty molecules that contain polar and nonpolar groups. Polar lipids include phospholipids and glycolipids, whereas nonpolar lipids include fatty acids and their esters, cholesterol and its esters, essential oils and wax esters. Lipids are important ingredients in the production of modern food and play key roles in physiological systems. Historically, TLC and GC have been used for the analysis of lipids. Due to the limitations of these techniques and the advances in HPLC detection technology, HPLC is gaining popularity for lipid analysis. The high temperatures used in the GC causes degradation of some molecules, whereas many fat molecules are not volatile enough to go through the GC. On the other hand, detection of fats on TLC is somewhat cumbersome.

Today, HPLC is the dominant analytical technique used for the analysis of most classes of compounds. The analyses can be carried out at room temperature and the collection of fractions for reanalysis or further manipulation is straightforward. The main reason for the slow acceptance of the HPLC technique for lipid analysis has been the detection system. Traditionally, HPLC used ultraviolet/visible (UV/vis) detection, which requires the presence of a chromophore in the analyte. Most lipid molecules do not contain chromophores and therefore would not be detected by UV/vis. Modern HPLC detection techniques, such as the use of a mass spectrometer as the detector, derivatization techniques to introduce chromophores, and the availability of pure solvents to reduce interference, have allowed HPLC to compete with and/or complement GC and other traditional methods of lipid analysis. In addition to analytical HPLC, preparative HPLC has been used extensively to collect pure samples of the lipids for the derivatization or synthesis of new compounds.

Triglycerides and Hydroperoxides in Oils

The composition of triglycerides is of great interest in food processing and dietary control. Owing to the slow stability of triglycerides containing unsaturated fatty acids, reactions with light and oxygen form hydroperoxides, which strongly influence the taste and quality of fats and oils. Adulteration with foreign fats and the use of triglycerides that have been modified by a hardening process also can be detected through triglyceride analysis. The HPLC method presented here is used to analyze triglycerides, hydroperoxides, sterols, and vitamins with UV-visible diode-array detection (UV-DAD). The HPLC method presented here is used to analyze triglycerides in aged sun flower oil.

Sample Preparation and Chromatographic Conditions

Triglycerides can be extracted from homogenized samples with petrol ether. Fats and oils can be dissolved in tetrahydrofuran.

Column	200 x 2.1 mm
	Hypersil MOS, 5 μm
Mobile phase	A = water
	B = ACN/methyl-tert, butylether (9:1)
Gradient	at 0 min 87% B
	at 25 min 100% B
Post time	4 min
Flow rate	0.8 ml/min
Column compartment	60°C
Injection volume	1 μl standard

UV absorbance

200 nm and 215 nm to detect triglycerides

240 nm to detect hydroperoxides

280 nm to detect tocopherols and decomposed triglycerides (fatty acids with three conjugated double bonds)

HPLC method performance

Limit of detection

for saturated triglycerides	>10 μg
for unsaturated triglycerides	>10 μg
fatty acids with 1 double bond	>150 ng
fatty acids with 2 double bonds	>25 nm
fatty acids with 3 double bonds	<10 ng

Repeatability of

RT over 10 runs	<0.7%
areas over 10 runs	<6%

Fatty Acids

Although gas chromatography is the dominant technique for fatty acid analysis, high-performance liquid chromatography has an important role to play in applications such as the handling of less usual samples, avoidance of degradation of heat-sensitive functional groups, and for micro-preparative purposes.

Sample Preparation and Chromatographic Conditions

The principles of the separation are well known, and the instrumentation is straightforward. The stationary phases used are almost exclusively of the octadecylsilyl ("ODS") type, with an octyl phase being recommended occasionally as an alternative. The mobile phase is either acetonitrile (mainly) or methanol containing some water. If free fatty acids are analysed, a little acetic acid can be added to ensure sharp peaks. These solvents are transparent to UV light at 205 to 210 nm, so UV detection at such wavelengths can be employed. However, much greater sensitivity is possible if phenacyl or related derivatives of fatty acids are prepared for detection at higher wavelengths. Then, the detector responds only to the ester moiety giving a quantitative molar response. Astonishing sensitivity is obtainable, down to femtomole levels, by using specific derivatives with fluorescence detection although quantification then presents problems.

In reversed-phase HPLC, fatty acids are separated both by chain length and by degree of unsaturation. The first double bond reduces the effective chain length by a little less than 2 carbon units, so an 18:1 fatty acid elutes just after 16:0. Second and further double bonds have smaller effects on retention so an 18:3 fatty acid elutes just before 14:0, for example. A separation of a standard mixture of fatty acids, as phenacyl esters, is illustrated in Figure 11.2.

Amino Acids

Amino acid analysis is used to quantitatively determine the amino acid composition of a protein. Amino acid analysis is widely applied in research, clinical facilities, and industry. In industry, it is used for quality control of products ranging from animal feed to protein pharmaceuticals.

Sample Preparation and Chromatographic Conditions

The protein sample is first hydrolyzed to release the amino acids. There are two major categories for amino acid analysis *i.e.* free amino acid analysis and determination of total amino acid content. Total amino acid content includes contributions from the free amino acids and the amino acids that are originally protein bound. These protein bound amino acids must first be liberated before chromatographic analysis. Amino acids are then separated using

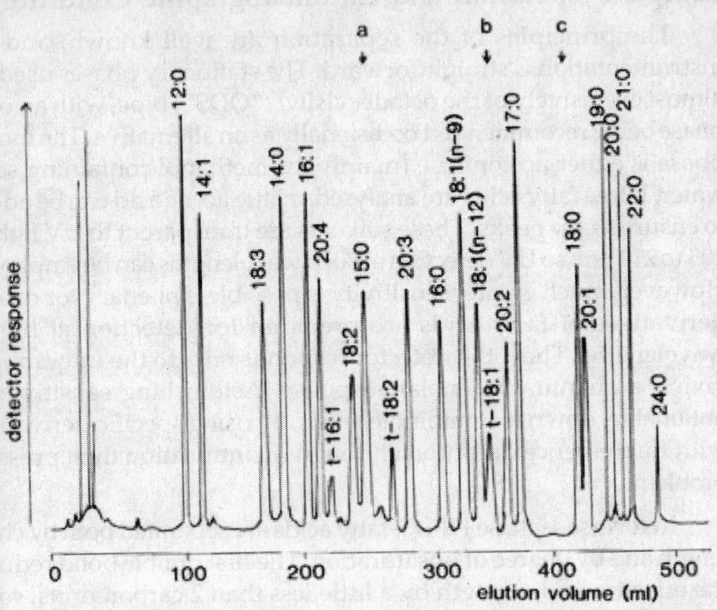

Figure 11.2: Separation of a Standard Mixture of Fatty Acids in the Form of the Phenacyl Esters by Reversed-Phase HPLC with Spectrophotometric Detection at 254 nm. The column (900 x 6.4 mm) was packed with µ-Bondapak C-18, and was eluted with acetonitrile-water in the proportions 76:33 (by volume) initially, changed to 74:26 at "a", to 4:1 at "b", and to 97:3 at "c", at a flow rate of 2 ml/min.

chromatographic techniques and quantified. Ion exchange chromatography, reversed-phase liquid chromatography, and gas liquid chromatography are three separation techniques and are commonly used.

The analysis of a polypeptide typically involves four steps: hydrolysis (or deproteination with physiological samples), separation, derivatization, and detection. Hydrolysis breaks the peptide bonds and releases free amino acids, which are then separated by side-group using column chromatography. Derivatization with a chromogenic reagent enhances the separation and spectral properties of the amino acids, and is required for sensitive detection. Pre-column derivatization is required for amino acid analysis. Dansyl chloride (5-dimethylamino-1-naphthalene sulphonyl chloride) is frequently used for this purpose, producing fluorescent dansyl derivatives that are separated by a reversed phase column chromatographic procedure. The column employs silica gel with attached non-polar hydrocarbon functional groups (*e.g.*, octadecyl moieties) as the stationary phase and uses a multi-step non-linear elusion procedure. Among other eluents, acetonitrile and water mixtures have been suggested for the separation of dansylated amino acids. These are then detected and measured by a fluorescence detector, which can provide detection limits in the picogram range. It has been demonstrated that HPLC, utilizing various non-polar stationary phases, is superior to ion-exchange chromatography for separating peptides.

Vitamins

Vitamins are biologically active compounds that act as controlling agents for an organism's normal health and growth. The level of vitamins in food may be as low as a few micrograms per 100 g. Vitamins often are accompanied by an excess of compounds with similar chemical properties. Thus not only quantification but also identification is mendatory for the detection of vitamins in food. Vitamins generally are labile compounds that should not be exposed to high temperature, light or oxygen. HPLC separates and detects these compounds at room temperature and blocks oxygen and light. Though the use of spectral information, UV-visible diode-array detection yields qualitative as well as quantitative data. Another highly sensitive and selective HPLC method for detecting vitamins is electrochemical.

Water Soluble Vitamins

The application of HPLC to the determination of water-soluble vitamins in foods has received far less attention than is the case with the fat-soluble vitamins.

HPLC method presented in the Table 11.2 for analysis of water soluble vitamins like thiamine, riboflavin, niacin and ascorbic acid in different foods.

Table 11.2: HPLC Systems for Analysis of Water Soluble Vitamins

Compound Determined	*Type of Sample*	*Sample Preparation*	*Stationary Phase*	*Mobile Phase (Proportions by Volume)*	*Detector*
Thiamine	Meat, potatoes	Extract with 0.25 M H_2SO_4, heat at 120°C incubate with takadiastase, incubate with papain, add trichloroacetic acid, heat and filter	20-30 μm silica gel	0.1 M phosphate buffer (pH 6.8) ethanol (90:10)	Post-column oxidation with potassium ferricyanide, flourescence, ex. 362 nm, em. 464 nm
Thiamine	Rice and rice products	Extract with 0.05 M H_2SO_4, autoclave. Incubate with takadiastase and papaion	μ-Bondapak C_{18}	Methanol-acetic acid-water (39:1:60) + 25 ml each of PICA and PIC7	UV 254 nm
Riboflavin	Components of meal	Extract with 0.125M H_2SO_4, autoclave, incubate with takadiastase (pH 4.6), filter	10 μm silica gel	0.1 M sodium acetate buffer, pH 4.6	Fluorescence ex. 457 nm em. 510 nm
Riboflavin	Rice and Rice products	Extract with 0.05 M H_2SO_4, autoclave, incubate with takadiastase + papain (pH 4.5), filter	μ-Bondapak C_{18}	Methanol-acetic acid-water (39:1:60) plus 25 ml each of PIC5 and PIC7	UV 254 nm
Niacin	Rice	Extract with 0.05M H_2SO_4, autoclave, incubate with takadiastase + papain, filter	μ-Bondapak C_{18}	Methanol-acetic acid-water (39:1:60) + 25 ml each PIC5 and PIC7	UV 254 nm

Contd...

Table 11.2–Contd...

Compound Determined	*Type of Sample*	*Sample Preparation*	*Stationary Phase*	*Mobile Phase (Proportions by Volume)*	*Detector*
Niacin	Foods	Extract with 0.125 M H_2SO_4, autoclave, incubate with takadiastase, treat with papain + trichloroacetic acid, centrifuge	10 µm Merckosorb SI 60	Acetate buffer containing 2.72% (m/v) sodium acetate and 1.2% (m/v) acetic acid	React with cyanogens bromide and p-amino aceto-phenone, fluorescence detection ex. 435 nm em. >500 nm
Ascorbic acid	Fruits, fruit juice, infant formula	Extract with 6% meta-phosphoric acid, homogenize, filter	µ-Bondapak C_{18}	Methanol-water (50:50, v/v) with 10^{-3} M tridecylammonium formate (pH 5.0)	UV 254 nm
Ascorbic acid	Fruits, infant foods, milk	Extract with 3% meta-phosphoric acid + 8% acetic acid, centrifuge, dilute with $5x10^{-2}$ M perchloric acid	LiChrosorb RP 18	Methanol -$8x10^{-2}$M acetate buffer + 10^{-3} M tlridecylamine (15:85, v/v), pH 4.5	Electro-chemical with carbon paste electrode at 800 mV versus Ag/AgCl electrode

Fat Soluble Vitamins

Fat soluble vitamins such as vitamin A, D, E and K have been analyzed by HPLC method. Vitamin A activity is shared by a number of compounds of which retinol, retinyl-esters and retinaldehyde are the most important for the food analyst. Certain carotenoids also possess vitamin A activity and of these β–carotene is the most widespread and biologically most active.

Retinol and its Derivatives

The use of HPLC for the determination of retinol is a vast improvement on the older methods. Owing to the extreme sensitivity of retinol to oxidation, it is important that all manipulations be performed in the absence of oxygen and shielded from direct sunlight and from the light of fluorescent lamps.

The HPLC method presented here is used to analyze vitamin A (retinol) in milk and milk based infant formula.

Sample Preparation and Chromatographic Conditions

Transfer 40 ml of ready-to-feed formula or fluid milk into a 100-ml digestion flask. Add 10 ml of ethanolic pyrogallol solution (2% pyrogallol in 95% ethanol) and saponify with ethanolic KOH (10% KOH in 90% ethanol) at room temperature for 18 hr or at 70°C using the reflux vessel.

Extraction of Digest- Pipette 3 ml digest into 15 ml centrifuge tube and add 2 ml of water. Extract with 7 ml hexane-diethyl ether (85 + 15). Repeat extraction 2x with 7ml portions of extractant. Pool extracts in a 25 ml volumetric flask. Add 1 ml of hexadecane solution [hexadecane + hexane (1+100)] and dilute to volume with hexane. Pipette 15 ml of diluted extract into a centrifuge tube and evaporate under nitrogen. Dissolve residue in 0.5 ml of heptane.

Chromatography Parameters

Column	15 cm x 4.5 mm packed with 3 mm silica (Apex 3 µm silica)
Mobile Phase	Isocratic, heptanes, and isopropanol (1-5%)
Detection	UV, 340 nm
Flow Rate	1-2 ml/min

(Exact mobile phase composition and flow rate are determined by system suitability test to give retention times of 4.5 and 5.5 min for 13-cis-retinol and all-trans-retinol, respectively).

Provitamin A carotenoids

Carotenoids may be extracted from dry samples by water immiscible solvents, whereas for wet samples water-miscible solvents such as mixture of acetone and methanol are used. Carotenes may be re-extracted from aqueous acetone extracts into chloroform or hexane in order to eliminate the water, which is difficult to remove the evaporation. Carotenoids have also been extracted from fruit juices by filtration through magnesium oxide which will absorb the pigments. Saponification is generally used to remove unwanted lipid material and is usually performed at room temperature with methanolic potassium hydroxide.

The HPLC method presented here for the analysis of α and β–carotenes in orange juice and tomatoes.

HPLC System Used for α and β-carotenes Determination

Compound Determined	*Type of Sample*	*Sample Preparation*	*Stationary Phase*	*Mobile Phase (Proportions by Volume)*	*Detection Wavelength (nm)*
α and β-carotenes	Orange juice	Absorb on magnesia extract, saponify, extract	Magnesia	n-Hexane-acetone gradient (99:1 to 80:20)	440
β-carotene	Tomatoes	Extract with acetone, saponify, extract	Partisil P X S 5/ ODS	Chloroform-acetonitrile (8:92)	470

Vitamin D

Vitamin D_3 (cholecalciferol) is the major form of vitamin D present in animal products but vitamin D_2 (ergocalciferol) may also be present in fortified food products. HPLC method has been used for such samples as fortified milk, margarine, butter, cod-liver oil and other fish products.

Sample Preparation and Chromatographic Conditions

Methods generally involve extraction, hydrolysis and sample clean-up before HPLC analysis. Hydrolysis (saponification with ethanolic potassium hydroxide) of the sample should precede the extraction. Saponification serves the purpose of freeing the vitamin D from the sample matrix and eliminating the bulk of the lipids, but further purification is usually needed before HPLC is applied. Purification by HPLC has the advantage that the resolution is much higher than with other older column chromatographic methods and retention volumes are more constant.

In application to food samples both normal and reversed-phase was able to resolve vitamins D_2 and D_3 with the result that methods which use absorption chromatography make no distinction between vitamin D_2 and D_3 and will report the total amount if both are present. Vitamin D_2 and D_3 may be separated from their corresponding pore-vitamins on most reversed phase or normal phase systems. Both vitamin D_2 and vitamin D_3 have absorption maxima at 265 nm which can be used for detection with variable wavelength detectors but owing to the inherent greater stability of fixed wavelength detectors, lower detection limit (1 ng vitamin D) may be obtained at their operating wavelength of 254 nm even though this is shifted from the absorption maximum.

The HPLC method presented here for the analysis of vitamin D_2 and D_3 in fortified milk and cod liver oil.

HPLC System Used for Vtamin D Determination

Compound Determined	*Type of Sample*	*Sample Preparation*	*Stationary Phase*	*Mobile Phase (Proportions by Volume)*	*Detection Wavelength (nm)*
Vitamin D_2, D_3	Fortified milk	Saponify at room temperature, extract, HAPS chromatography	5 µm LiChrosorb SI 60	Propan-2-o1-hexane (1: 99)	265
Vitamin D	Cod liver oil	Saponify at 70°C, extract, ppt with digitonin, Florex XXS chromatography	Partisil 10 Px S	Chloroform-hexane-acetic acid (70:30:1)	268

Vitamin E

Vitamin E, as it occurs naturally consists of eight compounds which belong to two series of methyl-substituted chromanols, with either a saturated (the tocopherols) or unsaturated (the tocotrienols) side chain in the two positions. Each of these compounds have different vitamin E activities and antioxidant properties.

The HPLC method presented here is used to analyze tocopherols and tocotrienols in rice bran oil.

Sample Preparation and Chromatographic Conditions

General food products: Add 10 ml of 6% (w/v) pyrogallol in ethanol to sample, mix, and flush with N_2. Heat at 70°C for 10 min with sonication. Add 2 ml 60% KOH solution, mix, and flush with N_2. Digest for 30 min at 70°C. Sonicate 5 min. Cool to room temperature and add sodium chloride and water. Extract with hexane (0.1% BHT) three times. Combine hexane extracts. Add 0.5 g of $MgSO_4$ and mix. Filter through a Millipore filtration apparatus (0.45 μm). Dilute to volume with hexane and inject 20 μl sample.

Margarine and vegetable oil spreads: Add 40 ml of hexane (0.1% BHT) to a 10 g sample and mix. Add 3 g of $MgSO_4$, mix, let it stand for 2 hr. Filter and dilute combined filtrate to volume with hexane (0.1% BHT) and inject 20 μl sample.

Chromatography Parameters

Column	Hibar RT, Lichrosorb S160 5 μm, 25.0 cm x 4.6 mm
Mobile Phase	0.9% isopropanol in hexane
Flow	1 ml/min
Detector	Fluorescence, ex. = 290 nm, em. = 330 nm

Preservatives, Artificial Sweeteners, Colorants and Flavours

Preservatives

Preservatives such as benzoic acid, sorbic acid, propionic acid, methyl-, ethyl-, and propylesters of p-hydroxy benzoic acid etc. inhibit microbial growth in foods and beverages. Various compound classes of preservatives are used, depending on the food product and the expected microorganism. PHBs are the most common preservatives in food products. In fruit juices, in addition to sulfur dioxide, sorbic and benzoic acid are used as preservatives, either individually or as a mixture.

Sample Preparation and Chromatographic Conditions

Sample preparation depends strongly on the matrix to be analyzed. For samples low in fat, liquid extraction with ultrasonic bath stimulation can be used. For samples with more complex matrices, solid-phase extraction, liquid/liquid extraction, or steam distillation may be necessary. HPLC and UV-visible diode-array detection (detection wavelength 260/40 nm) have been applied in the analysis of preservatives like benzoic acid, sorbic acid, propionic acid, PHB-methyl and PHB-propyl in food and beverages like white wine and salad dressing.

Artificial Sweeteners

Nowadays, low-calorie sweeteners are widely used in foods and soft drinks. Investigations of the toxicity of these compounds have raised questions as to whether they are safe to consume. As a result, their concentration in foods and beverages is regulated through legislation in order to prevent excessive intake.

Sample Preparation and Chromatographic Conditions

For sample preparation, same procedure as in case 7 preservatives may be used for artificial sweetners *i.e.* aspartome, saccharin and acesulfam. The HPLC method for the analysis of aspartame is based on automated on-column derivatization and reversed-phase chromatography. Detectors- UV-DAD (detection wavelength 338/20 nm) or fluorescence excitation wavelength 230 nm, emission wavelength 445 nm.

Colorants

Synthetic colors are widely used in the food processing, pharmaceutical, and chemical industries. The regulation of colors and the need for quality control requirements for traces of starting product and by-products have forced the development of analytical methods. Nowadays, HPLC methods used are based on either ion-pairing reversed-phase or ion-exchange chromatography. UV absorption is the preferred detection method. The UV absorption maxima of colors are highly characteristic. Maxima start at approximately 400 nm for yellow colors, 500 nm for red colors, and 600-700 nm for green, blue, and black colors. For the analysis of all colors at maximum sensitivity and selectivity, the light output from the detector lamp should be high for the entire wavelength range. However, this analysis is not possible with conventional UV-visible detectors based on a one-lamp design. Therefore, dual-lamp design based on one deuterium and one tungsten lamp is generally chosen. This design ensures high light output for the entire wavelength range.

Sample Preparation and Chromatographic Conditions

Turbid samples require filtration, solid samples must be treated with 0.1% ammonia in a 50% ethanol and water mixture, followed by centrifugation. Extraction is then performed using the so-called wool-fiber method. After desorption of the colors and filtration, the solution can be injected directly into the HPLC instrument.

Flavors

Three major classes of compounds are used as flavoring agents: essential oils, bitter compounds, and pungency compounds. Although the resolution afforded by gas chromatography (GC) for the separation of flavor compounds remains unsurpassed, HPLC is the method of choice if the compound to be analyzed is low volatile or thermally unstable.

Sample Preparation and Chromatographic Conditions

In this case also turbid samples require filtration, whereas solid samples must be extracted with ethanol. After filtration, the solution can be injected directly into the HPLC instrument.

Residues and Contaminants

Residues of Chemotherapeutics and Antiparasitic Drugs

In addition to several other drugs, nitrofurans and sulfonamides such as sulfapyridine, N-acetyl metabolite, chloramphenicol, meticlorpindol, metronidazol, ipronidazol, furazolidone, and nicarbazin are frequently fed to domestic cattle.

Modern intensive animal breeding demands permanent suppression of diseases caused by viruses, bacteria, protozoan, and/or fungi. A number of chemotherapeutics are available for the prevention and control of these diseases. After application, residues of these drugs can be found in foods of animal origin such as milk, eggs, and meat. These chemotherapeutics can cause resistancy of bacteria. Because of the toxic nature of chemotherapeutics, for example, chloramphenicol, government agencies in many countries, including the United States, Germany, and Japan, have set tolerance levels for residues of these drugs.

Sample Preparation and Chromatographic Conditions

Simple and reliable analysis methods are necessary in order to detect and quantify residues of chemotherapeutic and antiparasitic drugs in food products. After homogenization or mincing and pH adjustment, the samples are extracted using liquid/liquid extraction followed by degreasing, purification, and concentration.

HPLC method for analysis of residues of drugs in eggs, milk, and meat is based on reversed-phase chromatography and multisignal UV-visible diode-array detection (UV-DAD).

Mycotoxins

Mycotoxins are highly toxic compounds produced by fungi. They can contaminate food products when storage conditions are favorable to fungal growth. These toxins are of relatively high molecular weight and contain one or more oxygenated alicyclic rings. The analysis of individual mycotoxins and their metabolites is difficult because more than 100 such compounds are known, and any individual toxin is likely to be present in minute concentration in a highly complex organic matrix. Most mycotoxins are assayed with thin-layer chromatography (TLC). However, the higher separation power and shorter analysis time of HPLC has resulted in the increased use of this method. The required detection in the low parts per billion (ppb) range can be performed using suitable sample enrichment and sensitive detection.

Sample Preparation and Chromatographic Conditions

Samples were prepared according to official methods. Different sample preparation and HPLC separation conditions must be used for the different classes of compounds. The HPLC method for the analysis of mycotoxins in nuts, spices, animal feed, milk, cereals etc. is based on reversed-phase chromatography, multisignal UV-visible diode-array detection, and fluorescence detection.

Chapter 12

Atomic Spectroscopy

Introduction

Atomic spectroscopy is the technique of analyzing the energy emitted by atoms in order to determine the energy levels of the atom's electrons. Electrons can have only certain discrete energies. These energies are characteristic of each element; that is, every atom of an element has the same set of available energies. Normally, electrons in atoms are distributed in the lowest energy levels. This is called the "ground state" of the atom. If energy is added to the atom in the form of light, heat, or electricity, the electrons can move to a higher energy level. The electrons are said to be in an "excited" state. When the electrons return to their ground state distribution, they emit the excess energy in the form of light. The light carries the energy that is the difference between one energy level and another. The distribution of light energies is called a spectrum. The study of spectra is called spectroscopy. When light is emitted from an atom, the different colours of light can be seen after they are separated by a device like a prism or a diffraction grating. A line spectrum is very useful in identifying an element because no two elements have the same line spectrum.

In atomic absorption spectroscopy measurement is made of the radiation absorbed by the nonexcited atoms in the vapour state. In emission spectroscopy, measurement is made of energy emitted when atoms in the excited state return to the ground state.

Three important methods based on spectroscopy of atomic species are:

1. Flame Emission Photometry (FEP)
2. Atomic Absorption Spectrophotometry (AAS)
3. Inductively Coupled Plasma Atomic Emission Spectrometry (ICPAES)

1. Flame Emission Photometry (FEP)

Principle

Flame emission spectroscopy is a special area of emission spectroscopy in which a flame is used to excite the atoms. Flame emission techniques usually involve introduction of a sample solution in aerosol form into a flame. Solvent evaporation and vaporization of the salt occur prior to dissociation of the salt into free gaseous atoms. At the temperature of an air/acetylene flame (~2300°C) atoms of many elements exist largely in the ground state. When a beam of radian energy that consists of the emission spectrum for the element that is to be determined is passed through the flame, some of the ground state atoms absorb energy of characteristic wavelength (resonance lines) and are raised to a higher energy state. The radiant energy emitted when the atoms return to the ground state is proportional to the concentration and is the basis of flame emission spectroscopy. For example, at 589 nm,

$$Na \longrightarrow Na^* \text{ (energy from flame)}$$

$$Na^* \longrightarrow Na + h\nu \text{ (at 589 nm)}$$

The emitted radiant energy from flame emission is isolated by a monochromators and detected by a photomultiplier.

Theory

1. Sample solution sprayed or aspirated as fine mist into flame. Conversion of sample solution into an aerosol by atomiser (scent spray) principle. No chemical change in the sample in this stage. [NB atomiser does not convert anything into atoms].

2. Heat of the flame vaporizes sample constituents. Still no chemical change.
3. By heat of the flame + action of the reducing gas (fuel), molecules and ions of the sample species are decomposed and reduced to give atoms. *e.g.* $Na^+ + e^- \rightarrow Na$
4. Heat of the flame causes excitation of some atoms into higher electronic states.
5. Excited atoms revert to ground state by emission of light energy, hν, of characteristic wavelength; measured by detector. Flame spectra are mainly composed of ground state transitions, while higher energy sources give rise to transitions between excited states.

Atoms in the vapour state give line spectra (Not band spectra, because no covalent bonds hence no vibrational sub-levels to cause broadening). Coloured glass filter usually are able to isolate the line of analyte element if well separated from other emission lines. *e.g.* to measure sodium and potassium separately in samples containing both.

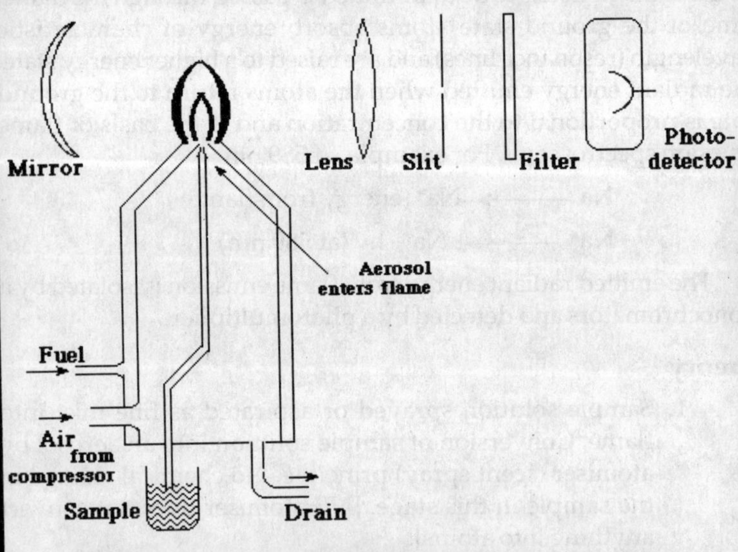

Figure 12.1: Schematic Diagram of Flame Photometer

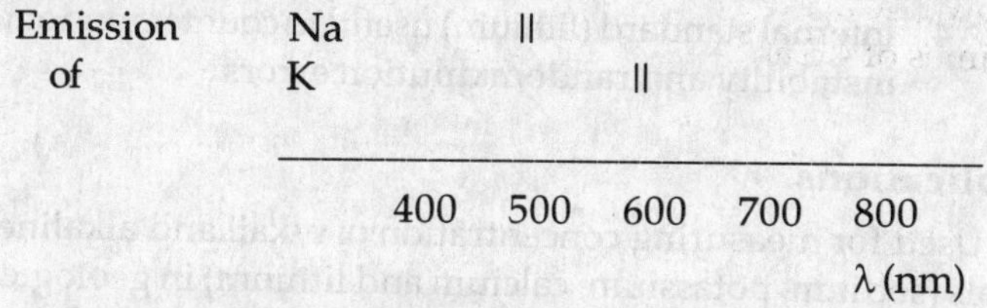

Atomic emission analyses are most commonly and routinely performed on solutions. Therefore the sample must be converted to liquid form prior to analysis. This is most conveniently done using a microwave to digest the sample, leaving a solution that can then be analyzed. There must be a sufficient concentration of analyte for the spectrometer to detect. Prior to performing atomic emission analysis, it is necessary to determine the minimum detection limit for the element of interest. The minimum quantifiable limit (the lowest concentration of analyte which can be quantitatively determined) is generally 3-5 times the minimum detection limit.

Flame photometry is largely an empirical method and is sensitive to experimental conditions. The signal intensity from a flame is dependent on the flame temperature, the rate of flow of liquid into the flame, the pressure and rate of flow of fuel gases, and any of many other variables which affect the character of the flame or atomizing of the sample. Thus, the compounds in which the ion is found and the viscosity of the solution have a great effect. A consequence of this situation is that reliable results can be obtained only after painstaking attention to details, with repeated checks of reproducibility and the effects of altering conditions.

Experimental Aspects of Flame Photometry

1. Propane-air or natural gas-air gives good flame *i.e.* strong heat and minimal background light emission. It is important to run a solvent blank for setting zero emission.
2. Solutions are diluted to fall within linear part of emission curve and can be calibrated with standards accordingly (*e.g.* from 0.05 -0.25 mM Na^+).
3. Anion and cation interference effects can cause errors (enhancement or suppression). "Radiation buffer" for dilution of standards and samples to swamp out inconsistencies.

4. Internal standard (lithium) useful to counter random flame instability and random dilution errors.

Applications

Used for measuring concentration of alkali and alkaline earth metals (sodium, potassium, calcium and lithium) in geological and agricultural soil testing, pollution monitoring and control, food and beverage testing and cement. In addition, it is also used to measure the concentration of the alkali and alkaline earth metals in coal, chemicals, ash, fuel and greases, crude oil, glass, acids, pharmaceutical and other industries. The method has also been applied, with varying degree of success, to determine of perhaps half the elements in the periodic table.

Sodium and potassium ions play an important role in a number of biological systems and their functions. Since these ions form few insoluble compounds and exhibit essentially no acidic or basic properties, they cannot be determined readily by conventional wet chemical techniques and are usually measured instrumentally. The usual techniques employed in determining these ions include atomic absorption spectroscopy (AAS), atomic emission spectroscopy (AES) and ion selective electrodes (ISE). All of these methods require that the sample exist as, or be converted to, an aqueous form. Choosing between the individual methods is based primarily on the sensitivity of the method required as well as the speed and convenience of the method. Since the detection limit for these ions is lowest by AES and AES is simple, this method is generally used for their determination.

2. Atomic Absorption Spectrophotometry (AAS)

Atomic absorption spectroscopy is a technique for determining the concentration of a particular metal element in a sample. The technique can be used to analyze the concentration of over 70 different metals in a solution.

Although atomic absorption spectroscopy dates to the nineteenth century, the modern form was largely developed during the 1950s by a team of Australian chemists. They were led by Alan Walsh and worked at the CSIRO (Commonwealth Science and Industry Research Organization) Division of Chemical Physics in Melbourne, Australia.

Principle

The technique makes use of absorption spectrometry to assess the concentration of an analyte in a sample. It relies therefore heavily on Beer-Lambert Law. The study of absorption spectra by means of passing electromagnetic radiation through an atomic medium that is selectively absorbing; this produces pure electronic transitions free from vibrational and rotational transitions. Atomic absorption methods measure the amount of energy (in the form of photons of light, and thus a change in the wavelength) absorbed by the sample. Specifically, a detector measures the wavelengths of light transmitted by the sample (the "after" wavelengths), and compares them to the wavelengths, which originally passed through the sample (the "before" wavelengths). A signal processor then integrates the changes in wavelength, which appear in the readout as peaks of energy absorption at discrete wavelengths. Any atom has its own distinct pattern of wavelengths at which it will absorb energy, due to the unique configuration of electrons in its outer shell. This allows for the qualitative analysis of a pure sample.

Theory

All atoms and their components have energy. The energy level at which an atom exists is referred to as its state. Under normal conditions, atoms exist in their most stable states. We refer to that most-stable level as the ground state. Although we cannot measure the precise energy state for an atom, we can usually measure changes to its energy relative to its ground state.

Certain processes can change the energy state for an atom. For example, adding thermal energy (heat) can cause an atom to increase to a higher energy state. This change in energy is written as ΔE. We refer to energy states which are higher than the ground state as excited *states*. In theory, there are infinite excited states, however there are decreasing numbers of atoms from a population that reach higher excited states.

The laws of quantum mechanics tell us that atoms do not increase their energy levels gradually. An atom goes directly from one state to another without going through intermediates. We refer to these "quantum leaps" as *transitions*. The transition from the ground state (written as E_o) to the first excited state (E_1) requires some form of energy input. This energy is absorbed by the atom.

That energy *absorption* is equal to $\Delta E_{0\rightarrow 1}$. When this energy absorption takes place in the presence of ultraviolet light, some of that light will be absorbed. This uv absorption occurs at a specific wavelength.

Each element in the periodic table will have a specific D E that will absorb a specific wavelength of uv light. The relationship between the energy transition and the wavelength (l) can be described by

$$\Delta E = h / \lambda$$

where, h is Planck's constant. Atomic absorption uses this relationship to determine the presence of a specific element based on absorption in a specific wavelength. For example, calcium absorbs light with a wavelength of 422.7 nm. Iron absorbs light at 248.3 nm.

In order to tell how much of a known element is present in a sample, one must first establish a basis for comparison using known quantities. It can be done producing a calibration curve. For this process, a known wavelength is selected, and the detector will measure only the energy emitted at that wavelength. However, as the concentration of the target atom in the sample increases, absorption will also increase proportionally. Thus, one runs a series of known concentrations of some compound, and records the corresponding degree of absorbance, which is an inverse percentage of light transmitted. A straight line can then be drawn between all of the known points. From this line, one can then extrapolate the concentration of the substance under investigation from its absorbance. The use of special light sources and specific wavelength selection allows the quantitative determination of individual components of a multielement mixture.

The process of atomic absorption spectroscopy (AAS) involves two steps:

1. Atomization of the sample
2. The absorption of radiation from a light source by the free atoms

The sample, either a liquid or a solid, is atomized in either a flame or a graphite furnace. Upon the absorption of ultraviolet or visible light, the free atoms undergo electronic transitions from the ground state to excited electronic states.

To obtain the best results in AA, the instrumental and chemical parameters of the system must be geared toward the production of neutral ground state atoms of the element of interest. A common method is to introduce a liquid sample into a flame. Upon introduction, the sample solution is dispersed into a fine spray, the spray is then desolated into salt particles in the flame and the particles are subsequently vaporized into neutral atoms, ionic species and molecular species. All of these conversion processes occur in geometrically definable regions in the flame. It is therefore important to set the instrument parameters such that the light from the source (typically a hollow-cathode lamp) is directed through the region of the flame that contains the maximum number of neutral atoms. The light produced by the hollow-cathode lamp is emitted from excited atoms of the same element which is to be determined. Therefore the radiant energy corresponds directly to the wavelength which is absorbable by the atomized sample. This method provides both sensitivity and selectivity since other elements in the sample will not generally absorb the chosen wavelength and thus, will not interfere with the measurement. To reduce background interference, the wavelength of interest is isolated by a monochromator placed between the sample and the detector.

Instrumentation

Atomic absorption spectrometers consist of the following components:

1. Radiation source- usually a hollow cathode lamp
2. Atomizer- uaually a nebulizer-burner system or an electrothermal furnace
3. Monochromator- usually an ultraviolet-visible (UV-Vis) grating monochromator
4. Detector-usually a photomultiplier tube (PMT)
5. Computer

The configration of a single-beam and double-beam atomic absorption spectrometer is illustrated in Figure 12.3 and 12.4. In double-beam instruments, the beam from the light source (hollow cathode lamp) is split by a rotating mirrored chopper into a reference beam and a sample beam. The reference beam is diverted around the sample compartment (flame or furnace) and recombined before

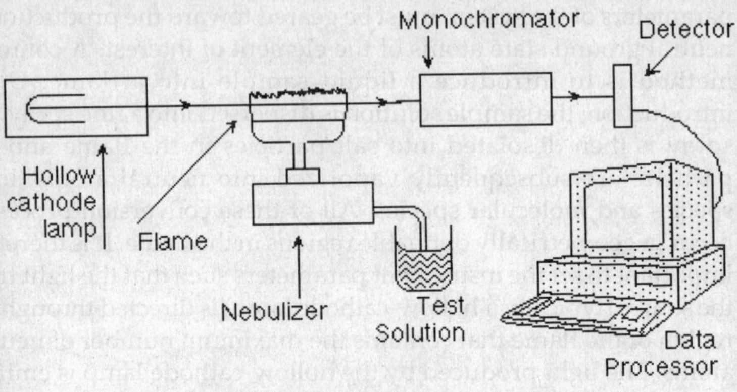

Figure 12.2: Basic AA Spectrometer Setup

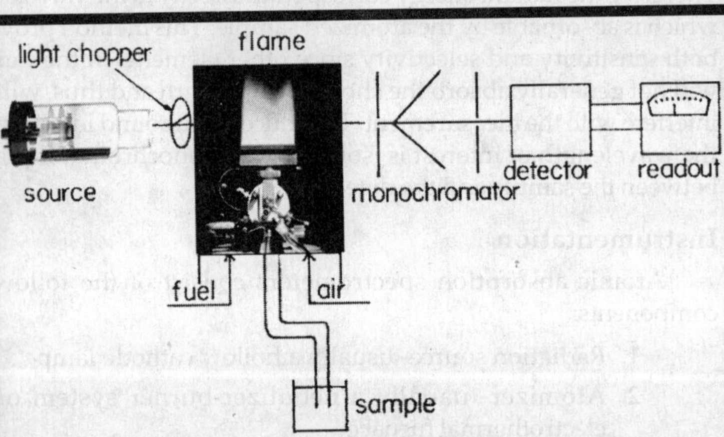

Figure 12.3: Representative Single Beam AA Instrument Setup

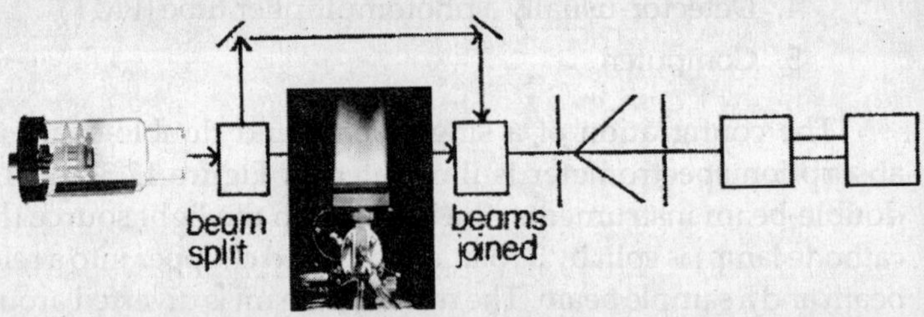

Figure 12.4: Representative Double Beam AA Instrument Setup

passing into the monochromator. The electronics are designed to produce a ratio of the reference and the sample beams. This way, fluctuations in the radiation source and the detector are canceled out, yielding a more stable signal.

The light source, called a hollow cathode tube, is a lamp that emits exactly the wavelength required for the analysis (without the use of a monochromator). The light is directed at the flame containing the sample, which is aspirated by the same method as in FP. The flame is typically wide (4-6 inches), giving a reasonably long pathlength for detecting small concentrations of atoms in the flame. The light beam then enters the monochromator, which is tuned to a wavelength that is absorbed by the sample. The detector measures the light intensity, which after adjusting for the blank, is output to the readout, much like in a single beam molecular instrument. Also as with the molecular case, the absorption behavior follows Beer's Law and concentrations of unknowns are determined in the same way. All atomic species have an absorptivity, a, and the width of the flame is the pathlength, b. Thus, absorbances (A) of standards and samples are measured and concentrations determined as with previously presented procedures, with the use of Beer's Law ($A = abc$).

Double beam instruments are also in use in AA. In this case, however, the second beam does not pass through a second sample container (it's difficult to obtain two closely matched flames). The second beam simply bypasses the flame and is relayed to the detector directly (*See* Figure 12.3). This design eliminates variations due to fluctuations in source intensity (the major objective), but does not eliminate effects due to the flame or other components in the sample (blank components). These must still be adjusted for by reading the blank at a separate time.

Radiation Sources

Hollow Cathode Lamp

As indicated in the previous section, the light source in the AA instrument is called a hollow cathode lamp. As stated before, the light from this lamp is exactly the light required for the analysis, even though no monochromator is used. The reason for this is that atoms of the metal to be tested are present within the lamp, and when the lamp is on, these atoms are supplied with energy, which causes them to elevate to the excited states. Upon returning to the ground state, exactly the same wavelengths that are useful in the analysis are emitted, since it is the analyzed metal with exactly the same energy levels that undergoes excitation. Figure 12.6 is an illustration of this point. The hollow cathode lamp therefore must contain the element being determined. A typical atomic absorption laboratory has a number of different lamps in stock which can be interchanged in the instrument, depending on what metal is being determined. Some lamps are "multielement," which means that several different specified kinds of atoms are present in the lamp and are excited when the lamp is on. The light emitted by such a lamp consists of the line spectra of all the kinds of atoms present. No interference will usually occur as long as the sufficiently intense line for a given metal can be found which can be cleanly separated from all other lines with the monochromator.

The exact mechanism of the excitation process in the hollow cathode lamp is of interest. Figure 12.5 is a close-up view of a typical lamp and of the mechanism. The lamp itself is a sealed glass envelope filled with argon or neon) gas. When the lamp is on, argon atoms are ionized, as shown, with the electrons drawn to the anode (+ charged electrode), while the argon ions, Ar^+, "bombard" the surface of the cathode (-charged electrode). The metal atoms, M, in the cathode are elevated to the excited state and are ejected from the surface as a result of this bombardment.

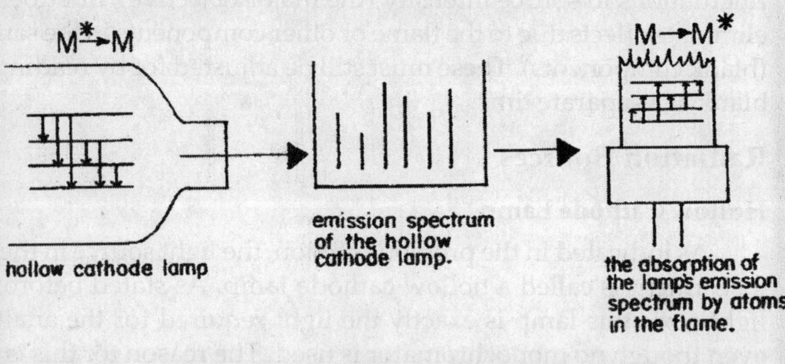

Figure 12.5: Illustration of How the Light Emitted by the Hollow Cathode Lamp is the Exact Wavelength Needed to Excite the Atoms in the Flame

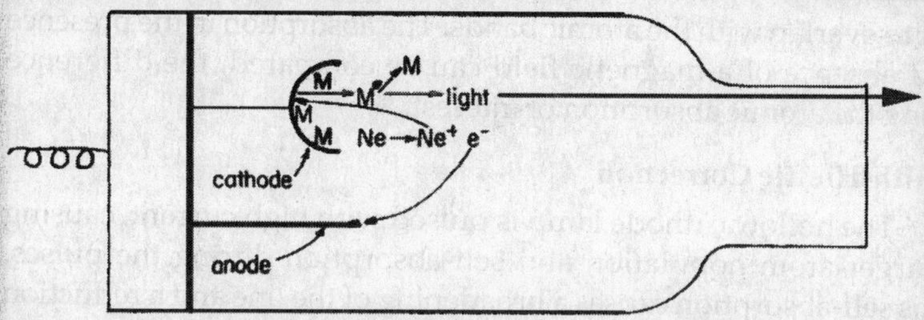

Figure 12.6: The Hollow Cathore Lamp and the Process of Metal Atom Excitation and Light Emission

When the atoms return to the ground state, the characteristic line spectrum of that atom is emitted. It is this light, which is directed at the flame, where unexcited atoms of the same element absorb the radiation and are themselves raised to the excited state. As indicated previously, the absorbance is measured and related to concentration.

Diode Lasers

Atomic absorption spectroscopy can also be performed by lasers, primarily diode laser because of their good properties for laser absorption spectrometry. The technique is then either referred to as diode laser atomic absorption spectrometry (DLAAS or DLAS), or, since wavelength modulation most often is employed, wavelength modulation absorption spectrometry.

Background Correction Methods

The narrow bandwidth of hollow cathode lamps make spectral overlap rare. That is, it is unlikely that an absorption line from one element will overlap with another. Molecular emission is much broader, so it is more likely that some molecular absorption band will overlap with an atomic line. This can result in artificially high absorption and an improperly high calculation for the concentration in the solution. Three methods are typically used to correct for this:

Zeeman Correction

A magnetic field is used to split the atomic line into two sidebands. These sidebands are close enough to the original wavelength to still overlap with molecular bands, but are far enough not to overlap with the atomic bands. The absorption in the presence and absence of a magnetic field can be compared, the difference being the atomic absorption of interest.

Smith-Hieftje Correction

The hollow cathode lamp is pulsed with high current, causing a larger atom population and self-absorption during the pulses. This self-absorption causes a broadening of the line and a reduction of the line intensity at the original wavelength.

Deuterium Lamp Correction

In this case, a separate source (a deuterium lamp) with broad emission is used to measure the background emission. The use of a separate lamp makes this method the least accurate, but its relative simplicity (and the fact that it is the oldest of the three) makes it the most commonly used method.

Comparison of AA and FEP

	AA	*FEP*
Process Measured	Absorption (light absorbed by unexcited atoms in flames)	Emission (light emitted by excited atoms in a flame)
Use of Flame	Atomization	Atomization and excitation
Instrumentation	Light source	No light source (independent of flame)
Beer's Law	Applicable	Not applicable I = kc
Data Obtained	A vs. c	I vs. c

Applications

One of the most important applications in the routine clinical chemistry laboratory is the determination of calcium and magnesium in blood serum and other body fluids. Another group of elements which is frequently determined by AA is copper, iron, and zinc in tissues and body fluids, and total iron- binding capacity.

Another frequently determined element is arsenic, and comparably harsh conditions have to be applied for acid digestion if total arsenic has to be determined. In occupational medicine, however, it is of particular interest to distinguish between the arsenic which originates from the exposure at the workplace, etc. and that which was ingested with marine animals. It was demonstrated that arsenic species relevant in occupational medicine are determined quantitatively in urine by AAS without an acid digestion.

3. Inductively Coupled Plasma Atomic Emission Spectrometry (ICPAES)

Inductively coupled plasma atomic emission spectroscopy (ICP-AES), also referred to as inductively coupled plasma optical emission spectrometry (ICP-OES), is an analytical technique used for the detection of trace metals. It is a type of emission spectroscopy that uses the inductively coupled plasma to produce excited atoms and ions that emit electromagnetic radiation at wavelengths characteristic of a particular element. The intensity of this emission is indicative of the concentration of the element within the sample

Principle

As illustrated in Figure 12.7, atoms emit electromagnetic radiation (hv) as they relax from an excited state to their ground state. The emitted radiation can be easily detected when it is in the vacuum ultraviolet (VUV, 120–185 nm), ultraviolet (UV, 185–400 nm), visible (VIS, 400–700 nm), and near infrared regions (NIR, 700–850 nm). Although atoms emit electromagnetic radiation in the infrared, microwave, and radiowave regions, the detection systems

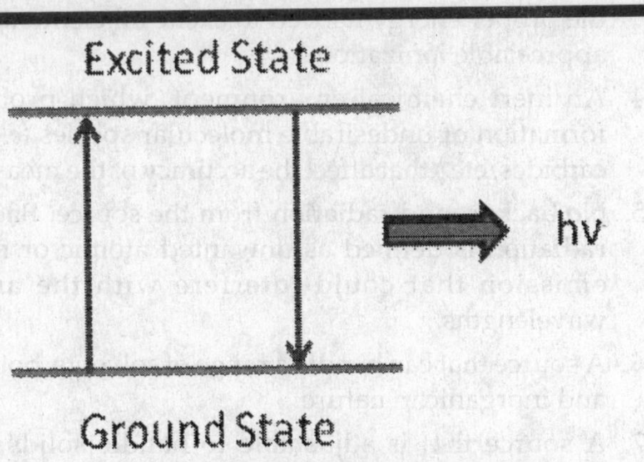

Figure 12.7: Emission of Radiation upon Relaxation from an Excited State

are less sensitive in these regions; therefore, the VUV, UV, VIS, and NIR regions are preferred. Of there only the VUV needs a special environment devoid of air. Nevertheless a portion of the VUV spectrum is used by analytical spectroscopists.

The basic aim of analytical atomic spectroscopy is to identify elements and quantify their concentrations in various media. The procedure consists of three general steps: atom formation, excitation, and emission. Before excitation, an element that is bound in a specific matrix must be separated from that matrix so that its atomic emission spectra is free from interferences. For UV and visible spectroscopy, the input energy must be sufficient to raise an electron from the ground state to the excited state. Once the electron is in the excited state, the atom emits light, which is characteristic of that particular element. This tutorial will compare the inductively Coupled Plasma (ICP) excitation source to other techniques while covering methods of sample interaction, detection and fundamental plasma processes.

The perfect atomic emission source would have the following characteristics:

1. Complete removal of the sample from its original matrix in order to minimize interferences.
2. Complete atomization but minimum ionization of all elements to be analyzed.
3. A controllable energy source for excitation, which allows the proper energy needed to excite all elements without appreciable ionization.
4. An inert chemical environment, which prohibits the formation of undesirable molecular species (*e.g.* oxides, carbides, etc.) that affect the accuracy of the measurement.
5. No background radiation from the source. Background radiation is defined as unwanted atomic or molecular emission that could interfere with the analytical wavelengths.
6. A source that can handle a range of solvents, both organic and inorganic in nature.
7. A source that is adjustable to handle solids, slurries, liquids, or gases.
8. Inexpensive to purchase and maintain.
9. Easy to operate.

Inductively Coupled Plasma-Atomic Emission Spectroscopy (ICP-AES) is one of several techniques available in analytical atomic spectroscopy. ICP-AES utilizes a plasma as the atomization and excitation source. Plasma is an electrically neutral, highly ionized gas that consists of ions, electrons, and atoms. The sun, lightning, and the aurora borealis are examples of plasmas found in nature. The energy that maintains analytical plasma is derived from an electric or magnetic field; they do not "burn." Most analytical plasmas operate with pure argon or helium, which makes combustion impossible. Plasmas are characterized by their temperature, as well as their electron and ion densities. Analytical plasmas typically range in temperature from 600 to 8,000 K. As a comparison, the temperature of the sun's interior is millions of degrees, while its surface temperature is approximately 10,000 K.

Following are the steps involved in determining the elemental content of an aqueous phase sample by ICP-AES:

1. *Sample Preparation*: Some samples require special preparation steps incuding treatment with acids, heating, and microwave digestion.
2. *Nebulization*: Liquid converted to aerosol.
3. *Desolvation/Volatization*: Water is driven off, and remaining solid and liquid portions are converted to gases.
4. *Atomization*: Gas phase bonds are broken, and only atoms are present. Plasma temperature and inert chemical environment are important at this stage.
5. *Excitation/Emission*: Atoms gain energy from collisions and emit light of a characteristic Wavelength.
6. *Separation/Detection*: A grating dispersers light that is quantitatively measured.

Instrumentation

The ICP Torch

The ICP is a radiofrequency-(RF, 27.12 MHz, 40 MHz) induced plasma that uses an induction coil to produce a magnetic field (H). The ICP operates between 1 and 5 kilowatts. The induction coil is wrapped two or three times around the ICP torch and has water flowing through it for cooling purposes. All ICPs have a capacitor bank that is continuously tuned to match the plasma's inductance. In order for the RF to travel along the surface of the hollow coil with minimum resistance, the coil is either gold or silver plated. Neither gold nor silver forms metal oxides upon contact with air. Although the RF power supply maintains the plasma, a tesla coil is used to ignite the plasma through the generation electrons and ions that couple with the magnetic field.

The most common ICP torch in use today has evolved over decades of development (Figure 12.8). The circular quartz tube (12–30 mm OD) has three separate gas inlets. The only gas routinely used is argon. The gas enters the plasma through the outer channel with a tangential flow pattern at a rate of 8–20 L min^{-1}. The auxiliary gas, which travels up the center channel, also has a tangential flow (0.5–3 L min^{-1}) pattern. The nebulizer gas has a laminar flow pattern (0.1 to 1.0 L min^{-1}) and injects the sample into the plasma. The

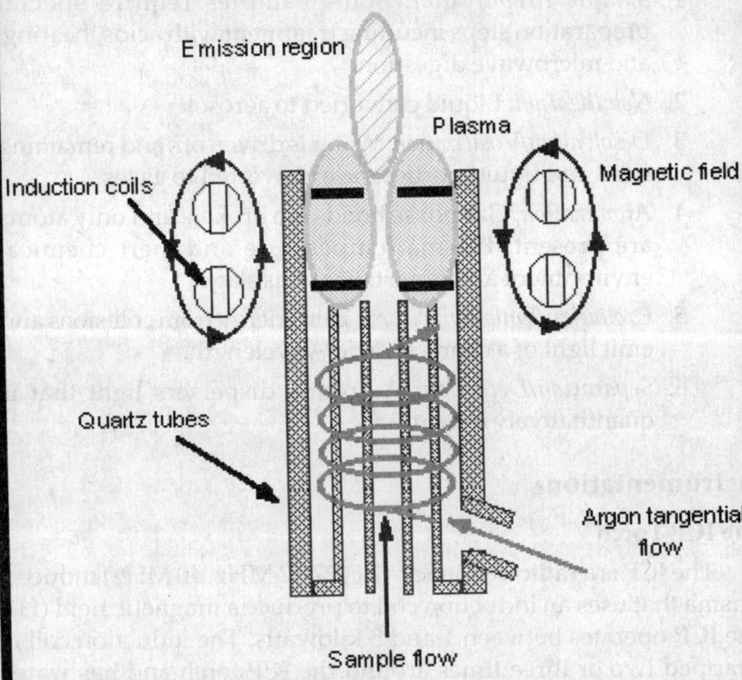

Figure 12.8: Schematic of an ICP Torch

analytical zone is approximately 1 cm above the coils and offers the best optical viewing area for maximum sensitivity. The plasma temperature in the analytical zone ranges from 5000–8000 K (the temperature varies with power, flow rate, etc.). The high temperature assures that most samples are completely atomized, although some molecular species (*e.g.*, N_2, N_2^+, OH, C_2, etc.) do exist and can be readily measured in the plasma.

Sample Introduction

All three states (solid, liquid, gas) have been successfully introduced into an ICP. Although both aqueous and nonaqueous solvents have been utilized, the most commonly analyzed sample is cations in solution. For solutions, a nebulizer is used to convert the liquid stream into an aerosol consisting of particles that are 1–10 mm in diameter. Direct injection of liquids into the plasma would either extinguish the plasma or cause the atoms to be improperly desolvated, making excitation and emission less efficient.

Dispersion and Detection Methods

There are three common devices used for the separation or dispersion of light: gratings, prisms, and Michelson interferometers. There are four basic types of detector systems: photomultiplier tubes (PMTs), photo diode arrays (PDAs), and charge coupled devices (CCDs). These dispersion and detection devices are typically combined in one of four configurations, which vary in sophistication: (1) Sequential; (2) simultaneous with single-point detection; (3) simultaneous with one-dimensional detection; and (4) simultaneous with two-dimensional detection.

Interferences

Any chemical or physical process that adversely affects the measurement of the radiation of interest can be classified as an interference. Interferences in ICP-AES may start in the sample preparation stage and extend to the plasma operating conditions. The first type of common interference involves two or more elements in the matrix emitting radiation at the same wavelength (*e.g.*, Cu at 515.323 nm and Ar at 515.139 nm). These spectral interferences can be minimized by using a high resolution system by using several analytical lines for the detection of a single element. A second type of interference involves the formation of undesired species (*e.g.*, ions, metal oxides). For example, some metals are extremely sensitive to small plasma fluctuations in terms of their relative neutral atom and ion densities. It is important to note that an atom of a specific element (*e.g.*, Fe) has a different emission spectra than one of its ions (*e.g.*, Fe+, Fe+2, etc.). Other interferences, such as the formation of metal oxides or metal carbides, have to be evaluated on an individual basis.

Applications

Examples of the application of ICP-AES include the determination of metals in wine, arsenic in food, and trace elements bound to proteins. In 2008, the technique was used at Liverpool University to demonstrate that a *Chi-Rho* amulet found in Shepton Mallet and previously believed to be among the earliest evidence of Christianity in England, only dated to the nineteenth century.

ICP-AES is often used for analysis of trace elements in soil, and it is for that reason it is often used in forensics to ascertain the origin of soil samples found at crime scenes or on victims etc. Taking one sample from a control and determining the metal composition and taking the sample obtained from evidence and determine that metal composition allows a comparison to be made. While soil evidence may not stand alone in court it certainly strengthens other evidence.

Chapter 13

Multivariate Calibration

Introduction

The multivariate calibration concerns how to get selective quantitative information from non-selective, multivariate chemical data. A mathematical relationship can be established to allow a quantitative determination of one or more variables from measured values of two or more other variables.

The parameters of this relationship or 'model' can be estimated statistically. Calibration is somewhat different from most of the established chemometric pattern recognition techniques, such as the classification and clustering methods. While these latter methods primarily are qualitative and often exploratory, calibration is quantitative and is usually applied to data which are already known to have interrelationships. But the qualitative and quantitative methods do overlap. Calibration methods can be used as an exploratory tool, and outlier detection in calibration can be regarded as a pattern recognition technique.

The method development in this quantitative direction of chemometric pattern recognition has been rather slow. One reason for this may be that calibration for a long time was treated as a statistical, rather than chemical, topic. The statisticians had well-known linear regression methods to offer. Since the traditional statistical regression methods worked reasonably well for simple calibration problems, there was little incentive for ploughing new land, and the number of statistically oriented papers focusing explicitly on multivariate calibration is surprisingly low. The main theoretical debate on calibration during the last 15 years has been on univariate linear modelling, concerning whether to regress instrument response on constituent concentration or vice versa. The two methods are called 'classical' and 'inverse' regression, respectively.

A considerable literature of relevance to multivariate calibration exists in the field of statistical prediction. However, only a few of these statistical prediction methods have been applied to chemical calibration, probably due to the lack of communication between statisticians and chemists.

Chemists have for a long time used univariate linear and non-linear calibration techniques with more or less thorough theoretical understanding of their mathematical foundations. In some applications even simple forms of multivariate calibration have been employed, such as the bivariate determination of protein based on ultraviolet absorbance at two different wavelengths. But new chemical instrumentation and methodologies were developed, for which univariate and bivariate calibrations were unsatisfactory. A variety of multivariate calibration techniques have, therefore, recently been developed.

Some new calibration techniques arose from established chemical concepts for modelling well-known phenomena such as the direct, multicomponent modelling of mixtures (direct and indirect 'unmixing'). Others were generalized from the so-called 'standard addition method' in analytical chemistry. Yet other linear techniques are extensions of more qualitative pattern recognition methods such as the regression on latent variables ('unscrambling'). The non-linear light scatter problems in near-infrared (NIR) reflectance instruments led to other calibration approaches consisting of univariate linear regression on non-linear transformations of the spectral data.

The calibration methods differ in a number of respects, but they all stem from attempts at using measured data that are non-ideal from the analytical chemist's point of view. Their potential is proven by the successful replacement of traditional 'wet chemistry' such as Kjeldahl-nitrogen by high-speed, low-selective multichannel NIR spectrometry in many applications.

Method development and new application of multivariate calibration require chemical knowledge about the samples analysed and the constituents determined, physical knowledge about the instruments and methods used for obtaining the data, mathematical and statistical knowledge about data analysis and, finally, computer knowledge in order to implement new methods in an applicable form.

This chapter is intended for chemists and we want to show how data analysis and multivariate calibration can be used to obtain quantitative information from non-selective measurements. Thus, irrespective of the type of measurement, the problems in data analysis are often quite similar and can be solved by similar methods.

Theory for multivariate calibration will be described in this chapter. Calibration by very restrictive ('hard') methods will be discussed as well as indirect multivariate calibration by 'softer' methods, *i.e.* flexible methods with very mild assumptions about the data generating process. Special emphasis will be placed on Partial Least Squares (PLS) regression. To illustrate various aspects of multivariate calibration, the determination of botanical components from autofluorescence spectra will be used as an example.

The Measurement for One Chemical Constituent

Very few measurements are selective for only the one chemical constituent to be determined. The solvent or other constituents may give similar signals, or they modify the signal of the constituent in question. The former type of interference is typically seen as overlapping peaks in fluorescence spectroscopy or overlapping chromatographic peaks in chromatography. The latter can be exemplified by shifts in the near infrared (NIR) water absorption spectrum resulting from the salt content of the sample. Such chemical interferences can cause serious errors. The term 'chemical interference' is here used for describing systematic errors in the quantitative determination of a certain constituent when these errors are caused by other chemical constituents in the sample. Most chemical samples, at least those of biological origin, are mixtures consisting of several different chemical constituents, and it can be difficult to find measurement conditions that are sufficiently specific for the desired constituent. The traditional approach has been to remove all major interfering constituents prior to the analysis. In some cases, however, this may be prohibitively expensive or physically impossible.

Most measurements are in addition affected by irrelevant physical phenomena. By physical interference in the samples is meant systematic errors in the determination of a chemical concentration caused by physical rather than chemical phenomena. Variations in sample structure, leading to changed light scatter properties in the samples, is an example of such 'physical interference'. As irrelevant physical phenomena in the samples can affect the measured signal strongly, they must be kept constant or compensation must be made for them.

The experimental condition of the actual measurement of the individual sample, such as the temperature of the sample or the instrument at the time of measurement, can often affect the readings. Thus, experimental interference concerns systematic errors due to variation in the way the measurement is made. Very few measuring instruments respond solely to the quality of the sample to be analysed. The condition of the individual samples at the time of measurement, and of the stability of the instrument, can also affect the readings.

In traditional univariate analytical techniques the interferences can cause serious systematic errors, making a certain measurement approach unsuitable for many types of samples. Sometimes interferences can occur unexpectedly to unknown samples. With univariate calibration (and with certain multivariate calibration methods as well) the resulting errors can pass unnoticed and cause grave mistakes. Taking replicates does not reduce or reveal this problem, because every replicate measurement will have the same systematic errors.

To make things worse, the measurement signals seldom change linearly with constituent concentration and, of course, random measurement noise usually contributes significantly to the measured data. These problems create additional difficulties in quantitative chemical analysis.

In analytical chemistry one has to usually rely on indirect measurements. But, like data from all other systems under indirect observations, such data present selectivity problems due to interferences, as we have just seen. Therefore, strict purity control is required if the determination is to be based on conventional univariate calibration.

By data pretreatment on a computer and multivariate data analysis it is often possible to reduce problems of interferences. Random noise can be reduced by digital filtering. Non-linear instrument response can be linearized in the computer and the new multivariate calibration techniques can combine many different measured variables into 'spectra' whose 'harmonic' properties can be analysed mathematically. This can be used to model and hence to eliminate the effects of well-identified, and sometimes even unidentified, interferences. It can also reduce the effect of random errors in the data and increase our understanding of the data and the phenomena which they represent. In addition, multivariate calibration allows automatic discovery of errors due to unexpected interferences, since such errors create a 'disharmony' that can be detected.

One aspect with potential consequence in analytical chemistry is that indirect multivariate calibration allows accurate concentration determinations from highly non-selective measurements. This makes it possible to replace expensive or slow 'wet-chemical' methods by cheaper and more rapid instrumental techniques for routine chemical analysis. The method replaced then just becomes a reference method for the more rapid multivariate instrument.

Multivariate calibration can greatly increase the speed of chemical analysis and allows new types of measurements but the results obtained should, like all analytical results, be regarded with some scepticism. Computerized data analysis can extend, but not replace, human insight and we must accept that some types of measurements do not contain enough information to be useful for quantitative analysis.

The Different Calibration Methods

The different calibration methods can be understood geometrically. One may envisage the multidimensional space having the spectral variables as axes. In this space, the spectrum of each

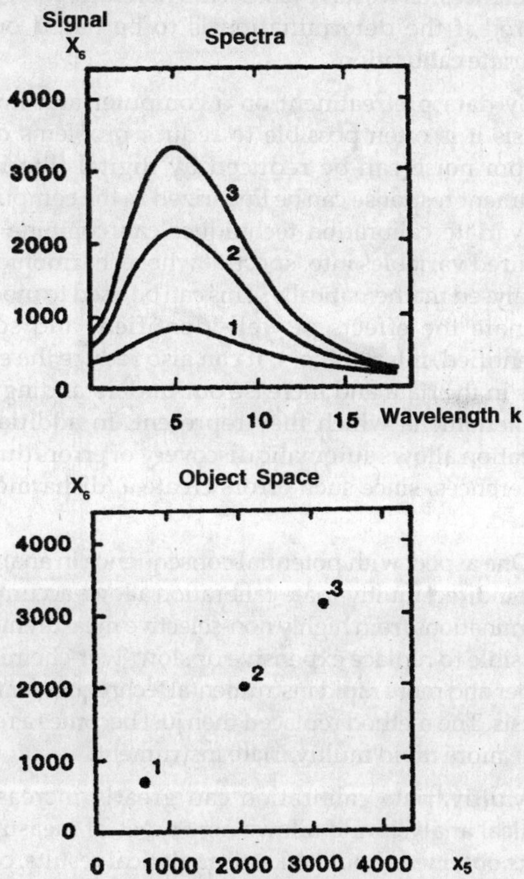

Figure 13.1: For Three Samples (Nos. 1, 2 and 3) Sepctra x_{ik}, $i = 1, 2, 3$ Expressed Versus Wavelength $k = 1, 2, \ldots 18$ and in the Object Space Using Only x_5 and x_6 for Illustration

individual sample (each object) represents a single point. It is therefore, often called the 'object space'. The direct multicomponent analysis described in the previous section requires the explicitly measured spectrum k_j of the constituents to be determined and, in addition, the spectra of all the interferences. These data are used to describe the geometrical locus of constant concentration of the constituent at different levels.

However, the spectra of some interferences cannot be adequately described analytically, either because some chemical constituents interact in the samples and therefore, change their characteristics, or because the instrument response is non-linear. Some types of interferences cannot be isolated for physical or economic reasons, or simply because we do not know that they are present. Indirect calibration then offers an alternative that seems to have quite general applicability.

Compared with the direct calibration approach discussed in the previous section, indirect calibration is more empirical. The modelling is 'softer', *i.e.* flexible and with very mild assumptions about the data-generating process. Indirect calibration requires spectral data x_{ik} from a set of calibration samples $i = 1, 2, \ldots l$, with known concentrations y_{ij} of the constituent in question. These data (x_{ik}, y_{ij}, $i = 1, 2, \ldots l$) are used for 'teaching' the computer how to predict the concentration of the desired constituent, in spite of interferences.

In indirect calibration the predictor, $\hat{Y} = f(X)$, is estimated statistically, based on calibration data from the known or explicitly measured concentrations of the constituents to be determined, Y. This entails computing the 'spectra' of all the main phenomena affecting the spectral input data, X, from the data of the l calibration samples. Neither the spectra nor concentrations of the different interferences need to be measured, as long as the calibration samples are chosen so that these interferences manifest themselves sufficiently well in the X measurements. However, every type of variability that can occur in future samples must be present among the l calibration samples.

Indirect multivariate calibration appears to have much interesting potential, but it requires several different conditions to be satisfied in order to function optimally.

The Indirect Calibration

Indirect calibration concerns the use of a set of samples with known content of the constituent(s) to be determined, so as to obtain a mathematical relationship that selectively converts the measured spectrum x_{ik}, $k = 1, 2, \ldots. K$ to the analyte concentration y_{ij}. The choice of calibration samples therefore, determines what type of unknown samples that can be analysed well with the calibration results obtained.

Two different aspects are important when it comes to choosing calibration samples:

The Calibration Samples must Span All Dimensions

All the main phenomena expected to affect the spectral data X of future unknown samples (the constituent to be determined, as well as the different types of interferences that one is aware of) must vary more or less independently of one another in the set of calibration samples. This is necessary in order for the mathematical calibration algorithm to be able to model and hence, compensate for the different interferences.

The exact levels of the different interference phenomena do not need to be known; it is sufficient that the level of each of them varies to some extent within the calibration set. The interferences must not correlate too strongly with the constituent-in-question nor with each other, unless they also correlate this way in all future samples.

If calibration samples are easily obtained and analysed, one can ensure that all relevant interference phenomena are modelled simply by including a high enough number of randomly selected calibration samples. This is known as 'natural' or 'random' calibration. If, on the other hand, calibration samples are difficult to obtain or expensive to analyse, then one should select the samples according to a more conscious experimental design; this is called 'controlled' calibration.

The Samples' Distribution Should be Representative

If the calibration data are noisy, or if the relationship between the measured spectra and the constituent concentrations cannot be modelled perfectly, linear calibration models give the best results when the model is developed on representative calibration samples. These are samples whose levels of the analyte and of the interferences have the same average variance, and the same intercorrelations, as the population of future unknown samples.

Figure 13.2 explains the main steps involved in many of the indirect multivariate calibration procedures.

One source of imperfection in linear calibration modelling is the existence of non-linear relationships between chemical and spectral data. If they cannot be explicitly linearized prior to the calibration, then the best linear approximation is found around the average sample. Another source of imperfection is the existence of a certain random variation in the relationship between spectra and concentrations either due to measurement noise in the data or to shortcomings in the final calibration model. Næs has shown

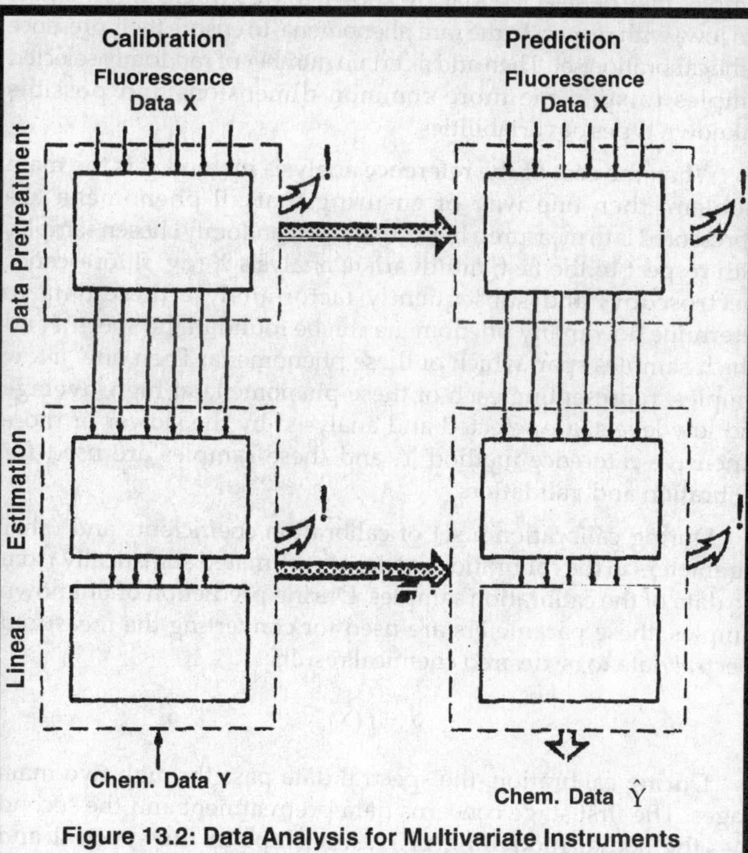

Figure 13.2: Data Analysis for Multivariate Instruments

theoretically that the best prediction results for normal samples in the long run can be obtained by using representatively distributed calibration samples.

The two desired qualities of the calibration samples (spanning all important dimensions of spectral variation, and having representative statistical distribution) can often come into conflict with each other. For instance, to obtain representative distributions of samples in natural calibration it may in some cases be necessary to use a prohibitively high number of calibration samples.

If some types of interferences occur rather seldom, while others are very common, then a mixed type of sampling can be used. Samples may be selected that are known to vary (high, intermediate and low) with respect to the rare phenomena, to ensure their presence in the calibration set. Then add a certain number of randomly selected samples to span the more common dimensions and possible unknown types of variabilities.

When the cost of the reference analysis method *Y* is the main problem, then one way of ensuring that all phenomena are represented is to measure a high number of randomly chosen samples with respect to the fast, multivariate analysis *X* (*e.g.* fluorescence spectroscopy) and subsequently factor-analyse these data to determine how many phenomena can be found in the spectra and which samples span which of these phenomena. Then only a few samples, representing each of these phenomena at high, average and low levels, are selected and analysed by the slower or more expensive reference method Y, and these samples are used for calibration and validation.

During calibration a set of calibration coefficients and other parameters in the calibration model are estimated statistically from the data of the calibration samples. During prediction of unknown samples, these parameters are used for converting the measured spectral data to be desired chemical results:

$$\hat{Y} = f(X)$$

During calibration, the spectral data pass through two main stages. The first stage concerns data pretreatment and the second one, the actual modelling of relationships in the spectral and chemical data.

1. Data pretreatment can be used to 'clean' the data before the multivariate analysis, *e.g.* by smoothing. In addition, various types of transformations are possible. A response linearization of x_{ik}, for instance, makes the spectral data suitable for subsequent linear modelling.

2. The second stage can be divided into data compression and calibration regression. Data compression concentrates all information in the spectral *X*-variables into the most important phenomena [factors $T = (t_1, t_2, \ldots t_A)$] that appear to affect these spectra via a function *w*( ): $T = w(X)$. In calibration regression, the transformed and compressed spectral variables $T = (t_1, t_2, \ldots t_A)$ are used to build a mathematical model that predicts the chemical constituents in question, via some function:

$$\hat{Y} = q\,(T).$$

In some calibration methods, the different phases are performed simultaneously. With scanning NIR instruments data pretreatment, data compression and calibration regression are sometimes performed simultaneously by forming a ratio of spectral derivatives in an iterative manner. In the linear calibration, methods based on extensions of 'Beer's Model' the data compression and parts of the calibration regression are done as one single stage. PLS regression distinguishes between data compression and calibration regression, but allows the two phases to influence each other in order to assure that both are performed optimally. In other methods, all the stages are treated independently.

During subsequent prediction, the parameter values obtained from the various calibration stages are applied to *X*-data from new samples. The measured spectra are passed through similar stages with these parameter estimates, producing statistical estimates of the compressed variables $T = w(X)$ and of the desired constituent's concentration in the last prediction phase ($\hat{Y} = q(T) = q(w(X)) = f(X)$). This can be done on independent samples with known *Y*-levels, to validate the calibration results and to check the optimal degree of complexity of the calibration model. It can then be done to predict the *Y*-level in unknown samples.

Several other types of information are also generated in the calibration and in the predi ion; these can be used for automatic reliability control and for improved understanding. One important aspect of this is the detection of outliers–samples that for some reason do not fit in the same calibration model as the other samples.

An additional stage in the calibration concerns the update of the estimated calibration parameters. At regular intervals some samples with known constituent concentrations must be predicted to validate the calibration results $\hat{Y} = f(X)$, to check that neither the spectral instrument nor the general sample quality has changed since the time of the calibration.

If systematic drift in the analysis is detected by this running evaluation check $(Y - \hat{Y})$, then the calibration parameters can be subjected to minor adjustments to compensate for this. The update can most easily be done by including an extra stage that relates the chemically determined concentration data of control samples to their more or less incorrectly predicted concentrations. This allows future conversion of the incorrectly predicted concentrations to more correct values.

Other relevant variables can also be included in this updating relationship using linear or non-linear regression techniques. This implies an additional multivariate calibration computation that can remove bias, proportional errors, curvature errors, etc., in the final concentration predictions. In this way, the control samples are put to more efficient use than just a yes/no checking of the prediction results. The updated parameters, however, should not be used uncritically; their statistical precision and their relevance must be weighed against those of the old parameters. For instance, it is not correct to ignore a very precise offset, originally estimated on 200 calibration samples, replacing it by a new, but imprecise, offset estimated by the bias from only 10 prediction control samples. On the other hand, if there is unavoidable drift in the instrument or sample quality over time, then the newer results are more relevant than the older ones. A weighted average of the old and the new updated parameters is probably the best alternative, with weights determined by the statistical uncertainties and the relevance of the old and new parameters. Alternative calibration update algorithms have recently been developed.

Multivariate calibration aims at reducing the prediction error by modelling chemical and physical interference phenomena that would otherwise destroy concentration determinations. Each independent interfering phenomenon requires an independent linear factor dimension in the multidimensional calibration model. Even non-linearity phenomena can often be approximated in this way, but again at the cost of extra factors. Why does the prediction error often increase at a certain number of calibration factors? This phenomenon is fundamental to modelling of data and will be discussed in some detail. It concerns statistical aspects of analytical chemistry.

The various statistical methods for indirect multivariate calibration have one problem in common: how to determine the optimal complexity of the calibration model – in other words, how to choose the number of dimensions or regression factors to be used in subsequent predictions?

The Model Complexity in Multivariate Calibration

All methods for indirect multivariate calibration require a choice of model complexity. This depends on the complexity of the samples, the quality of the data and the type of calibration method. In the case of calibration by Stepwise Multiple Linear Regression (SMLR), the model complexity roughly corresponds to the number of wavelengths to be used as regressors (predicting variables). But it is also a function of the number of alternative model choices having been tested and rejected. In PLS regression and other related 'full-spectrum' methods for collinear X-data, it approximates the number of regression factors. Ideally, the computer software should be able to determine this optimum automatically. In practice, outliers and other unexpected difficulties in the data make some human control desirable. This can be done by various model validation techniques such as cross-validation or prediction tests, supplemented with the user's interpretation of model parameters, residuals, etc.

The prediction error can, for simplicity, be regarded as a sum of two main contributions, the remaining-interference error and the uncertainty error. The former is the systematic error due to unmodelled interferences in the spectral data of the prediction samples, while the latter is caused by random measurement noise of various kinds.

The two contributions to the prediction error have opposite trends with increasing complexity of the calibration solution. Provided that the calibration samples are sufficiently representative for the new samples to be predicted, the remaining-interference error should decrease with increasing number of interferences being modelled and hence eliminated. The statistical uncertainty error,

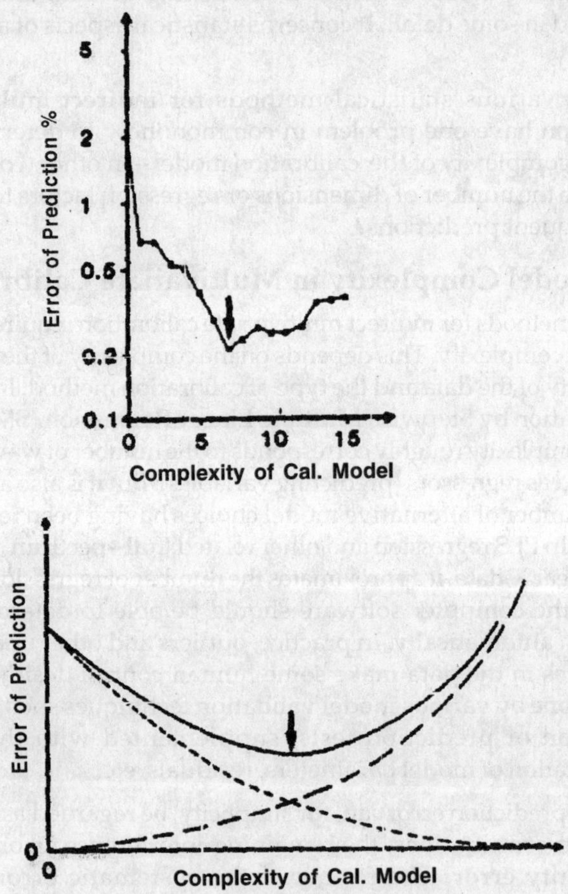

Figure 13.3: Prediction Error as a Function of the Complexity of an Indirect Multivariate Calibration Model

however, increases at the same time due to the increased number of independent model parameters estimated from the more or less noisy data available.

Biological material consists of thousands of chemical constituents with different, but overlapping, fluorescence spectra. How is calibration then possible? Clearly, such spectral data are too complex for univariate modelling using only one wavelength; multivariate calibration is required. But does every constituent require its own statistical parameter? That would require a prohibitive number of calibration samples.

Luckily, there are usually intercorrelations between many interfering constituents, and groups of constituents whose concentrations vary together can be modelled by the same latent variable. Also, many constituents contribute so little to the total spectrum measured that they can be ignored. Thus, only a limited number of main phenomena have to be modelled for a given class of samples in order to eliminate the interferences. This is important because only a limited number of independent parameters can be estimated with precision from a given set of calibration data. Conceptually, minimal prediction error is obtained when the remaining-interference error and the uncertainty error equal each other. Modelling too few interference phenomena is called 'under-fitting' and modelling too many is called 'over-fitting'.

For a given number of spectral variables and calibration samples measured at a given precision, the under-fitting versus over-fitting compromise determines the minimal prediction error and the degree of complexity that yields this minimal prediction error. When the number of interferences is high, the prediction ability cannot be as good as when the number of interferences is low.

Validation of Calibration Modelling

Calibration is an empirical scientific activity requiring action on the basis of incomplete prior insight.

A more or less self-modelling method is used for extracting a calibration model from empirical data. Additional insight can then be gained during the actual calibration and prediction work. However, the combination of incomplete prior physical/chemical knowledge, measurement noise in the calibration data and the human mind's impressive ability to form unwarranted

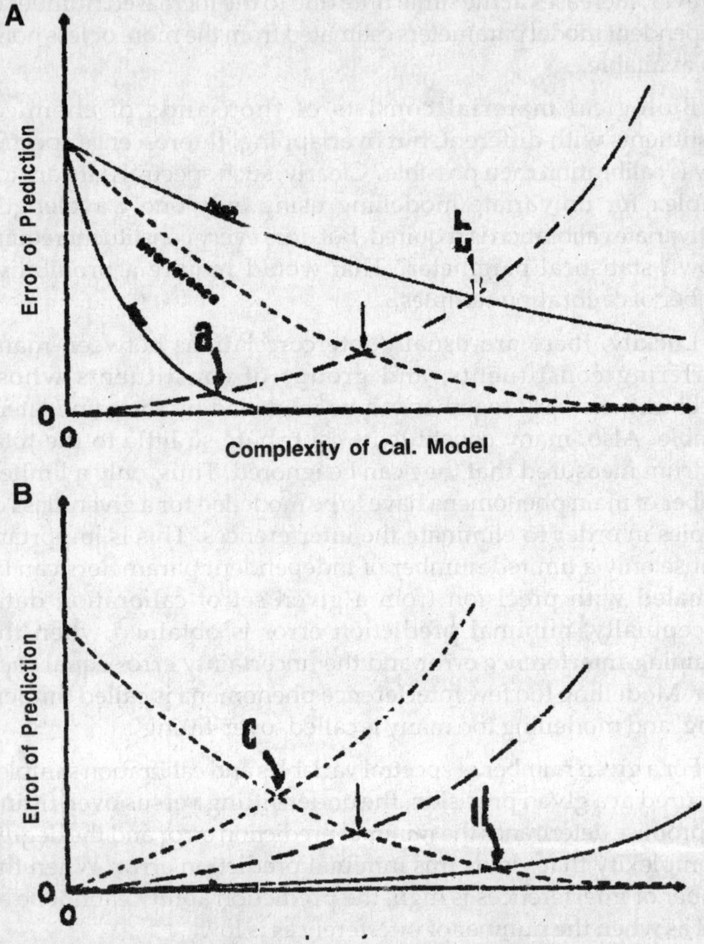

Figure 13.4: The Main Contributions to the Prediction Error, the Remaining-interference and the Random Noise Effect, Expressed as Functions of the Complexity of the Calibration Model

'explanations' from strange observations makes it important to be cautious, guarding against mistaken over-optimism. The calibration modelling must be validated.

One way to validate the results is to try to understand the resulting mathematical model. This is usually easy and sufficient for validation of simple calibration systems with linear relationships and few phenomena. For more complicated problems it is not sufficient, but it is still important. How can it be done?

The PLS regression can be written in terms of function: q( ), *w*( ) and *f*( ) = *q*(*w*( )): $\hat{Y} = f(X) = q(T) = q(w(X))$ where $T = w(X)$. This is a self-modelling process that gradually expands the calibration model in order to describe more and more of the interrelationships in the data. The mechanism for expanding the model is to include an increasing number of PLS factors $t_1, t_2, \ldots, t_a, \ldots$ in T. These PLS factors a = 1, 2,......are intended to describe the various variation phenomena in the spectra X that are relevant to the prediction of information variables Y. These relevant phenomena include the spectral effects directly related to the analytes, as well as physical and chemical effects clearly interfering with these desired effects. The apparently most relevant phenomena are modelled by the first factors; later factors model the less relevant phenomena. The last factors may just model random, irrelevant measurement noise, and these should not be used in the model.

The interpretation problem is first to find possible flaws in the calibration data (outliers). The PLS regression, as implemented in the UNSCRAMBLER program, gives outlier warnings based on various types of abnormalities detected in X and Y. The user has to decide which of the outliers are errors and which are especially informative data.

The next problem is to decide how many factors to accept into the final calibration model. The relevant phenomena have to be modelled, otherwise we get 'under-fitting'. The irrelevant noise phenomena, however, should not be modelled, because this may lead to 'over-fitting', which again decreases the predictive ability of the model. How can we determine A_{opt}, the optimal number of factors?

One way is to look at the successive factors and try to interpret them physically. This may be helpful, but it can be difficult. The successive PLS factors t_a, a = 1, 2, ... span the systematic variabilities or 'subspace' of the relevant phenomena in a mathematically efficient way. However, it is important to note that the individual factor t_a usually does not reflect the effect of a single physical phenomenon.

What it does is to span the contrast between high and low levels of some linear combination of the relevant phenomena.

Therefore, the factor scores t_{ia}, $i = 1, 2, \ldots I$ for factor no. a represent a combined concentration variation around the average composition, and the corresponding loading spectrum $p'_a = (p_{ak}, k = 1, 2, \ldots K)$ represents the difference spectrum between high and low levels of this factor. Consequently, for continuous fluorescence spectra it is useful to look at the loading spectra p'_a for 'acceptable', interpretable features or for 'non-acceptable' noise spikes or random patterns etc. Likewise, 'maps' of scores may give valuable clues to the understanding of what is going on in the spectra. Non-linearities and other unforeseen effects can give rise to important, but odd-looking, PLS loading spectra and score plots, so interpretation alone is not enough.

Another approach to model checking is to look at the lack-of-fit residuals between the data and the model. The PLS regression gives two types of residuals, for X and for Y. The respective residuals after a factors are termed $E_a = X - $ 'TP' and $F_a = Y - TQ'$. These estimated residuals can be assessed statistically in various ways; usually they are squared and summarized for each object i over the variables as well as for each variable k and j over the objects.

The simplest form for 'statistical' assessment is to inspect the residuals to check if 'on the average' they are higher than the noise level known or expected to be present in the input data X and Y, the contrary indicates more or less harmful over-fitting, To be more efficient, such residual inspection ought to be done in a proper statistical way. However, the conventional statistics based on *F*-tests and *t*-tests may not always be appropriate; in part because we do not want to make too strong distributional assumptions, in part because PLS regression is a systems analysis for which exact conventional 'significance' tests have yet to be developed. This is not a problem, however, because the statistical testing can be based instead on the estimated predictive ability of the model, which is the goal of the calibration process anyway.

In order to obtain optimal prediction ability for future samples of the kind calibrated for, only the information of relevance to future prediction should be modelled. Thus, PLS factors describing only measurement noise or other incidental errors pertaining only to the calibration data themselves should be kept out of the model. These irrelevant variabilities should be instead be described by the estimated residuals' *E* and *F* variances and their summary variance statistics.

Thus A_{opt}, the number of factors to be used in the calibration model, has to be decided, based on some estimate of how well the model will predict the *Y*-variables from future *X*-data when different numbers of factors $a = 0, 1, 2, \ldots A_{max}$ are used (Using $a = 0$ factors means representing the calibration data by the average values only).

Ideally, one ought to have a large, representative, independent test set of *N* future samples with known *Y*-levels for this estimation. The mean-square error, estimated variance including bias, in the prediction of *y*-variable no. *j* would then be:

$$V_{yj} = \sum_{i-1}^{I} (y_{ij} - \hat{Y}_{ij})^2 / I$$

It is important that this test set is large and heterogeneous enough to ensure that the predictive ability is really tested. This approach is rather wasteful, because these test samples are not used in the calibration modelling.

A better alternative is to estimate the predictive error from the actual calibration data. This can be done in different ways. To guard against over-fitting, it requires some additional mathematics, but it works well in practice. Internal validation is based on one simple, but important, aspect of experimental design. For empirical multivariate calibration, it is sensible to demand that the user ensures that every important spectral variation phenomenon is represented by at least two independent calibration samples, one higher and one lower than the average level of the phenomenon, or for example two that are higher than the average level.

The Full-Spectrum Calibration

In the full-spectrum calibration, the 'average' error of prediction for the three botanical components is about 4 per cent when calibrations are performed separately for each variety, and about 6 per cent when the three different varieties are combined.

The prediction ability can be improved by selecting a narrower subset of samples. When the calibration is performed for endosperm rich samples only, the error of prediction is reduced to approximately

2 per cent and there is very little difference in prediction ability between the separate calibrations and the combined calibration. Therefore, it is not surprising that an attempt to level out the differences between the varieties by normalizing the spectra does not result in more precise predictions. When a subset of samples is selected, it is important to remember that every type of variability that can occur in future samples must be present among the calibration samples, and the choice of calibration samples determines what type of unknown samples can be analysed well with the calibration results obtained.

Selection of a few discrete wavelengths to allow for simpler instrumentation seems possible, but some kind of response linerization is necessary. The use of polynominal terms facilities modelling of non-linearities and improves the prediction ability considerably. When six wavelengths are used and derivatives included in the calibration, the errors of prediction are only about 3 per cent. However, further attempts should be made linearize the spectral data prior to the calibration. The use of chemical information as extra X-variables might also improve the precision.

The study clearly shows that the botanical composition can be estimated from autofluorescence data, and that it is possible by PLS calibration to establish one general model applicable to wheat and wheat fractions of different varieties. However, at regular intervals samples with known constituent concentrations must be analysed to validate the calibration results to check that neither the spectral instrument nor the general sample quality has changed since the time of calibration. A continuous update of the calibration is necessary to compensate for drift in the instrument.

Because the calibration is based on manually dissected samples, which cumbersome and time-consuming to prepare, the update of the calibration is a problem which has not yet been solved. The extended used of chemical data, as indicators of botanical composition, in the calibration is a possibility which needs to be explored. In the end, the combination of fluorescence and NIR reflectance spectroscopy might prove useful.

The preceding section illustrates the potential of multivariate calibration as a general tool for determining combinations of chemical constituents from non-selective data. Quantitative chemometrics open new research possibilities, and computerized data analysis can give better use of chemical data. In particular, multivariate calibration allows us to replace slow, imprecise, or expensive measurements by faster, more precise, or cheaper measurements. Thereby, we can spend less time on the actual measurement and more on problem formulation, experimental design, data analysis, and interpretation. New types of on-line instruments using multivariate calibration can probably improve process control in industry and medicine.

This shift from 'wet chemistry' to computerized technology will also have some non-technical implications. Multivariate instruments and software must be designed for people, and people must be educated to use them correctly. Data analysis should be taught at every level of technical education to avoid alienation. Semi-automatic computerized instrumentation can lead to monotonous jobs. This can be avoided by giving the operator wider responsibilities for sample selection and data interpretation.

Bibliography

Aeschbacher M., Reinhardt C.A. and Zbinden G. 1986. A rapid cell membrane permeability test using fluorescent dyes and flow cytometry *Cell Bioi Toxicol* 2: 247–55.

Arthur C.L., Belardi R.P., Pratt K.F., Motlagh S. and Pawlislyn J., 1992. Environmental analysis of organic compounds in water using solid phase microextraction, *J. High Res. Chromat.* 15:741.

Arthur C.L., Chai M. and Puwliszyn J., 1993. Solventless injection technique for microcolumn separations, *J. Microcol. Sep.* 5:51.

Arthur C.L., Killam L.M., Buchholz K.D., Pawliszyn J. and Berg J.R., 1992. Automation and optimization of solid-phase microextraction, *Anal. Chem.* 64: 1960.

Arthur C.L., Killam L.M., Motlagh S., Lim M., Potter D.W. and Pawliszyn J., 1992. Analysis of substituted benzene compounds in groundwater using solid-phase microextraction, *Environ. Sci. Technol.* 26:979.

Aug-Yeung C. and MacLeod A., 1981. A comparison of the efficiency of the Likens and Nickerson extractor for aqueous, liquid/ aqueous, and lipid samples, *J. Agric. Food Chem.* 29:502.

Berg J.R., 1993. Practical use of automated solid phase microextraction, *Am. Lab. (Nov.)*: 18.

Bornman J.F., Bomman C.H., Bjorn L.O. 1982. Effects of ultraviolet radiation on viability of isolated *Beta vulgaris* and *Hordeum vulgare* protoplasts Z *Pflanzenphysiol* 105: 297–306.

Boyer Rodney F., 1993. *Modern Experimental Biochemistry*, 2nd edn. Benjamin/Cummings Publishing, California, USA.

Broekaert J.A.C., 1998. *Analytical Atomic Spectrometry with Flames and Plasmas*, Third Edition. Wiley–VCH, Weinheim, Germany.

Buchholz K.D., Pawliszyn J., 1993. Determination of phenols by solid-phase microextraction and gas chromatographic analysis, *Environ. Sci. Technol.* 27:2844.

Buchholz K.D., Pawliszyn J., 1994. Optimization of solid-phase microextraction conditions for determination of phenols, *Anal. Chem.* 66: 160.

Burguera, J.L., Burguera, M., Rivas, C., de la Guardia, M. and Salvador, A., 1990. *J. Flow Inject. Anal.*, 7: 11.

Chai M., Arthur C.L., Pawliszyn J., Belardi R.P., Pratt K.F., 1993. Determination of volatile chlorinated hydrocarbons in air and water with solid-phase microextraction, *Analyst* 118:1501.

Chai M., Pawliszyn J., 1995. Analysis of environmental air samples by solid-phase microextraction and gas chromatography/ion trap mass spectrometry, *Environ. Sci. Technol.* 29:693.

Chang S., Vatlese F., Hwang C., Hsieh O., Min D., 1977. Apparatus for the isolation of trace volatile constituents from foods, *J. Agric. Food Chem.* 25:450.

Christian, Gary D., 2004. *Analytical Chemistry*, 6th edn. John Wiley and Sons Inc., New Jersey, USA.

Cornel D., Grignon C., Rona J.P., Heller R. 1983. Measurement of intracellular potassium activity in protoplasts of *Acer pseudoplatanus:* origin of their electropositivity *Physiol Plant* 57: 203–9.

de Bruyn J., Schogt J., 1961. Isolation of volatile constituents from fats and oils by vacuum degassing, *J. Am. Oil Chem. Soc.* 38:40.

Eisert R., Levsen K., 1995. Determination of organophosphorus, triazine and 2,6- dinitrounilillc pesticides in aqueous sample via solid-phase microextraction (SPME) and gas chromatography with nitrogen-phosphorus detection, *Fresemius J. Anal. Chem.* 351:555.

Eisert R., Levsen K., Wunsch G., 1994. Element-selective detection of pesticides by gas chromatography-atomic emission detection and solid-phase microextraction, *J. Chromatogr.* A 683: 175.

Fluher E.N. 1987. Characterization of new spectroscopic molecular probes of membrane potential (Ph.D. Thesis) *Diss Abst Int* 47: 3213.

Galbraith D.W., Mauch T.J., 1980. Identification of fusion of plant protoplasts II: conditions for the reproducible fluorescence labelling of protoplasts derived from mesophyll tissue Z *Pflanzenphysiol* 98: 129–40.

Hahne G., Herth W., Hoffmann F., 1983. Wall formation and cell division in fluorescence-labelled plant protoplasts *Protoplasma* 115: 217–21.

Hahn-Hägerdal B., Hosono K., Zachrisson A., Bornman C.H. 1986. Polyethyleneglycol and electric field treatment of plant protoplasts: characterization of some membrane properties *Physiol Plant* 67: 359–64.

Hawthorne S.B., Miller D.J., Pawliszyn J., Arthur C.L., 1992. Solventless determination of caffeine in beverages using solid-phase microextraction with fused-silica fibers, *J. Chromtogr:* 603: 185.

Heslop-Harrison J., Heslop-Harrison Y., 1970. Evaluation of pollen viability by enzymatically induced fluorescence: intracellular hydrolysis of fluorescein diacetate *Stain Technol* 47: 115–20

Ho C.T., Manley C.H., 1993. *Flavour Measurement*, Marcel Dekker, New York, eds.

Huang C.N., Cornejoo M.J., Bush D.S., Jones R.L., 1986. Estimating viability of plant protoplasts using double and single staining *Protoplasma* 135: 80–7.

Jayatilaka A.P., Poole S.K., Poole C.F., 1995. Solid phase microextraction of flavor compounds from cinnamon and their separation by series coupled-column GC for the identification of botanical origin of cinnamon of commerce, Abstr. of the 1995 Pittsburgh Conf., #472P, New Orleans, March 5–10, 1995.

John, L.W. and Wainer, I.W., 1995. *High Performance Liquid Chromatography: Fundamental Principles and Practices.* CRC press, Baltimore, Maryland, USA.

Johnson B., Walter G., Burlingame A., 1971. Volatile components of roasted peanuts: basic fraction, *J. Agric. Food Chem.* 19: 1020.

Jones K.H., Senft J.A., 1985. An improved method to determine cell viability by simultaneous staining with fluorescein diacetate-propidium iodide *J Hislochem Cytochem* 33: 77–9.

Kanchanapoom K., Boss W.F., 1986. The effect of fluorescent labelling on calcium-induced fusion of fusogenic carrot protoplasts *Plant Cell Reports* 5: 252–5.

Katz, E.D., 2009. High performance liquid chromatography: Principles and methods. In: *Biotechnology*. Wiley-India. www.wiley.com/wileyCDA/-/productcd.html.

L'vov, B.V., 1997. Forty years of electrothermal atomic absorption spectrometry: Advances and problems in theory. *Spectrochim. Acta B*, 52: 1239–1245.

Larkin P.J., 1976. Purification and viability determinations of plant protoplasts *Planta* 128: 213–16.

Leahy M., Reinecciux G., 1984. "Comparison of Methods for the Isolation of Volatile Compounds from Aqueous Model Systems," in *Analysis of Volatiles, Methods, Applications* (P. Schreier, ed.), de Gruyter, New York, p. 19.

Louch D., Motlagh S., and Pawliszyn J., 1992. Dynamics of organic compound extraction from water using liquid-coated fused silica fibers, *Anal. Chem.* 64: 1187.

Maarse H., Belz R., 1981. *Isolation, Separation and Identification of Volatile Compounds in Aroma Resarch*, Akademic-Verlug, Berlin.

MacGillivray B., Pawliszyn J., Fowlie P., Sagara C., 1994. Headspace solid-phase microextraction versus purge and trap for the determination of substituted benzene compounds in water. *J. Chromatogr. Science* 32:317.

Macrae, R., 1982. *HPLC in Food Analysis: Food Science and Technology* (A series of monographs). Academic Press, London.

Manning, T.J. and Grow, W.R., 1997. Inductively coupled plasma: Atomic emission spectrometry. *The Chemical Educator*, 2(1).

McCann J., Yamasaki E., Ames B.N., 1975. Detection of carcinogens as mutagens in Salmonella/microsome test: assay of 300 chemicals *Proc Natl Acad Sci USA* 72: 5135.

McCully M.E. 1970. The histological localization of the structural polysaccharides of seaweeds *Ann NY Acad Sci* 175: 702–11.

Montaser, A. and Golightly, D.W., 1988. *Inductively Coupled Plasmas in analytical Atomic Spectrometry*. VCH Publishers, New York.

Motlagh S., Pawliszyn J., 1993. On-line monitoring of flowing samples using solid phase microextraction-gas chromatography, *Analytica Chim. Acta* 284:265.

Moyler, D.A., 1984. Carbon dioxide extracted ingredients for fragrances, *Perf. Flav*. 9:109.

Nickerson G.B., Likens S.T., 1966. Gas chromatographic evidence for the occurrence of hop oil components in beer, *J. Chromatog.* 21: 1–3.

Nollet Leo, M.L., 2000. *Food Analysis by HPLC*, 2nd edition (Revised and expanded). Marcel Dekker Inc., New York.

Olesik, J.W., 1991. *Anal. Chem.*, 63: 12A.

Otu E., Pawliszyn J., 1993. Solid phase micro-extraction of metal ions, *Mikrochim. Acta* 112:41.

Page B.D., Lacroix G., 1993. Application of solid-phase microextraction to the headspace gas chromatographic analysis of halogenated volatiles in selected foods, *J. Chromatogr:* 648:199.

Paolillo D.J., 1964. Acridine orange fluorescence in shoot tips of *Ephedra Acta Histochem* 18: 276–82.

Parliment T., Stahl, H., 1995. "Formation of Furfuryl Mercaptan in Coffee Model Systems," in *Developments in Food Science V37A Food Flavors: Generation, Analysis and Process Influence* (G. Charalambous, ed.), Elsevier, New York, p. 805.

Parliment, T.H. and Stahl, H.D., 1994. "Generation of Furfuryl Mercaptan in Cysteine-Pentose Model Systems in Relation to Roasted Coffee," in *Sulfur Compounds in Foods* (C. Mussinan and M. Keelal, eds.), American Chemical Society, Washington, DC, p. 160.

Parliment, T.H., 1986. A new technique for GLC sample preparation using a novel extraction device, *Perf Flav. I:* 1.

Potter D.W. and Pawliszyn J., 1992. Detection of substituted benzenes in water at the pg/ml level using solid-phase microextraction and gas chromatography-ion trap mass spectrometry, *J. Chromatogr.* 625:247.

Potter D.W., Pawliszyn J., 1994. Rapid determination of polyaromatic hydrocarbons and polychlorinated biphenyls in water using solid-phase microextraction and GC/Ms, *Environ. Sci. Technol.* 28:298.

Potter, Geoffrey W.H., 1995. *Analysis of Biological Molecules: An Introduction to Principles, Instrumentation and Techniques.* Alden Press, Oxford, UK.

Risch S., Reinecciux G., 1989. "Isolation of Thermally Generated Aromas," in *Thermal Generation of Aromas* (T.H. Parliment, R.J. McGorrin. and C.T. Ho, eds.), American Chemical Society, Washington, DC, p. 42.

Rocks, B.F., Sherwood, R.A., Turner, Z.J. and Riley, C., 1983. *Ann. Clin. Biochem.*, 20(2): 72.

Rotman B., Papermaster B.W., 1966. Membrane properties of living mammalian cells as studies by enzymatic hydrolysis of fluorogenic esters *Proc Natl Acad Sci USA* 55: 134–41.

Sarna L.P., Webster G.R.B., Friesen-Fischer M.R., Sri Rajan R., 1994. Analysis of the petroleum components benzene, toluene, ethyl benzene and the xylenes in water by commercially available solid-phase microextraction and carbon-layer open tubular capillary column gas chromatography, *J. Chromatogr.* A 677:201.

Sawhney, S.K. and Singh, R., 2001. *Introductory Practical Biochemistry.* Narosa Publishing House, New Delhi.

Schreier P., 1984. *Chromatogaphic Studies of Biogenesis of Plant Volatiles*, Huthig, New York.

Schultz T., Flath R., Mon R., Eggling S., Teranishi R., 1977. Isolation of volatile components from a model system. *J. Agric. Food Chem.* 25:446.

Schultz W., Randall, J., 1970. Liquid carbon dioxide for selective aroma extraction. *Food Technol.* 24: 1283.

Shepard J.F., Totten R.E. 1977. Mesophyll cell protoplasts of potato: isolation, proliferation and plant regeneration *Plant Physiol* 60: 313–16.

Sherwood, R.A. and Rocks, B.F., 1989. *In: Flow Injection Atomic Spectroscopy*, (Ed.) J.L. Burguera. Marcel Dekker, New York, pp. 259–291.

Van Gijzel P. 1971. Review of the UV fluorescence photometry of fresh and fossil exines and exosporia. In: Brooks J., Grant P.R., Muir M.D., Van Gijzel P., Shaw G. (eds) *Sporopollenin* Academic Press, London.

Van Gijzel P. 1975. Polychromatic UV fluorescein microphotometry of fresh and fossil plant substances with special reference to location and identification of dispersed organic matter in rocks. In Alpern B (ed) *Petrographic Organique et Potential Petrolier* CNRS, Paris.

Wan H.B., Chi H., Wong M.K., Mok C.Y., 1994. Solid-phase microextraction using pencil lead as sorbent for analysis of organic pollutants in water, *Anal. Chim. Acta* 298:219.

Wilson, K. and Walker, J., 1996. *Practical Biochemistry: Principles and Techniques.* Cambridge University Press, Cambridge, UK.

Wittkamp B., Tilotta D.C., 1995. Determination of BTEX compounds in water by solid-phase microextraction and raman spectroscopy, *Anal. Chem.* 67:600.

Yang H.Y., 1986. Fluorescein diacetate used as a vital stain for labeling living pollen tubes *Plant Science* 44: 59–63.

Yang X., Peppard T., 1994. Solid-phase microextraction for flavor analysis, *J. Agric. Food Chem.* 42:1925.

Zhang Z., Pawliszyn J., 1993. Analysis of organic compounds in environmental samples by headspace solid phase microextraction, *J. High Res. Chromatogr:* 16:689.

Zhang Z., Pawliszyn J., 1993. Headspace solid-phase microextraction, *Anal. Chem.* 65:1843.

Zhang Z., Pawliszyn J., 1995. Quantitative extraction using an internally cooled solid phase microextraction device, *Anal. Chem.* 67:34.

Zhang Z., Yang M.J., Pawliszyn J., 1994. Solid-phase microextraction: a solvent-free alternative for sample preparation, *Anal. Chem.* 66:844A.

Zybin, A., Koch, J., Wizemann, H.D., Franzke, J. and Niemax, K., 2005. Diode laser atomic absorption spectrometry. *Spectrochimica Acta B*, 60: 1–11.

Sherwood R.A. and Rocks B.F. [illegible] In: [illegible] Spectroscopy (2nd) [illegible] Marcel Dekker, New York, pp. 259-291.

Van Gijzel P. 1971. Review of the UV fluorescence photometry of fresh and fossil exines and exosporia. In: Brooks J., Grant P.R., Muir M.D., Van Gijzel P., Shaw G. (eds) Sporopollenin. Academic Press, London.

Van Gijzel P. 1975. Polychromatic UV fluorescence microphotometry of fresh and fossil plant substances with special reference to location and identification of dispersed organic material in rocks. In: Alpern B. (ed) Pétrographie de la matière organique [illegible] CNRS, Paris.

Wan H.B., Chi H., Wong M.K., Mok C.Y. 1994. Solid phase microextraction using pencil lead as sorbent for analysis of organic pollutants in water. Anal. Chim. Acta 298:219.

Wilson K. and Walker J. 1996. Practical Biochemistry: Principles and Techniques. Cambridge University Press, Cambridge, UK.

Wittkamp B., Tilotta D.C. 1995. Determination of BTEX compounds in water by solid-phase microextraction and Raman spectroscopy. Anal. Chem. 67:600.

Yang H.Y. 1986. Fluorescein diacetate used as a vital stain for labeling living pollen tubes. Plant Science 44: 59-63.

Yang X., Peppard T. 1994. Solid-phase microextraction for flavor analysis. J. Agric. Food Chem. 42:1925.

Zhang Z., Pawliszyn J. 1993. Analysis of organic compounds in environmental samples by headspace solid phase microextraction. J. High Res. Chromatogr. 16:689.

Zhang Z., Pawliszyn J. 1993. Headspace solid-phase microextraction. Anal. Chem. 65:1843.

Zhang Z., Pawliszyn J. 1995. Quantitative extraction using an internally cooled solid phase microextraction device. Anal. Chem. 67:34.

Zhang Z., Yang M.J., Pawliszyn J. 1994. Solid-phase microextraction: a solvent-free alternative for sample preparation. Anal. Chem. 66:844A.

Zybin A., Koch J., Wizemann H.D., Franzke J. and Niemax K. 2005. Diode laser atomic absorption spectrometry. Spectrochimica Acta B 60:1-11.

Index

A

B

C

D

Q

R

S

T

V